RETURNING TO MEMBERSHIP IN EARTH COMMUNITY:

SYSTEMIC CONSTELLATIONS WITH NATURE

EDITED BY
FRANCESCA MASON BORING & KENNETH EDWIN SLOAN

WITH CONTRIBUTIONS FROM
JOHN CHENEY, ZITA COX, ANDREAS DEMMEL,
PETER DEVRIES, SARA FANCY,
DAAN VAN KAMPENHOUT,
KIRSTEN LOVE LAUZON, CHRISJAN LEERMAKERS,
FRANCESCA MASON BORING, BETH MURRAY,
SNEH VICTORIA SCHNABEL, SUSAN SCHLOSSER,
KENNETH EDWIN SLOAN AND BERCHTHOLD WASSER

First Published in the United States in 2013 by
Stream of Experience Productions, Pagosa Springs, Colorado
www.stream-of-experience.com

Library of Congress Control Number: 2013945216

Black and White Interior Version ISBN: 978-0-9826-077-5-6

Color Interior Version: ISBN: 978-0-9826-077-6-3

Ebook Version: ISBN: 978-0-9826-077-7-0

Proofreading: Ruby Webber ruwebber27@gmail.com

Cover and Frontispiece art by Jane Kiskaddon janekiskaddon.com

The online community and resources for this book are at www.nature-constellations.net

This book on Facebook
www.facebook.com/NatureConstellations

Dedication and Appreciation

To our ancestors, our parents, our teachers, our fellow explorers,
and all the members of Earth Community who have helped us along the path,
often in ways we did not even notice.

Thank you!

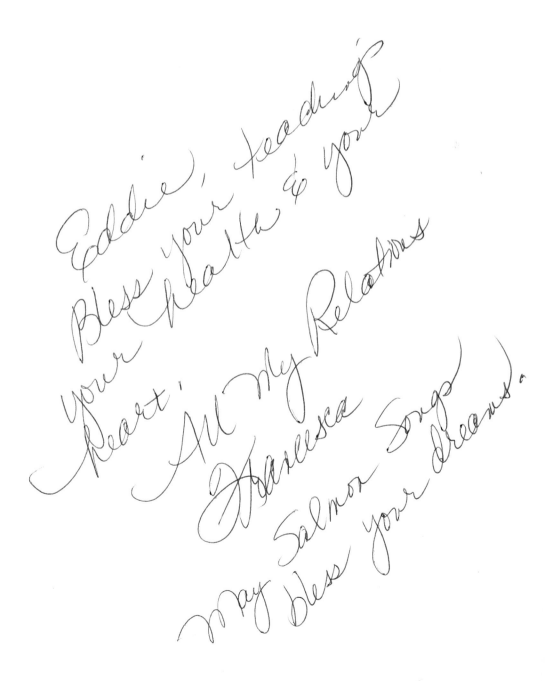

Eddie, teaching
Bless your
your health & your
heart,
All My Relations
Francesca
May Salmon Songs
bless your dreams

CONTENTS

Introduction

Four Streams Flowed Together

This book exists because of the fruitful confluence of four streams of development: deep ecology, shamanism, consciousness research, and systemic constellation work. A loose network of individuals have pioneered, discovered each other, learned from each other, and then explored the fascinating realm where these four currents merge: "systemic constellations with nature." Fourteen of them have contributed chapters to this book about how they came to this work, what they have discovered, and how their way of working has enabled them and the people they work with to deeply experience and better understand their membership in Earth Community. Before we present their contributions, here are a few words about each of the four parallel streams of development on which this work is based.

Deep Ecology

In 1988 John Seed - in collaboration with Joanna Macy, Pat Fleming, and Arne Naess - published the seminal book Thinking Like a Mountain: Towards a Council of All Beings (Seed, 1988). The book was only 122 pages long but contained a rich collection of drawings, poetry, quotations and writings associated with the Council of All Beings group process that John and Joanna had developed in Australia in 1985. An important part of the ritual involves each participant taking the role of a specific animal, plant, species, or any other aspect of the ecosystem and speaking for that part. The work spread around the world and continues to this day to be an important part of what Macy and her colleagues refer to as "The Work That Reconnects." (Macy and Brown, 1998)

In a 2002 blog post on her web site (www.joannamacy.net) Joanna Macy summarizes the process and its value as follows:

> *The Council of All Beings is a communal ritual in which participants step aside from their human identity and speak on behalf of another life-form. A simple structure for spontaneous expression, it aims to heighten awareness of our interdependence in the living body of Earth, and to strengthen our commitment to defend it. The ritual serves to help us acknowledge and give voice to the suffering of our world. It also serves, in equal measure, to help us experience the beauty and power of our interconnectedness with all life.*

When we experience our interconnectedness with life, and to the natural environment, we begin to operate from a different set of perceptions and values. And this is exactly what we must do - individually and collectively - if we are to slow, stop, and reverse the historical trend of the industrial age in which decisions are made solely from the position of narrowly-defined cost/benefits for some group of humans which result in severe damage to the natural world, and damage the health and well-being of the many beings living now and in the future.

Systemic constellation work with nature is exciting and useful because it supports the goals of deep ecology in a new way: this work enables us to come into coherent direct dialogue with the elements of nature, so that we can gather much more information about how our actions or lack of action, or even our attitudes, are perceived by other elements of nature - animals, plants, landscapes, whole ecosystems or even the planet as a whole - and affect them. And we can of course also hear their ideas about what should and what should not happen, including learning what is valuable to them, which is often quite different from what we may have imagined from our anthropocentric point of view. This is what it means to be a member of Earth Community: to recognize and consider the perceptions, needs, values, and proposals of the other non-human participants in life here on earth versus solely our own, or those of only humans or groups of humans.

Shamanism and Native Wisdom

In Thinking Like a Mountain, John Seed referenced the deep wisdom and competence of native peoples and their shamans in not just understanding but experiencing directly their oneness with nature and interdependence with all beings. His quote from Gary Snyder expresses this aspect precisely:

> The shaman speaks for wild animals, the spirits of plants, the spirits of mountains, of waterheads. he or she sings for them. They sing through her....the whole society consults the non-human powers and allows some individuals to step totally out of their human roles to put on the mask, costume and mind of Bison, Bear, Squash, Corn or Pleiades, to re-enter the human circle in their form and by song, mime and dance, convey a greeting from the other realms. (Snyder, 1977)

Michael Harner's publication in 1980 of his ground-breaking book The Way of the Shaman (Harner, 1980) and his subsequent founding and expansion of the Foundation for Shamanic Studies with his wife Sandra brought new attention to both the preservation of shamanic wisdom among First Peoples and an approach to passing this wisdom on in the form of training. In the western world there was a fresh and appreciative view of what wisdom and power shamanism could offer.

The wisdom of native people's, even outside the framework of shamanism in its many forms, has always emphasized the importance of respect for and consideration of all other creatures and the elements of nature itself. This was the very foundation of the people's ability to survive and thrive in peace with the natural world. It is exactly this that we have lost.

Corbin Harney, Shoshone Elder, used to tell a story. He told many stories that had been told for generations. He told how it used to be that we always talked with everything. We prayed for everything. We were connected to everything.

Corbin's example, taken from the teachings of old, was the conversation we had with the water. It used to be that we had good manners. When we saw the water in the creek, we took the time to say, "You are so beautiful today; it feels so good to stand with you." Or, when we took a drink of water we would say, "Water, thank you for what you do for my body. Thank you for being here for me and helping to keep me healthy." When we washed and the water touched our skin, we would say, "Thank You. It feels good to be refreshed by you today." And this is how it was.

This soft spoken elder who carried the wisdom of ages in his memory shared something which may be relevant for modern man who suffers from a pandemic sense of depression, anxiety and isolation. Corbin would say, "People now days wonder, and worry. What can we do? What is wrong with the water? The water is sick and we want to know how to take care of it." He would tell us, "We want to help the water and we worry. I can tell you what is wrong with the water. We no longer talk with the water. What is wrong with the water? The water is lonely." (Harney, 2009)

As systemic constellations expand to include environmental topics and explore enlisting nature as a resource for family and community systems which are injured, we remember again being in conversation, being a part of, being included, returning to Earth Community. We remember how easy it is to be in direct communication with the nature around us. And, when we stand as a representative for some aspect of that nature, and experience its perspective, we are ourselves changed.

Perhaps, when we have done this, when we are again in conversation, we will find that no longer is the water lonely. And perhaps the greatest discovery we will find, when the water is no longer lonely, will be that neither are we.

Consciousness Research

Although quantum theory and the experiments that verified it had transformed traditional Newtonian-Cartesian physics long before, it was not until the 1950's and the availability of LSD that serious scientific researchers in the west began asking questions about the validity of the human "I" as merely a skin-encapsulated ego (to use Alan Watts' term). Many spiritual systems had long maintained that it is consciousness that underlies apparent reality and is the causal element behind the physical world, in direct contradiction to the western materialist view that consciousness is a transient phenomena arising from and dependent on specific configurations of matter. Further, many spiritual systems assert that human beings (like all beings) have the capacity to connect with that network of consciousness and experience a much broader identity, including gaining information that is not available through normal material means. Might these spiritual systems be right? Stanislav Grof (Grof, 2012), Ervin Lazlo (Lazlo, 2007), Rupert Sheldrake (Sheldrake, 2007) and many others did their research, collected data that could only be explained by a radical revision of theories of consciousness, and began to hypothesize and test what this new vision of consciousness might look like in scientific terms. They then asked other scientists to examine the evidence, hoping that others would join in the exploration. But, as Thomas Kuhn so eloquently documented in his 1962 book, The Structure of Scientific Revolutions (Kuhn,1962), the defenders of an established paradigm do not give way easily to a new one, regardless of evidence that contradicts the established paradigm, since for them to abandon or significantly revise what they have learned, taught to others, and proclaimed as "truth" is to lose some aspect of self-identity. That is, new evidence that contradicts the old paradigm throws them into a form of identity crisis. In a paradigm shift that demands a new definition of what it means to be human, the crisis is especially severe.

In the context of this book we are interested in the hypothesized existence of what Ervin Lazlo terms the "Akashic Field" which is trans-temporal and trans-spatial (Lazlo, 2007). Stanislav Grof has coined the term "holotropic" (Grof, 2012) to refer to the state of consciousness in which we are in direct contact with and participate in this field. This field underlies and is (potentially) available to all consciousness, thereby providing an explanation for phenomena routinely encountered in constellation work that are inexplicable or bluntly "impossible" in the traditional materialistic Newtonian-Cartesian world view of consciousness. (But which, ironically, appear to depend on underlying mechanisms that are already proven and tested in quantum physics.)

Systemic Constellation Work

Beginning in 1993 with Gunthard Weber's publication of Zweierlei Glück about Bert Hellinger and his development of family constellation work, a growing number of psychotherapists, especially in Europe, became interested in "Family Constellations" and the larger category of "Systemic Constellations" in which participants in a group process (in service to a specific client or focus) represent individuals or elements of a specific system, whether a family system or organizational system or any kind of system with inter-related parts.

The foundation of all constellation work is the experience that human beings have the capacity - given the intention, the appropriate setting, and support - to experience body sensations, emotions and thoughts that do not belong to them personally but reflect the experiences, emotions, and thoughts of some other element of a larger system which they represent, or even of the system as a whole, of which they had no prior knowledge.

That is, systemic constellations are an application of and provide a direct and personal experience of the larger field of shared consciousness that deep ecology, shamanism, and consciousness research describe and also in their own ways explore.

This book is specifically about systemic constellation work applied to our relationship to natural systems, both in us and around us.

Earth Community

The listing of the sources and foundations for this book would not be complete without deep thanks to David C. Korten for his 2006 book, The Great Turning: From Empire to Earth Community (Korten, 2006). In this book Korten builds on the work from deep ecology to describe the importance of establishing or re-discovering our individual and collective relationship to the Earth, as felt experiences in our bodies and the potentially transformative effects of such a shift, both individually and collectively. We have used his term Earth Community in our main title.

How This Book Came into Being

At the United States Systemic Constellations Conference in October of 2011 in San Francisco, Francesca Mason Boring talked to Kenneth Sloan about her idea of a book which would collect the approaches developed by early practitioners of systemic constellations with nature. Francesca herself was such a practitioner and teacher, and there was a loose network of others involved. John Cheney, Sara Fancy, and Kirsten Love Lauzon were also at the conference, and Francesca introduced each of them to Kenneth as good representatives of the work being done, and each one was ready to write a chapter for the proposed book. Kenneth himself had been involved in the work since 2003, mostly in collaboration with Berchthold Wasser of Switzerland. The material was there, for sure, but it would be a lot of work to bring it together into a presentable book. Francesca was insistent and persistent. In the end Kenneth had no choice but to promise to assist in putting the book together. And for Francesca a long-held dream of sharing more of this way of working moved a step closer to reality. Soon other contributors were added to the list, and the process of gestation, growth, and eventually birthing the book began.

How this Book is Structured

The first section of the book contains three chapters under the heading Origins. The three contributors there - Francesca Mason Boring, Sneh Victoria Schnabel, and Daan van Kampenhout - represent the elders of the work, both in terms of their personal contributions and the traditions which they represent. They have also collaborated from time to time in offering conferences on the theme, have been teachers to many, and have inspired many of the others represented here through these conferences and the writings, trainings, and workshops that they offer.

The second section is called Explorations and provides "reports from the field" from various facilitators of systemic constellations with nature. There is a broad range of approaches and applications, writing styles, and vocabulary. We have sought to present these reports in the contributor's own voice as much as possible, although using a common structure for the information. We have found that there is strength in this diversity: the cumulative effect of the chapters is to enable us to step back and see what elements of the work are specific to a particular facilitator versus being fundamental.

The third section is Opportunities and briefly describes categories of application in which we have experienced that this way of working is useful.

The fourth section is Resources and describes where additional related information can be found.

Our Wish

Our wish for you dear reader is that you enjoy this collection and are also in some way helped to rediscover or reaffirm your own membership in Earth Community, therefore becoming more fully present, aware, in balance, connected and whole in your life. Further we hope you will feel encouraged to embark on some explorations of your own, whatever form they take. If you want to share your experiences and/or questions around this topic or related topics online with us and the other contributors we have set up a simple online community, at www.nature-constellations.net, where you can do so.

Francesca Mason Boring
Great Basin person living in the
Cascadia Bioregion

Kenneth Edwin Sloan
Cross Timbers person living in the
Black Forest Ecoregion

July, 2013

References

Grof, Stanislav. Healing Our Deepest Wounds: the Holotropic Paradigm Shift, 2012.

Harner, Michael. The Way of the Shaman. 1980 (many later editions).

Harney, Corbin, The Nature Way: Wisdom from a Western Shoshone Elder, University of Nevada Press, 2009.

Lazlo, Ervin. Science and the Akashic Field: An Integral Theory of Everything, 2007.

Kuhn, Thomas. The Structure of Scientific Revolutions, 1962 (several later editions).

Korten, David C. The Great Turning: from Empire to Earth Community, 2007.

Macy, Joanna and Brown, Molly. Coming Back to Life: Practices to Reconnect Our Lives, Our World, 1998.

Seed, John, et al. Thinking Like a Mountain: Towards a Council of All Beings, 1988.

Sheldrake, Rupert. Seven Experiments That Could Change the World: A Do-It-Yourself Guide to Revolutionary Science, 2007.

Snyder, Gary. The Old Ways, 1977.

Weber, Gunthard. Zweierlei Glück, 1993.

PART I

Origins

Francesca Mason Boring is an international facilitator and teacher of Systems Constellation, including: Family Systems Constellation, Nature Constellation, Community Constellation, Organizational Constellation and Constellation as Ceremony.

Author and contributing writer to several books, her most recently published: Connecting to Our Ancestral Past: Healing through Family Constellation, Ceremony & Ritual (North Atlantic Books, 2012) is a pragmatic, spiritual journey that introduces a variety of specific rituals and conversations in connection with Constellations work, an experiential process that explores one's history and powerful events of the past to understand and resolve problems of the present. A range of voices from around the world—leaders in the fields of systems constellations, theoretical physics, and tribal traditions—contribute to this exploration of aboriginal perspectives that will benefit facilitators of Constellations work, therapists, and human beings trying to walk with open eyes and hearts.

Francesca writes for, and serves on the Advisory Board for The Knowing Field, the International Systems Constellation Journal published in England.

Mason Boring has served on Faculty of the International Intensive Constellation Training in Southern Germany since May, 2007; and has trained with Masters of Family & Human Systems Constellation as well as her own Elders and aboriginal teachers.

Website: www.allmyrelationsconstellations.com

CHAPTER ONE

Nature Constellations:
An Ancient Walk with Knowing and Healing

by Francesca Mason Boring

Abstract: What are the broader applications of Nature in constellation work and what is the benefit of standing in the "knowing field" of the Natural world? Is this experience new, or is it the most fundamental and ancient relationship that resonates with all of our ancestral field and deepest cellular memories? My hope is to share some experiences, observations, cautions, and indigenous thought in a way that could encourage the impulse of your heart to find a space where you might experience Nature Constellation and respect for this field which holds such promise.

Systems Constellation came to me in the form of Sneh Victoria Schnabel coming from Freiburg, Germany to the rural town of Colville, Washington to teach Family Constellation. One of life's miracles was that Sneh was one of the few facilitators teaching at the time who had a certainty that if the "field" included any element that seemed essential in a constellation it should be given a place.

The "knowing field" came to me as an infant in the form of trans-generational history of work with this field of connection and listening. On my mother's side I come from the Shoshone, an indigenous native tribe in the United States. My maternal grandmother was a Dreamer; her aunt had always worked with this way of "knowing" before her. My mother would say, "It's just the way we are."

Sitting with my maternal grandfather, I learned that the wind, the dust, the birds, everything around us is in conversation with us. The tragedy began to be clear as I became an adult: most people were ignoring the conversation.

My father, the grandchild of immigrants, had an easy way of being in nature, fishing, camping, gardening, and giving us a sense that play and the outdoors went hand in hand.

For more than a dozen years, I have been fortunate to facilitate and/or teach constellation work in the US, Canada, Germany, Switzerland, Holland, Italy, Singapore, Australia, and South Africa. Family Constellations opened the door to Organizational Constellation, Constellation as Ceremony, Community Constellations and Nature Constellations. Life took me to places that led me to conclude that there is something which we might call a Universal Indigenous Field and I wrote about this in Connecting to Our Ancestral Past: Healing through Family Constellations, Ceremony & Ritual (North Atlantic Books, 2012). This ancient and ever present field is connected to Nature. It is of the Earth.

At one time, ethnocentricity and limited life experience led me to believe that North American Tribes had a singularly unique connection to Mother Earth. Then, an elderly man, (in his 80's perhaps) shared something with me. It is always an honor when an elder shares. They have been given by the Creator time on the Earth and if they have listened they have learned from mankind and all that is not "human." He had bright eyes and was fit in his body. His energy was high. He spoke about his Uncle and how he had gathered herbs with his Uncle in the hills. He had been just a boy when he walked with his Uncle. His Uncle had known healing songs and had a relationship with plants and listened to what they had to tell him. When someone was ill, singing and listening, and walking in the hills until he was led to the particular plant that was willing to heal…all of these things came together; he would pick a plant that was committed to contributing to the healing of someone in his village who was ill.

This man who spoke with me was from the mountains in Europe. This could have been the story of my own indigenous Native American relatives. I began to realize, some version of this same story is told in the mountains and rural areas internationally, and in virtually all indigenous cultures throughout the world. That nature is a reliable healer with whom we can converse and interact is not a new concept. Perhaps it is a component of the Universal Indigenous.

This indigenous field greatly influenced my integration of working in "the knowing field" as one aspect of Ceremony. That this work in "the knowing field" had to be done with respect, prayer, and permission of every soul, being and person was for me a very organic and cultural given. Certainly, in the classic western approach, training makes one the expert-treatments plans, prescriptions, and a wide spectrum of therapies are directive. This mind set and approach is changing by the minute. Spiritual Psychology, Integrative Health Care, and consumer choices are following a different stream.

Family Constellation, as introduced by Bert Hellinger has expanded to include a multiplicity of "systems." The place of Nature in Systems Constellation is a reflection of "what is." We are a part of Nature; Nature is a part of us.

The conversation with Nature in indigenous culture is different from clinical observation. It is an exchange. This reciprocity is the fiber of indigenous thinking. It is not that we (humans) have a corner on the market of consciousness and awareness of the other. In many tribal traditions Nature is an active conversant, a generous participant in relationship with us. Everything in Nature has a complex, conscious, influential place in our system. In addition to being conversant, Nature is known as a teacher, benevolent, and a Healer. As one Shoshone Elder, Corbin Harney wrote:

> "Sometimes we, the people, don't realize all the living things out there have got a voice, they've got a spirit like we do…They were put here for us to use, but we, the people, have to ask them to continue to support us and we must support them…So when you see a tree, it was put here for a lot of reasons: to beautify the Mother, for the birds to use so they will build their nest in the tree, and the animal life uses the tree to rub itself against it. And then we sit under a tree to get away from the sun and to get in the shade. Sometimes when you don't feel good, you lean up against a tree. That tree can heal you, it can give you strength, it can give you energy." (Harney, C., 2009, p.81)

In constellations which introduce nature as a resource, constellations which invite one to experience the "field" of individual aspects of nature in a personal way, we "remember" the conversation. In terms of constellation structure, we may have elements of Nature represented in a family constellation, for instance when one has been so traumatized or abused that there are no "human" resources which can be identified within the system. We have often seen that representatives placed for the "ancestors" provide support for many who cannot easily identify immediate family members who support them. But there are those for whom all human beings are suspect and not to be trusted. When this is the case, there are "resources" available within the panorama of nature which can at times represent something solid, safe, and reliable.

It may be that the "turtle" teaches one about self-defense, not as pathology but natural healthy reflex. Or perhaps "willow" teaches one about self-care, quenching one's own thirst and moving with the winds of life. When elements of nature are invited into the Circle of constellations, they often come as gentle yet powerful mentors.

It is also possible to have constellations done outdoors. If the constellation is highly personal, (i.e. a family constellation), it becomes very important that the location is protected. Foot traffic going to and fro is not a safe environment, but at a secluded private place, where one will not be assaulted by the interference of strangers, it becomes possible for humans to feel, through constellation, the healing touch of Nature. The wind, the birds, even the rain can quickly become willing and valuable participants in the constellation.

Being in Nature does not bring comfort to everyone. For some, this is a place of too much physical exposure, so as with everything in constellation work, it is a responsible thing to give people a choice. If it is clear that the work will occur out-doors in advance, then participants are usually eager and have chosen that forum. However, if there is a situation where the movement or invitation of Nature calls the work outdoors spontaneously, it is good to give space for those who are not comfortable, to step back without shame.

There is a growing body of research and applications of using Nature in response to deep trauma. The use of Nature in healing was described by Anngwyn St. Just, an internationally recognized systemically oriented social traumatologist:

Wilderness settings and time spent in the natural world, can serve as an important catalyst and therapeutic setting for reorienting traumatized people…More and more, I came to understand the degree to which natural settings present an opportunity for temporary re-immersion into a holistic and integrated state of consciousness. In nature, one can reclaim, and renew half-forgotten physical and emotional knowledge. (St. Just, A., 2006, p. 85)

The elements of Nature, introduced in Constellation may have the identical impact of actually standing in the forest, by a creek, being at peace and listening to the trees. However, it has been clear that even in a "nature" constellation there are points of vulnerability for some participants.

There are two dynamics which have been observed as possibly traumatic for some who participate in "nature constellations."

1. I have found a couple folks who were very urban, educated, and felt that Nature was not conscious. They experienced a rather deep grief and sense of loss when they stood as representatives for aspects of Nature and found it to be conscious, wise, and interactive. They felt deeply that they had missed something profound for so much of their life- 40, 50, 60 years of loss. It is not a forbidding issue, but it is something which a facilitator will want to be prepared to take time for. It is a reason to celebrate- such a dramatic change of view - and in the same moment, there can be a very penetrating sense of loss for one who has a dramatic paradigm shift accompanied with a grief of understanding how much was lost to them through their previously limited perspective.

2. The other point of possible momentary destabilization for some participants can occur when someone has felt that Nature needed saving. If they have a huge missionary zeal and hate polluters, and feel morally superior, it has taken a minute for people to recover when they find that our interest in protecting nature is "self" interest. In one example a woman who was a strong environmental activist stood as a representative for a river that was being polluted. The river was not worried and said to the humans, "You may not last, but I will. I have been here forever and when you are gone, I will be here still." The woman standing as the river was representing something (a knowing) which was very far outside of her

own belief or concepts. It really took some adjusting and was a bit surreal because she was compelled to represent something which was in direct conflict with her own belief. This is something facilitators will want to make time for -if someone experiences distress as a result of something in the constellation coming into conflict with their belief.

Naturally, you have these same challenges in family constellation, but occasionally when people are doing Nature Constellation these integration challenges can catch them off guard if they are not prepared. Knowing that just as with Nature, there is room for play, but a greater mandate for healthy respect, seems to be a good foundation for both facilitating and participating in Nature Constellations. There always has to be enough time and attention allocated to support those who become unexpectedly fragile when they face a truth that their body struggles to find a place for.

In addition to the possibility of client vulnerability, there is another point of caution a facilitator should be aware of. There are those who have a connection to the wounding of the environment, and with that a great pain and presentation of drama in the constellation process. In psychology there are those who begin to discuss the possibility of a pathology which is identified by a crippling empathetic sympathy with the perceived vulnerability of the environment. This impact of perception is still in flux in terms of definitions.

"Psychosocial consequences result not only from the direct psychological effects of toxicological effects (analogous to the psychological consequences of physical illness) but also increasingly from their perceived impact and risk to health. Indeed, the impact of episodes in which there is no actual environmental hazard at all but only the perception of such a threat can be as damaging as those in which there is at least some chemical exposure. These episodes tend to be overlooked and are often reported under the label of mass psychogenic illness—referring to a dramatic increase in similar symptoms among affected individuals. It is an unsatisfactory term but preferable to mass hysteria. No terminology exists for the long-term effects of perceived exposures." (Page, Petrie, Wessely, 2006)

Some participants in Nature Constellation have a conscious and unconscious identification with the pollution and perceived trauma to the Earth. Their field, knowing, or perception may interfere with the development of pragmatic solutions and understanding. It is a voice that must be heard, but it is also a voice that can derail constellations which are seeking solutions and new insight. These representatives often end up portraying the Earth as failing, injured, without strength. They also tend to represent only the toxic aspects of environments. The representation is often agonizing for the representative as well as for those present in the Circle and has a distracting affect.

In Nature, there is the gentle wind, and there is the tempest; one experience which can be a bit jarring in a Nature constellation is the visceral presence of predator. In one constellation, when the group was invited to see who would invite them to stand as a representative, a Disneyland scene began to evolve:

I stand for the butterfly.
I stand for the baby fawn.
I stand for the swan.
I stand for the sunshine.
I stand for the rainbow.
Each representative took their place in the Circle, experiencing the field of the being which had invited them and began an idyllic dance. Before long, the representative for the baby fawn began to look fearful, and began shaking.
I approached the fawn and asked, "What is happening for you?"

The representative for the fawn, shaking, pointed at another representative, someone who was standing for some lovely aspect of nature. There, on the back of his T-shirt was a scene of a wolf pack.

The field had inserted the predator.

It has become evident in working with Nature in many aspects of the constellation field that Mother Earth- "terra firma" is always solid. If you set up a nature constellation and the representative for the Earth is upset or weak, this represents the geopolitical or local ecological aspect of the Earth…it is just the soil, not The Earth. Geological time and the ability of the Earth to repair herself are deep and old; the blood of the historical conflicts does not trickle far into the core. If a facilitator has the Mother Earth or "place" begin to fall to the ground, the contrast is seen when "terra firma"- the Great Mother Earth is placed beside the less stable representative of the Earth or a place. This coincides with the concept of "Gaia." The most jarring definition of Gaia supposes that we are like lice on the body of the living Earth. Maybe a little extreme. But it is good to remember that she does survive without us, but not we without her. Many species have come and gone. In fact, by some estimates 99% of all species which have inhabited the Earth have become extinct. (Walsh, Bruce, 1995) The Earth is stable. Nature Constellations provide a gentle introduction to humility.

Including Nature in constellation, both as resource and topic brings a hope that Constellation work may be one vehicle which truly provides a new and valuable tool in understanding some of the environmental compromises which exist today.

The world over, many farmers, bee-keepers, environmentalists, and conscious citizens are aware and concerned that the honey bee is in decline. In one "Community Nature Constellation" one possible component of the decline was revealed through constellation. In the Community Nature Constellation, each person present is encouraged to go within and listen to see if any being in Nature asks one to stand on its' behalf; does the being "give permission" to be represented in the constellation? Only when one is invited by a particular element does one stand and state, "I stand for Crane." …"I stand for wolf." I stand for Dragon Fly."

The listening, and waiting for permission is fundamental in this constellation. It is quite different from being "assigned" a role or "taking" a representation. This journey is by agreement. It is a conversation between the representative and the element of nature, as well as a gateway to understanding in the group.

To illustrate the potential of this type of constellation the following is a brief summary of a Group Nature Constellation which was done in a coastal community. A variety of other beings were represented in the collective constellation, but of exquisite interest was this particular component of the group movement:

After inviting all in the Circle to a time of silence and open listening one representative felt invited to represent a particular bush in the area.

Another representative felt invited to represent a bee.

As a facilitator I became nervous because no one felt drawn to represent a flower. I asked the bee representative…"Do you need a flower?"

The representative for the bee said, "No, I am very strong when I stand by this bush."

When we closed the constellation I shared that we do not always understand everything in a Nature Constellation. I shared that I did not understand why the bee did not need a flower and felt so secure beside the particular bush.

Of course- it just happened that someone in the circle was a biologist with a specialty in botany. He said he was astounded and absolutely understood. He explained to us that the bush was native to the area and was quickly disappearing. You cannot find the bush at any commercial plant nursery because it is considered unattractive. Further, most landscapers remove the bush if it is standing on a construction development site. So, as a "weed-tree" this bush is becoming very rare in the area.

What he further explained was that this particular bush has the highest protein content of any plant in the area, so in the spring when the bees are beginning to come to life in this cold area, they can quickly find the most efficient fuel through this bush. The constellation showed that the bee needs this bush. The local extraction of this necessary nutrition for the bees is certainly not happening with any questions regarding what the ripple effect may be in the greater ecosystem.

As a result of this constellation experience, in advance of facilitating a Nature Constellation I now solicit group agreement that we waive confidentiality for the constellation in the event there is anything which occurs which would have public benefit or provide a valuable insight that should be more widely shared.

There are a host of other constellations through which tremendous insight can be gained in regard to Nature: looking at re-forestation, bug infestations, the development of utilizing green spaces in architecture, among them.

Providing constellations which help clarify the systemic dynamics of community or environmental issues involving nature has become a pragmatic possibility which can support architects, community development projects and conscious communities wanting to know how they can best support nature, and how they can construct communities in a way which integrates elements of the natural world into every day ways of living.

Nature Constellations can teach us and remind us in regard to nature and communities and ourselves. As Gregory Cajete, author of Native Science: Natural Laws of Interdependence writes:

Learning from nature directly moves us beyond the everyday, socially conditioned flow of life in which we are immersed in our homes and malls. The "mediated pulse," that window through which we know nature today, is largely only a fantasy created through words and images describing nature. Only by truly touching the Earth can we honor and enable the vision and action necessary to recapture the feeling and understanding that we have always been a part of a living and "conscious" Earth. (Cajete, G.,2000, p. 289)

Nature Constellations and the placement of aspects of nature in family constellation provide a path to connecting with nature, and a vastness of support that was all but forgotten in the rush to become modern mankind. Supported by our own Universal indigenous field, (from where ever that comes), and walking with respect and care, this application of the work proves to have a healing impact for participants in constellation work. When Nature is included, within the safety of the Constellation container, we again remember what it is to be in conversation with Nature, and each other, with all our hearts.

Bibliography

Cajete, Gregory. Native Science: Natural Laws of Interdependence, Clear Light Publications, Santa Fe, New Mexico, 2000.

Harney, Corbin. The Nature Way: Wisdom from a Western Shoshone Elder, University of Nevada Press, Reno, Nevada, 2009.

Page, Lisa A., Keith J. Petrie, Simon C. Wessely. Psychosocial responses to environmental incidents: A review and a proposed typology. *Journal of Psychosomatic Research* 60 (2006) 413– 422.

St. Just, Anngwyn. Relative Balance in an Unstable World: A Search for New Models for Trauma Education and Recovery, Carl-Auer, Heidelberg, Germany, 2006.

Walsh, Bruce. University of Arizona Syllabus, 1995., Department of Ecology and Evolutionary Biology.

Sneh Victoria Schnabel. Internationally known constellation facilitator, trainer and conference speaker. Faculty member of the annual International Training Intensive in Bernried, Germany. Co-creator and creative director of three conferences on constellation work and spirituality. Creator and director of the School of The Path Less Traveled. Published article: Chaos-Constellations in The Knowing Field magazine, and others. Co-author of the German constellation book: Derselbe Wind Läßt Viele Drachen Steigen.

She holds a B.A. in Art and Art History, and has seven years experience teaching and counseling in high school. She co-directed and acted in an experimental theater, and did three years pro-bono work counseling in prison.

During the 1980s, she spent time in India, three years in Italy and one year in the United States training in breath-awareness and other therapies. During her stay in Italy, she lived and worked in a meditation and therapy center in the hills of Tuscany.

In 1993, she met Bert Hellinger, with whom she learned constellation work.

Her current work interests include rituals, "coyote medicine," and chaos constellations.

She enjoys organic gardening, gathering wild herbs, creating wall paintings, and watching movies with her American husband who is also the organizer of her work, and with whom she lives in Freiburg, Germany.

Website: www.victoria-schnabel.com

CHAPTER TWO

Talking Trees, Whispering Rocks

by Sneh Victoria Schnabel

In the Beginning...

I had the good fortune to grow up at the edge of a small city with plenty of sloping fields and a mountain that was the beginning of many walks into Germany's Black Forest. Its hillside was wooded with old and gnarled trees providing a great invitation to climb high out of sight of the occasional passerby. These ancient trees had mysterious hollows and caves at their roots, seemingly leading straight into the fairylands where elves and Hobbits reside, who many times, I swear, I saw disappear out of the corner of my eye!

Another of my many childhood's gifts was that both my parents believed nature to be a good place for a child to be; my mother trusted my natural instincts to bring me home when hungry! That meant a big dose of freedom and much time for expeditions into the wild behind the house.

Growing older, with the new influences of school and homework, television and boys, my time spent in the woods behind the house grew shorter. And yet, whenever I needed time to be alone, to find safety in the turmoil of my growing into womanhood, I looked to nature: to find the rock or tree to lean against, and to feel home again. Nature had become a reliable resource whenever I was in need.

The Butterfly Experience

In my work as a counselor and constellation facilitator, I believe that who we are ultimately attracts the people to whom we can be of help. And so I trust that the people who come to my workshops and trainings are open to the idea of nature providing powerful resources, and are therefore willing to expose themselves to nature, to wind and weather.

But before I ever considered doing constellations outdoors, I received powerful help from nature itself. For quite a while, I had used representatives to stand in for a mountain, a landscape or whatever appeared to be important in a client's narrative, but it took a real encounter with nature before I started to uncover the strength and magic of nature when it is present in person. And the following is how I remember it to have happened.

I was in Italy leading a four-day section of a training outdoors under the roof of an open tent. As I was working with a mother who was worried about her teenage son, unexpected help came from nature itself. The constellation seemed to go well, with the representative for the young man finding a good place in the constellation and feeling well. But the representative for the mother still felt uneasy and not quite trusting the situation, which (again) had a diminishing and negative influence on the son. Even after an exchange where a representative of her grandmother, together with a son who died as a child, had given their blessings to the present mother and son, the energy in the field seemed not totally restored, and the real mother seated beside me still looked worried.

I did not know what she would need, so asked her to take her place in the constellation, hoping that some miracle would happen. And it did, in the form of a bright yellow butterfly, appearing out of nowhere and starting to circle around her. When she became aware of it, she let out a surprised little sound and then started to cry softly. We all waited, sensing something was shifting with the tears, and watched the butterfly settle down on the woman's right shoulder. After the butterfly left, she told us how this same kind of butterfly had danced around her at a time when she was pregnant with her son and very fearful that something bad might happen to the baby. When the butterfly finally settled on her right shoulder, she knew that all would be well with the birth. And so it happened that her son was healthy. And now this same kind of butterfly had come again in a time of trouble; she took it as sign and finally relaxed.

During this ongoing group, we had more helpful encounters with the flying kind. One time it was a bee which seemed to be crawling straight for the feet of a barefooted representative, who then stopped in her tracks. The person whose constellation it was, witnessing this, decided to slow down a project she was working on and had wanted insight into its dynamics. When I later met her at another section of the training, she told me that the slowing-down actually had helped the project to move in another and much better direction.

Another great moment was witnessed by me in a break, when a bird dropped a little gift right on my head. This happened after I felt especially smug about an intervention I had just done earlier that had left me feeling rather half-enlightened.

And all the while as we were working under the tent, the fir trees around us provided us with moments of simply listening to the wind and hearing the quiet. Later, much later, I was to use that memory and have participants actively listen to trees representing their voice.

Outdoor Constellations: The Framework, The Structure and The Resource of Stepping-In-And-Out

Once a year, in each of my trainings, I take the group for a week long retreat into the mountains of the Black Forest. There, we are free to work either inside the house or outdoors. Nature and the elements are all around us, a constant inspiration to be included in the work.

When working outdoors, we need to switch from our fast-paced daily life of doing, to one of slowing down and being. Silence is oftentimes the key to this; therefore, I advise the group to walk in silence to our chosen clearing in the woods.

I had come across a particular place in the forest on my first morning at this seminar center, and it later became the home of many summers workshops and retreats. I was alone; the group would not arrive until afternoon, so I had ample time to walk and to explore. Soon I had left the established paths and went inside the woods by following a pair of buzzards that circled above me. They were hidden from sight by the dense foliage of the treetops, but they were in constant communication with one another through their distinctive cries. I followed them by ear, and when I was finally able to see them, they circled a long time above my head. I had come to a little hidden clearing, a perfect place in which to do our work.

When I was leading the first group to this place, the two buzzards appeared again and we all felt blessed by them, and ready to enter a different and quite magical world. In the opening ceremony we addressed these magnificent birds, telling them about our work and thanking them for their appearance. We promised to be respectful towards their home.

On our way back to the house after the work was done, we found a feather on our path, a gift that was not there before. This feather, I keep to this day as a reminder that nature will guide you, if you are ready to follow.

From then on, whenever I bring a group to this magical place, the first thing we do is stand in a circle. The silence will be broken only by the sounds of nature, until we begin to work.

I start with a ritual, perhaps bowing down to all the trees, and asking them to kindly help us in our learning. The ritual always follows the need of the moment. If the buzzards appear, they will be included; if our work will be with the rock-people, we talk to them. And always we will thank all that surrounds us, ask for protection and promise to give respect in return. Sometimes a song wants to happen, sometimes a story, or a prayer. The important thing for me is that we are constantly learning to become aware of what it is that needs to happen.

After that, I use a participant's issue as a demonstration of how to lead structured constellations with elements of nature as resources.

For this, I often choose the following structure:

• a person for the client's current focus

• a person for the goal that they hope to achieve

• a person for the block, or what stands in the way

• a person for the resource, in our case, something of nature: a rock, a plant, an animal, a tree

First, the whole group moves to the place where the resource is situated; they had taken time earlier to look for it. Next, the roles are distributed or volunteered by themselves, depending on the client's preference. Then, I start beating a drum, and the players set out to find their place. A drum, if used with care, can be a great device to help a person or a group to enter a mild waking trance in which it is easier to forget oneself, and enter roles and states beyond the boundaries of one's self.

The only role that has a designated place is the resource. The person representing it will go to where the chosen tree is located and will then, while touching it, become the voice for this resource. After the players have found their place, each one shares how they feel. There will be a second round of drumming, during which they can adjust or change positions, which is followed by another round of sharing. Should the emerging picture and the words be all that is needed for the client, we end the constellation, giving thanks to the tree, rock, or stream.

Sometimes more is needed, and if so, I continue, suggesting movements which I sense are needed. It sometimes can be as simple as adding another resource, or it might prove to be so complex that many steps are needed. If the situation is stuck, I use a procedure I know from my theater days, when breaking a role was the means to better grasp it. I tell the representatives to simply step out of their roles and move a few paces to the side. From there, as themselves, they look back at the place of the role they had just represented, remembering what it was that was missing. I will then ask them to find which one of their very own resources could be beneficial for the role. Some time is given while I beat the drum until they all are ready to step back in. The resulting constellation will be different this time, because they bring with them a gift: a resource from their own lives.

The movements that become possible now will change the whole gestalt, most of the time helping the stuck or frozen constellation to move forward in a healing way. As before, we end with the client thanking the tree, rock or stream.

Once the group has seen the demonstration, they will divide in groups of five and do the work amongst themselves. I will circulate, seeing where help is needed, and sometimes give an extra boost of drumming. They all had been encouraged weeks before to bring a drum or rattle to the woods to find out whether it helps them to do the work. After their first constellation, for which I suggest more-or-less thirty minutes, we meet again to talk about what happened, to clear up misunderstood information, and to find suggestions for how to proceed.

The work will then continue amongst themselves. The timing of the whole unit has proven to be more easily adjustable if a long lunch-break provides an extra hour for groups that need more time. When all are done, we take a good amount of time for sharing and for supervision questions.

(Systemic Structural Constellations - www.syst.info/english - were introduced by Mathias Varga von Kibéd and his wife, Insa Sparrer, in the early nineties. They created a rich choice of various formats that are very helpful in tackling difficult issues. I have taken the liberty to fit them to my own preferences, sometimes to a degree that their origins might not be recognizable! Nevertheless, I owe the inspiration for my own format to this wonderfully creative couple.)

Examples of Nature Constellations

In the following, I will present two examples from training groups, and two from open workshops.

A Tree's Answer: A Constellation for a Single Person in a Group of Trainees

One of the trainees, a woman of about thirty-eight years, wanted to understand what stood in the way of her having a lasting relationship. She always felt, after some months of honeymoon, she had become disillusioned, bored, destructive, and ruined the relationship. Several examples of this in her past showed the same pattern.

The first representative I had her choose was the voice for the nature resource, her tree. Then she chose someone for herself; someone for her goal; someone for the destruction. The whole group moved together with her to the tree which she had sought out. There, she presented herself to the tree, stated her issue again, and asked the tree to help her with her endeavor.

In this constellation, the person standing for the voice of the tree sat down on its prominent roots, the back against the trunk. The client's representative stood close to the tree, looking at destruction, which stood between her and the goal. When asked, she said, "All I can see is you. I do not even know I have a goal." The goal stood far away from the scene looking at the client and, when asked, said that she felt quite neutral. The person standing for destruction said, "I need to be here; I am important and this is all I know."

When the voice of the tree was asked for feedback, we could observe a struggle to find words. This is what the tree finally said, "It is not the right time!" Hearing this, the client started to cry softly, and said, "I do not know why, but to hear this is a great relief."

We agreed to stop the constellation here, and sat on the floor in a circle to see what needed to be talked about. During the sharing, the person standing for the goal said that she also felt relief when she heard the tree's answer and now felt really interested. Even though none of us had any idea what the deeper meaning of the fir tree's answer was, we all could feel the truth of it.

At a conference five years later, I met the woman again. She was in the company of a friendly-looking man whom she introduced as her partner of four years. And she told me how she had come to understand the tree's answer: On one of her visits home, she told her mother about the constellation, and how puzzling and, at the same time, calming the tree's answer had been. At that, her mother exclaimed, "This makes a lot of sense! Your grandmother at age eighteen had lost her mother, your great-grandmother, to sickness. This mother asked her daughter, your grandmother, on her deathbed to take care of her two younger sisters and to not marry herself, not until the two younger sisters had found husbands. Fortunately, after quite a long time, they did get married. Your grandmother had to wait all that time, and finally got married herself at age forty-three, which in those days was considered very late."

The former trainee had found the man she was now with a year after her constellation, at age forty-three. It was the right time.

Grandfather's Way

The trainee who presented his issue was a middle-aged man who owned a small company; having to make decisions was required of him on a daily basis. He was currently experiencing a time in which he felt rather stuck. He described it as not knowing how to make any decisions and was rather afraid that if he continued this road, that he would seriously harm his company.

His constellation happened at a place where a big solitary rock provided a platform big enough for a person to stretch out upon it. The players that he needed were: the goal (comfortable making decisions); his focus; the block (difficulty with making decisions); and the voice of his resource (the rock).

The roles of the latter two were given to women; both the goal and the focus were represented by men, the focus being the youngest man in the group, and the goal the oldest one. Later on, this proved (as it often does) exactly fitting, but at this early stage he could not have been aware of it.

During the drumming period, the goal (comfortable making decisions) placed itself at a great distance, always looking at the focus, who had placed himself close to the rock, following the block (difficulty with making decisions) with his eyes. The block moved around without being able to stand still, restless and as in search of something. The voice of the rock was laying belly-down, one ear close to the rock.

And this is what was communicated:

• the goal was genuinely interested in the focus, but felt held back

• the block experienced herself as being very unstable, in need of something, and with a longing to finally come to a stop

• the focus, feeling small and helpless, was mesmerized by the movements of the block

• the voice of the rock, asked last, said, "Do it your grandfather's way!"

This last statement hit home, and the client needed extra time before being able to tell the group the following:

As a child, his grandfather would take him on cherished walks behind the house in nature. They would always rest at a certain rock formation, where, after sharing grandfather's wonderful sandwiches, they would sit close together and have those important talks about the nature of all things, how rocks and trees have grown and how to ask for a wish from a cloud. He remembered how much he loved the talks, but what he loved best was when it was finally the time for rock talk.

His grandfather had once shown him how to put his ear against the rock in order to listen for an answer, after having him voice an important question. He had talked to him about how the rocks know everything, they being the oldest people in the world! And if he were ever in trouble and needed help, they would listen and let him know what they think sometimes by planting a solution in his head.

While these memories were shared with the group, the block came to a halt, saying she was not needed anymore, and stepped out of her role. The focus now was able to see the goal and he felt himself growing small as a child. And, pointing at the goal, he said, "I know this one."

The client whispered that it was his grandfather. The representative of the goal agreed and smiled, opening both arms wide, and the focus, now a young boy, went for a hug, overwhelmed with feelings.

The client had tears in his eyes, and looked with tenderness as the boy turned to him from the arms of the grandfather. And now it was they being drawn to each other: the grown man and the small boy. During a long hug, they embraced, and arm-in-arm, they turned towards the grandfather and bowed down. The client thanked him for having been his beloved grandfather, who taught him so much. The grandfather replied, "I was, and always will be, watching over you, and you can always find me with the rocks."

Did the constellation end with a hug of the client, grandfather and boy? Did I do a little ritual to let the boy and man unite again to become one? I do not remember. But what I do remember is thinking that, in the future, I needed to bring more tissues with me! We ran out of them in those woods, because there was not one dry eye in the group.

Months later, at our next section of the training, the man told the group how he had started to go for walks again, mainly to a place where he had found listening-rocks almost as good as those of his childhood.

When we asked him how his decision-making had come along, he laughed and said that it was not really different on the outside, but a lot better on the inside. He also felt much more relaxed, and with this, he easily could live and take the proper time to make a good decision. A rock moves very slowly, he added. And we all agreed.

How Beautifully You Danced: A Constellation on Top Of a Tower

I had advertised a Constellations in Nature workshop for women around our city. We would go to a nearby park with great old trees, large meadows and a lake, and we would climb on top of a hill with a tower open to the public. The format of the workshop was such that on each of the 4 days, one of the four elements would be explored as resources in constellations.

Early one morning, we were climbing the hill with the tower in order to get a good experience of the morning mist and the wind. It was clear that whoever would like to have the element air as their resource would get a constellation. We climbed to the tower's platform, and stood in a circle for an opening ceremony, with a gentle wind blowing through our hair.

The participant, a middle-aged woman, came forward with her issue; she stated that the secret dream in her life was to dance, but that she did not feel able. Exploring the matter together, she told us that her father, when she was little, had ridiculed her every time she danced, telling her that she was too clumsy. Now, many years after his death, she still could feel the sting of his words. What she wished for was feeling the freedom to actually dance when she felt like dancing.

I let her stand in the middle of the circle, choose one person to represent 'the dance', and have the rest of the group stand with their hands held high. The hands began to dance with the wind, and soon voices could be heard, humming or singing along. In no time, the participant who stood for the dance started moving to this melody, and almost immediately, the client joined in the rhythm her body swaying with such delicate and yet strong flowing movements that we were all entranced by the sheer beauty of it.

In that moment, an old man who obviously liked the early morning hour as much as we did stood at the entrance of the platform, clearly surprised by what he found. Trusting my intuition I did not ask him to leave, but rather made some space so he could enter the circle. I whispered to him that we were doing a little celebration. The woman in the middle had not seen the old man arrive as she was dancing with her eyes closed.

When her dancing came to an end, she stood with her body facing in the old man's direction. The singing had stopped and she had opened her eyes, and the man, clearly touched, made a little bow in her direction, saying with a shaken voice, "How beautifully you danced! Thank you that I was allowed to watch. I wish you all a happy celebration." Then he bowed to us all, and left.

During the sharing, the women told her what they felt the wind, the air, would want for her: to keep dancing, to make dance her home, that dance was her way of expressing herself. One of the women said, "I'll bet that your father, wherever he is now is happy. This old man came in his place!" And the woman herself, with a radiant smile, said, "Maybe I have permission now."

Even though I have not heard from her in all these years, in my mind's eye, I see her taking every opportunity to dance.

One other thing about that day that I will never forget: not only she, but the whole group, looked transformed. On the way back to the center of town, the women all walked with the flowing grace of dancers, and all with heads held high.

The Bird on the Water: A Constellation in the Park

The following account of a constellation is not complete. I do not remember the details, not even what the issue of this young woman was, but the circumstances that carried the teaching are worth being shared.

I had brought the group to one of our city parks which had a good-sized lake. The shoreline in some places is curved in ways that form a gentle creek. Such a place was the background for our work. If I remember correctly, we were exploring water as resource. We stood right at the edge of it, with someone standing barefoot in the water, to catch the information. While I was drumming, something floated around the corner and was carried into view. It looked like some sort of debris, perhaps some tangle of leaves and twigs. Suddenly, a current underneath turned it. We all gasped in shock. What had come into view was a dead bird, floating on the water, with its wings spread wide.

This is not exactly what I, or anyone else, had envisioned to be a resource! One young woman was much shaken, and, with tears streaming down her face told us that her father had drowned in the ocean. She was only seventeen years old at the time and felt very left alone and forsaken. "Just when I needed him the most, he was suddenly gone!" She also said that she was aware how much she, after all these years, still held the pain (and shock) inside her body, heart and mind.

I stood immediately behind her while she talked. When she had finished, I felt her back, as if by chance, touching me. I stayed where I was and, looking over her shoulder to the water, we both watched the dead black bird spread out on the water. It seemed to rest in utter peace, being gently swayed by the small ripples. I asked her what she saw. He looks so peaceful, is what she said. I pondered aloud that fathers who are no longer present in their body might find other ways to signal to their daughters that they are at peace and that she, too, may be allowed to find her peace with missing him. I felt her weight relax against me a bit more, tears still running. We stood quietly for some time, together with the group until, with a deep sigh of relief she moved a step ahead and waved at the bird, which by now was gently drifting towards the other shore.

Thoughts and Insights

The experience of leading nature constellations, and seeing the outcome of them all unfold, has taught me to continue on this path. Therefore, whenever there is an opportunity, I will take my group outdoors. And it is amazing how many of them appear, once we allow the opportunities to guide the way. A forgotten key to the workshop room can lead to a splendid morning with the trees in the park; the sudden opening of the clouds after many days of rain can inspire a whole group to go outside and do a constellation with the sun.

Today, looking back at my experience with constellations done outdoors, I know, while leading them, my own constellations have happened alongside those that I have led. They have helped me to again find that precious part inside of me that always knew that a tree can talk if you listen to it; a rock is alive but moves very slowly; the wind knows your name wherever you go; and that stretching out on the grass can make one feel at home and whole.

And the elves and Hobbits? The other day I swear I saw them disappear again out of the corner of my eye!

Daan van Kampenhout, born 1963, studied with teachers from various cultures. His most important shamanic teachers were of the Lakota, Southern Ute and Sami. Daan's shamanic teachings have been developed over 20 years of teaching experience in many different countries and cultures, and are based on the wheel of the four directions and the guidance that comes through dreams. He is the author of seven books about shamanism and his work has been translated into ten languages.

Website: www.daanvankampenhout.com

CHAPTER THREE

The Queer Breath of the Universe Reclaiming Membership in Earth Community for Gay, Bi and Transgender Men

by Daan van Kampenhout

Systemic work comes in a variety of different forms. What makes all of them systemic is that they all see an individual as an interactive part of a larger system. How such a larger system is defined will depend on the paradigms on which the systemic method is based or is determined by the purpose of the session done: it can be a nuclear family, an extended family, a group of colleagues, a religious group, a social class or something else. The method and the facilitator who offers it are also influenced by the larger systems they are part of, since these two together embody all kinds of ideas and values of the culture(s) to which they belong. Each culture is based on paradigms which may be seen as universal but in fact are cultural: each culture has very distinct assumptions about reality and about (what is considered) the natural order of things.

Something that is seen as right and sane in one culture can be considered strange in another and even be violently rejected and repressed in yet another. Cultures, nations and tribes vary considerably in their conscious and unconscious attitudes towards all facets of life. An individual belonging to any given culture's mainstream group (which is usually the largest, the most powerful and the most influential) will usually be able to identify completely with the general cultural rules and ideas. Those who belong to one of the minority groups within the larger culture will however find themselves in a less straightforward position. Any given minority has its own separate group identity, which comes with its own codes and behavior, and each minority has its own ideas about what is right and wrong, about what is normal and what should be seen as deviant. Still, the mainstream will dictate many or most aspects of the lives of those who belong to minorities. Those who belong to a minority must by necessity internalize thoughts, behaviors and codes which come from the dominant culture, otherwise they could not function in the larger society and would not be tolerated. Even when a minority does not choose to participate fully in the mainstream culture or is denied the right and possibility to do so, a certain amount of unconscious internalization of the ideas of the majority will always take place, and this creates a specific tension in the soul.

In Systemic Ritual, the method I have developed over the years, aspects of this tension can be made visible and some options for a better balance can be offered to the individual. The method is based on elements of family constellations and shamanic teachings. I started studying shamanism in the early eighties of the last century, and more than 20 years ago I started my personal studies with shamanic healers and ceremonial leaders from the Lakota and the Southern Ute (USA), the Sami (Europe) and others. In 1998 Bert Hellinger became an important source of inspiration during the last phase of the development of what are now often called "classical family constellations" (up to 2001). Having a mixed Jewish/non-Jewish background myself, Judaism also influenced me and I was especially touched by reb Zalman Schachter, a hassidic rebbe. Almost all of my most important teachers come from minorities with a history of exclusion, persecution and genocide. All of them had a direct or indirect influence on the creation of Systemic Ritual.

As I mentioned earlier, various kinds of systemic work all have their own flavor. Systemic Ritual brings awareness of some of the complex and often unconscious victim-perpetrator dynamics that are related to majority-minority dynamics, and gives the individual a larger perspective in which his/her personal story can be recognized as a manifestation of a larger, tribal or cultural dynamic. As soon as the personal can be seen as interwoven with an archaic process, the details of the story become less important. Support and healing can then be found in the embrace of precisely set up archaic images of balance and wholeness.

Each minority faces its own particular challenges. Each group has its own history and its own inner tensions that are the result of historical events that have left their mark on the collective memory and of internalized mainstream opinions and behaviors. The minority that I would like to focus on in this writing is the group of queer people, which consists of gays, lesbians, bisexuals and transgenders. Queers have one thing in common that sets them apart from the people belonging to most other minorities. When you are born black in a western country, you have black parents or at least a black single mother who, like you, is black in a predominantly white world. You know you are black and you know where you come from. A child born in a Christian family in a Muslim country will learn what it means to be Christian in the Islamic world from it's parents. The child knows "I am a Christian". In these examples family members function as role models for the young, role models who know what it means to be member of a specific minority. But when a boy is gay, he grows up in a family that is straight. True, nowadays there are some exceptions to this rule, but they are really very few. A girl who finds out she is transgender only rarely finds a positive role model in her family. Queers typically have to go through a very personal and often lonely process of gradually recognizing that they are somehow very different from the rest of their family and environment. In their family, they hear no words and see no examples about who they are.

If you, reader, are straight, then imagine for a moment growing up in a world where everybody and everything is queer. You have two mothers who are lesbians, a biological father who donated his sperm, he is gay. Your doctor is a transsexual, your school teachers are lesbians, the members of the national football teams are lesbians and bisexual women. In this world, the few male football teams are not taken very seriously. Your hairdresser, ballet teacher and stylist, of course, are gay. All your friends in school are gay, lesbian or transgenders. All movies, all TV series, each book you read, each pop song, each advertisement for coffee or a new washing powder reflects the themes, issues, dynamics, seductions and challenges of the queer world. Try and imagine this for a while. And then, while you are growing up in this world where nobody would even consider you being something else than queer, it gradually dawns on you that this is somehow not true for you. Mysteriously you feel at home in your own male or female body, you are not transgender. And, much more radical: you are attracted to the opposite sex, so you can not be lesbian or gay! But how to get clear about such feelings when the culture does not offer you any functional role model? Maybe in some TV show there is one straight person, acting as a laughable sidekick, not to be taken serious in any way. That can not offer you a real point of reference. Certainly you are not like that person. Maybe you are not even aware of the words "straight" or "heterosexual", or if you did, they have no helpful meaning for you. How to see yourself? How to define yourself? How to value yourself when the culture seems to have no place and no words for that what you are? This is a challenge for any child or teenager. Consider for a moment that just one generation ago in the western world queers did not even have a normal language to describe their own reality to themselves, the only words that were known to them were coming from the world of psychopathology which described them as ill, or the words were insults, meant only to be used in a demeaning and shaming way. Each minority integrates ideas and opinions from the mainstream. Queers start out not even knowing they are part of a minority, and have to face their "otherness" on their own without support. For them this dynamic of internalization of the mainstream's rejection of many or all things queer is particularly present.

The term "coming out" describes the end result of a process of self defining, the final step in taking on a new identity, the choice to become recognizable as a member of one of the queer minorities. Earlier I have mentioned that each culture has its own history, its own ideas, its own definitions of what identity is or should be. "Coming out" is a process that queers go through in most of the western world, which is a world in which the influence of Christianity is still strong. The monotheistic religions have a world view in which queers have no place, and the more orthodox its members are the more aggressive their attitude towards queers is. When there is just one single god, there can be just one way, one model. Cultures whose images of the divine and the forces or creation are pluriform and multi-faceted usually have a much larger tolerance for otherness. So, is "coming out" a universal process? In many parts of the non-western world, the coming out process does not exist. For various reasons. In most of the Islamic and African world it is not an option because to be recognized as queer means to be ostracized or, more likely, to be killed. No coming out process there, obviously. Elsewhere there is no coming out because it simply is not really necessary. There are cultures that have their own words, names, places and roles for queers. Those cultures, on the world scale, are themselves minorities. But many first nation cultures in for example Polynesia, Siberia and North America and many cultures in Asia see queers as part of the system and have names and places for them. There, they are not seen as mistakes, they are part of the natural order, bringing a gift to the community at large, just like all other members bring their gifts to the circle to make it complete. A queer child in Uganda and many other places on this planet can not really permit himself to ask the question who he is, since to know the answer is far too risky. Youngsters in some first nation and Asian cultures simply do not need to ask themselves this question, they know who they are and have a place in their society.

In the western world, the essential question for queers is: "Am I part of the natural order, or am I some kind of mistake?" Science can provide the answer. It is: "Yes, you do belong, you are part of the natural world." The zoo in Amsterdam has a yearly project during gay pride week. People can listen to a lecture, get a tour through the zoo and then have lunch together. The zoo provides the basic facts: "Homosexuality does not limit itself to just the sexual act. Animals seduce members of their own gender and sometimes raise young together. Homosexuality in the animal kingdom has been registered for 1500 species of birds and mammals." People who would like to know more can read Biological Exuberance: Animal Homosexuality and Natural Diversity by Bruce Bagemihl. In this study hundreds of animal species are presented with fascinating details, all information coming from scientific research about the ways they choose partners, mate, have sex and raise their young. The completely straight model is really less prevalent in nature than the biology lessons in school have told you.

But even when nature itself says "Yes, you belong," mainstream western culture does not agree easily. I visited some websites on which the yearly program of the Amsterdam Zoo is presented and I checked the responses. The majority of posts that can be found on these websites are negative. The word "unnecessary" shows up often, and in the light of the rest of responses it should be considered a friendly term. "Gays are rich enough to afford this tour because they have no children and they both work". Prejudice is at work here, but it is not a direct attack, not yet. Many people express denial ("For animals it is not sexual, it is just affection") Others are convinced that the tour in the Zoo is a manifestation of the "totalitarian homo regime under which Amsterdam is living." This is already more aggressive in tone but still is considered friendly enough to keep it on the site. Many other posts had to be removed, because they were considered offensive. All except one or two posts express irritation, unease, denial and/or anger. The current political support from some parties for queers and their rights is historically a very recent phenomenon, socially and historically it is still too new for it to be truly integrated in the western collective. Not so deep down, western culture does not yet see queers as truly belonging.

Each Systemic Ritual that I have developed over the years is always determined by the precise needs and challenges of the client in relation to the group, culture, sub-culture or minority they belong to. The Systemic Ritual I would like to describe now was developed specifically for queers. It addresses the issue of belonging in several steps through meetings with successive groups of ancestors. I have offered this ritual to groups on several occasions, with slight variations dictated by the context and conditions in which I was working.

The version I will present now was offered to a group of about 30 gay, bisexual and transgender men. The voices of some of these men are added to the description. The ground plan used for the ritual was simple: seven rows of people standing behind each other, all facing the same direction. Row 1 looked away from the rows behind them, row two looked over the shoulders of row 1 etc. Each row had about four to six men in it.

<pre>
          00000
          0000
          00000
          0000
          00000
          0000
          000000
</pre>

In the first row stood the men who represented themselves and the queers of today, in the western world.

In the second row stood the men who represented the queers belonging to the families of those in row 1. These were the queers of the recent few generations, some of them known, some of them suspected to be queer, but most of the people represented in this row would have lived lives in which their queerness was hidden or suppressed. Some exceptions may have been there though.

In the third row stood the ancestors of the men in rows 1 and 2: queers who have been living in western (or monotheistic) culture throughout time. Most of them will have been leading hidden lives, some will have committed suicide, some have been hanged or burned because they were queer. There will also have been some who managed to find some kind of balance or happiness.

The men in the fourth row represented the queers of the human family throughout time, of cultures in which queerness was seen as a variety of the natural order, belonging to and wanted by creation, including the pre-Christian earth oriented cultures of Europe.

In row 5 the men represented queers of the animal kingdom, in all their many different manifestations.

In the 6th row the men represented the queer element of the earth itself. So many animal species know forms of queerness, so queerness must be an intrinsic part of the natural order which has created all these variations.

In the last row, the men represented "the queer breath of the universe". This is the life giving element that has made the earth possible, and most likely also many planets with other life forms throughout the universe. And since the earth has so many forms of queerness build into the sexuality of its children, the animals, it is likely that in places where other life forms exist there will be yet more versions of queerness. The "queer breath of the universe" is the parent of them all.

After explaining the setup of the seven rows, I let the men who were participating choose in which row they wanted to stand. Soon the seven rows were in position. At the start of the ritual none of the men in any given row could look the men in other rows in the eye, since they were all looking in the same direction. They could see just the back of the heads of the men in the row in front of them. After a moment of centering and concentration, I asked the men in the first row to repeat out loud a few sentences that I gave them. "We are the queers living today, living in the western world that has started to recognize our rights but is often still uneasy with us. Some of us enjoy the freedom we now have, for others there are still restrictions of all kinds. We are the queers of this time, this culture." After saying this, and after giving them a bit of time to let the words sink in, I asked them so slowly turn and face those in the row behind them: their queer relatives of the last few generations. To the men in the second row I suggested the repetition of lines like: "We are the queers of the generations that came before you. We are your uncles, aunts, fathers, grandfathers, grandmothers, great uncles and others. Some of us could find a way to embrace our queerness. Some of us did not know how to, or were not allowed to embrace it. Some of us lived in shame, fearing to be found out. Some of us stepped out of life because we could not face ourselves. Some of us found happiness. We are those who came before you, of the recent generations. Look at us now, as we look at you. You belong to us, as we belong to you. Come to us. We are your ancestors."

It is hard to describe what happens in a ritual like this after sentences like these are spoken. Each participant is going through an individual process, in each meeting between two pairs of eyes something different happens. Slowly, without further words, tentative steps are taken. Hands reach out, an embrace happens. Feelings and images of the representatives themselves or belonging to those they represent make themselves felt. Often, in the start of the ritual, when the first few rows meet, memories of family members and of recent history come up.

"My thoughts drifted to my father who passed away today exactly seven years before. I am sure, he was gay or at least bisexual and - as far as I know - never did live it. And if he wouldn't have married my mom, would I be here at all or would I have be born elsewhere? Did he sacrifice a part of himself for me and my siblings?"

"I was in row two, representing the relatives of those in row one who could not express their queerness in the times they lived in. A sudden thought came into my head and I decided to 'be' the uncle of the man directly in front of me. When the men in row one were asked to turn around, I saw this man looking at me with tears in his eyes. After the ritual he told me that in fact he had been thinking of his uncle when he looked at me – an uncle who was gay, something the family knew but did not talk about."

"You know, I don't believe much in a world ghost or whatever, neither in a queer spirit. I decided very clearly to be in the first row because it felt right to meet my uncle and also all the

gays that lost their lives in concentration camp Mittelbau-Dora. Two different stories, but of the same generation. In the real Mittelbau-Dora I once had the opportunity to participate in a meeting of gay historians and sociologists. I learned that especially in that place many gays lost their lives. There I had first the feeling of 'these men are my ancestors'. And now, in this ritual, it was the time for a meeting with them."

The first and second rows gradually mingled and became one single row. Then I asked the men who had originally been in row 1 to say to those who had made up row 2: "Turn around, and together with us look at those who stand behind you." The men who had been in the second row turned, and together they faced the men in the third row. The men in row 3 spoke. "We are those who came before you. We are the queers of western and monotheistic culture throughout the ages. A few of us found happiness, others found only shame. Some were killed, others ridiculed, most of us lived our lives in the shadows. Some of us found creative solutions that allowed us to be true to our nature, some of us never found a way to live our queerness, not even for a single moment. Look at us now, as we look to you. You belong to us, as we belong to you. Come to us now, we are you ancestors."

"I was standing in row two, part of the generations just before us. When the first row turned to us I was deeply touched. I thought: At last! At last they turn, they look at us, they see us! It felt to me that this was an important step for them and it touched me. When all of us together turned to row 3, the queer ancestors of the western world, I was suddenly in the position of the younger ones who finally turned to see who came before them. I was deeply touched to be welcomed and embraced in all of my queerness by the older generations."

All kind of silent interactions followed between the men who had turned and the men of row 3. And again, after a while, a new row had formed in which all three first rows were integrated. Then those who had been part of row 1 and 2 spoke to those of row 3: "Turn, and look with us to those who came before us. Let us look at our ancestors together." The men in row 4 said: "We are those who came before you, we are the queers of mankind who were welcomed. Many of us knew joy and acceptance. We are black, yellow, brown, red, and white. We may have been outcasts in some places, but we were also given places elsewhere, in some places we were sacred. We were ridiculed or killed here, but we were honored and dignified elsewhere. We are all of this. You belong to us, as we belong to you. Come to us, we are your ancestors."

"I stood in the line where we embodied the energy of tribal ancestors. It felt so beautiful to stand in that energy, to be bathed in an energy that was timeless and had no conception of right or wrong, just a sense of Being, standing in love. I felt as if I were a Native American, with no shame, no pride either, but complete, unquestioning self acceptance, and acceptance of others."

Again a process of turning, looking, recognizing, being welcomed. The looking, holding, embracing, crying and laughing happened each time another row had formed that then turned to face the next. In one meeting between two individuals sadness was felt, in another shame had to be overcome, in yet another pride and joy stood out. With each meeting between the rows, the group that faced the older ones grew bigger as row after row integrated in the group that slowly moved to be taken in by the queer breath of the universe.

"We are the animals who know their own versions of queerness. We are older than you humans. You are our younger relatives, we are your ancestors. We are part of nature, as you are. Come to us, you belong to us."

"We embody the queer spirits of the earth itself. Animals, humans, all of you are younger than us. We are your true ancestors, you are there because we have been here from the very beginning. Come to us now, take strength from us, we hold all of you. We are your ancestors."

"I am the oldest. I am the queer breath of the universe that moves through each and every one of you. Before the beginning, I was there already. After the end I will still be there. Each of you is my child – now let me hold you. Rest in my embrace. Let me breathe through you. I am the oldest, your true ancestor – I am the queer breath of the universe."

At the end of the ritual, all men formed a single entity, one breathing and humming organism. Each of them had made a very individual journey. For most, there was a deep sense of belonging, a relief, a merging into something larger that welcomed them strengthened their essence. For some, tears or tensions were there still. In a ritual like this, where historical wounds are touched that are as much individual as collective, it is not possible to dry each tear, to heal each wound. Generation after generation of hidden lives, and now suddenly openness, connectedness, a welcome. The soul can not always take in all of that so easily at once.

"I was participating at the ritual in the second row, representing the ancestors of the gays, queers, transgenders of today. As the first row addressed us and turned to look at us I felt a lot of shame, first not knowing where it resulted from. I couldn't look into the eyes of the ones in front of me, although I had the urge to do so. I had the strong feeling of representing a transgender woman hiding behind the walls of her little home, with little or no chance to get in contact with the world. As we all turned around to address the third row, I experienced for the first time a strong feeling of togetherness. A feeling of being united and, as often as we turned, the feeling became stronger and stronger until we were facing the last row. There was so much power there that I was afraid of it, I could not trust it yet – it was too big. I needed to hide behind all the others, in order not to be rejected again, for not being able to live the life I wanted to."

In the ritual, the men who participated could experience a welcome as queer beings. Different kinds of "ancestors" called them forwards, welcomed them to step into their world, layer after layer, until each one was permeated by the queer element of creation itself. In this structure, the question about belonging dissolves. "Belonging" is no longer an issue, no abstraction or puzzle. From an existential question it is transformed into a directly felt sense of knowing who one is, a sense of being part of something larger, of being a manifestation of a larger historical reality and a spiritual energetic continuum.

"The ritual was very impactful. Some months before it I had a long overdue conversation with a family member and calmly and clearly asserted the naturalness of my being gay. I said it from a deep space that I knew was also speaking to the part of me that still didn't accept this. The ritual took that realization of the naturalness of being queer to an even more profound level."

"I stood in the line of the earth. The moment the first of the seven rows turned, the tears started rolling over my cheeks. I had thoughts like "This is strange… Why would the old wise energy of the earth need to cry? It is probably a part of myself that is crying…" The crying repeated itself with each row that turned. It was coming from so deep that I started to sense it was really coming from the earth energy itself, from the part of the earth that I represented. When the row of the animals met the group of humans I was touched even deeper and I started to make a sound, a deep humming and grunting from joy coming from my center, my earth part. Simultaneously I was aware of the universal queer spirit behind me, I felt a

vibration coming from there – this vibration translated itself into the sound I was making. As if it was through me, the earth, that something could be made heard, could be made manifest that otherwise would have stayed in the silence, the unmanifest. In the last part of the ritual I was aware of an all encompassing connectedness, having access to and being a carrier of the wisdom of creation itself. I could sense that queers have their own part in that, we have a specific role to play, a function."

"The day after the ritual we took a silent walk, early in the morning when it was still dark outside. The man next to me pointed out a bright light in the dark sky and said 'Venus'. Then he pointed to another: 'Jupiter'. Right then, I had a most amazing experience. I felt with all my soul and all of my body that these two were a part of me and that I was part of them, nothing was separating us. There was no distance between me and the stars and planets, and no difference between our essence. I felt with my whole being the truth that the "queer breath of the universe" was inside me and that it was inside those planets too. It was this spirit that was uniting us. We come from the same source. It was not an abstract idea or insight but a kinesthetic knowing. Never before did I have his kind of direct, utterly simple and undivided experience, looking at the night sky."

"I was deeply affected when I could recognize that between feelings of being incomplete, being alone (as was represented by the group in front of me) and the feeling of being connected and being grounded in queerness (as was palpable in the rows behind me) there is just my own choice that determines where I stand. My blessings and love were there for the row that turned to face me, I could support them to be true to themselves, to be who they are. The row behind me carried me, held all the fear and loneliness, they absorbed me in the field of those whose queerness was an expression of their essence. I understood that I have the choice, that it is up to me in which row I will stand. And I can make that choice now, because I could feel both sides. I now stand side by side with those who are connected with the long tradition of living their gayness. I stand next to those who are committed from the depth of their hearts to live their sexuality, to live their life."

The silent voice of the universe is always whispering to its queer children. In dreams, visions and through rituals like this, its timeless message can be heard.

"You were there in the past. You are here now. Because of me, you will always be there in the future, however cultures may respond to you.
I have created you. You belong to me.
Stand in dignity."

PART II

Explorations

Berchthold Wasser is the married father of two daughters. For over twenty years he has been the owner and head of a small engineering office in Thun, Switzerland. Since finishing his studies as a forestry engineer at the ETH in Zürich, the forest has been his most important field of interest, especially protection of the forests of the European Alps.

"I grew up on a farm at the border of a stream close to the forest and enjoyed lots of freedom there. Nature has influenced me and my life directly and effortlessly. Studying forestry engineering was yet another step towards nature for me. And indeed, this career choice has enabled me to work in and for the forest for three decades."

"In my work I have developed a lot of interesting projects and solved challenging issues for forest owners in several Swiss cantons and especially for the federal environment agency ("Bundesamt für Umwelt") in Bern. The consulting service for forest rangers and administration is still my main work today. During my studies, I realized that we are able to answer a lot of questions using the traditional analytic scientific approach. However, in practice I have found that a strictly rational analytic approach often contributes more to the problem than provides solutions, because the "objectivity" disconnects what essentially belongs together. This realization led me to search for ways that bring things together versus separate them. My work with nature constellations is a direct result of that search."

E-Mail: wasser@naturdialog.ch

Website: www.naturdialog.ch

Offers: Training "Naturaufstellungen" in German
                         Seminars and Workshops
                         Consulting for relevant issues and questions.

CHAPTER FOUR

Experiencing Ecosystems

by Berchthold Wasser

Abstract: In nature constellations, we can see the unfolding of living systems. That which flows between people, animals, plants and landscapes becomes visible. We can see where this flow is interrupted and how to get it going again. Because of this, the method is perfectly suited for diagnosis and discovery of possible solutions concerning questions about ecosystems, as well as everywhere that humans are influencing their environment and it is influencing them.

Audience:

This method is well-suited to resolve problems encountered in all phases of projects involving ecosystems. Therefore it can be a useful tool for architects, building engineers, forest rangers, horticulturists, farmers, planners and nature conservation experts. It also offers great potential for those who deal with the impact of such projects, such as the responsible administration offices, private nature conservation organizations and other non-profit organizations.

Issues:

The range of meaningful applications of nature constellations is very broad and still not yet clearly defined. I will try to provide a sense of the possibilities by sketching a framework for possible questions and problems and then listing some examples.

A question or a problem is always located within a system. In nature constellations this is often an ecosystem, for example a forest, a certain landscape, or waters. Experience shows that nature constellations are also suited for systems that are predominantly influenced by humans, like a farm or a garden, or for partial systems, like the industrial area in a city or weeds in a garden. Relevant insights also reveal themselves in constellations at the intersection of naturally and humanly influenced systems, like questions about conflicts between farm and wild animals or about the meaning of plants for the health of humans. It is important that the relationships of the constellated elements, either through common experiences in the past or the present situation, are obvious and strong enough.

Generally it is possible to make a constellation for any of the mentioned systems, but I suggest nature constellations only if at least one of the persons present is connected with the system in a way that his or her actions have a significant direct influence on the system itself. For example, in a building project, if the project leader, the building owner, the responsible person in the administration department or a representative of the local environment organization is involved. Experimental constellations have demonstrated that this work can also be effective if the focus does not have direct and obvious influence on the system. Since the effects of such constellations still remain unclear and the danger of manipulating or leading the system in an already determined direction is high, I would advise not doing a constellation under these circumstances unless there is a special situation and even then to treat it as an experiment.

The intention can be very well-meant (for example: I want oil drilling in the deep sea to be forbidden). But in such a situation if no one involved in the constellation has a direct connection with the issue it has the feeling of an outside "director" which for me is diametrically opposed to the essence of nature constellations. That is, nature constellations for me are not about getting what I or some client "wants," but rather to look deeply together into what is happening in the system, including our part in it, and to see if there are options or alternatives for movement that come from within the system itself, not from outside it.

Examples of nature constellations about ecosystems:

- A valley is heavily damaged through a flood. This leads to an intense conflict between the residents who want a re-creation of the area as it previously was and an environmental conservation agency that wants to allow the natural dynamic of things to play out. The leader of the project is searching for a way that is ideal both for the residents and the biodiversity of the area (see case study 1)

- A student writes her master's thesis about her research into the physical and spiritual meaning of water in countries with a surplus and countries where water is scarce. She wants to test her research hypotheses through the help of a nature constellation (see case study 2).

- A garden becomes more and more shaded because of tree growth. Since there is less light for the humans and the plants there, the residents want to know which trees are very important for the overall quality of living – for them and for the garden - and which they can cut down.

- A re-naturation project for a river meets the resistance of many stakeholders and it is uncertain if the project will achieve the expected improvement for the biotop. The project leader wants to know what he should propose to do so that the impact on nature is positive and at the same time how a sustainable consensus of the stakeholders can be found.

- In a nesting box on a farm, house barn owls are gradually replaced by kestrels. The farmer's wife wants to know if and how it is possible for both bird species to keep the house as a nesting site.

Desired Outcomes for the Work:

Clarifying the Question. The focus of the constellation (for example the project leader) has to formulate his or her question as succinctly and clearly as possible. The introductory talk helps him or her to concentrate on the essence. Often the focus only discovers what the actual question is through this talk.

Change of Perspective. One of the greatest benefits of constellation work is the view of the focus from the outside, on the system in which one is embedded. Just this change of perspective leads to a shift as unrecognized, overlooked and overrated aspects become visible. And of course for each representative standing for some system element there can be a major change of perspective, especially when the person stands for some element of nature rather than some person or human group.

Diagnosis. A view on the movements of the system shows obstacles and blockages instantaneously. By small rearrangements it is possible to check which situation leads to a specific blockage, and which directions support softening. If this is used, for example, for project planning, consensus seeking and permit procedures can be considerably shortened.

Evaluation. Usually there are several possible variants for projects. With nature constellations it is possible to check the effects of the different variants on certain elements (example:

Impacts of certain hydraulic-engineering methods on a rare reptile species)

Solution Steps. The issue provided by the focus gives the system its direction. The dynamic in the constellation shows then if the system succeeds with this direction or which steps are needed for it to succeed. (Example, case study 1: Only after the environmental conservation agency takes its place and defends it is the project leader able to realize his actual function.)

How the Work is Done:

Seminars with Co-facilitation. Most of the nature constellations I facilitated so far have been in the context of seminars/workshops with eight to twenty participants. Usually I do this together with another facilitator, often Kenneth Sloan, also a contributor to this book. I experience the shared leadership as helpful in several respects. There is initially the mutual development of ideas and exercises during the preparation, the allocation of responsibilities during a constellation, the feedback from a second perspective and last but not least the mutual evaluation during the midday and evening breaks.

Nature Constellations on Request. When I get a request to facilitate a constellation outside of a workshop, I first clarify what it is about and ask myself only then if constellation work is the proper approach in this case. If a constellation is appropriate, I think about who and what it would need at the minimum. If it is an issue with a certain relation to a place, I try to do the constellation at that location. The direct relation to the place makes the involvement of the representatives with the real elements stronger and provides the possibility that spontaneous elements previously unobserved can show themselves. (Example: In a constellation concerning an old right-of-use on a farm, suddenly the farm dog enters the constellation and begins to dig inside of the circle at the feet of the representative for the municipal administration representative. Later, as the owner of the property effectively "dug out" the relevant original documentation he had never actually seen before, it turned out that the circumstances were quite different than asserted by a neighbor and the supposed problem was resolved.)

Procedure of Constellations. Important characteristics of nature constellations as I conduct them are:

The Represented Elements. We have not yet discovered elements that couldn't be embodied through representatives. There are no limitations concerning the attributes of the elements. One should take care that the elements are involved in the question, so that there is enough energy in the constellation itself.

Organizing Principles. Hierarchies, as we know them from man-made, human societies (and often transferred to other systems), are not, or only under certain circumstances, valid in nature constellation work! For facilitators of nature constellations it is always a challenge not to force their own preconceptions on the system they are working with. For example, whoever thinks he or she has a standpoint from which he or she can judge and decide about "good" and "evil" in natural systems should not in my opinion facilitate nature constellations.

Emphasis on the phenomenological approach. More than in family or organizational constellations, nature constellations follow what reveals itself from moment to moment. This is especially relevant for those moments when we as facilitators think that we know, based on former constellations or our preconceptions, which movements or adjustments should happen now. Because of the meticulous care taken in determining each step forward, nature constellations often last one or even two hours.

Outdoor Constellations. From the beginning I facilitated constellations outdoors, although many facilitators at that time (1999) had asserted that the energy level is too low outdoors and the influence and disturbances of the surroundings are too high. Needless to say, nature constellations can also be conducted inside. But constellations outdoors have the advantage that certain elements and energies appear that cannot, or not in this quality, show themselves indoors (for example: the dog that runs between the elements in the constellation and digs a hole). But outdoor nature constellations offer more than just the occasional appearance of phenomena that "accidentally" fit what happens in the constellation. I realize more and more that the qualities of the phenomenological approach are able to more fully unfold themselves outdoors. The greater my readiness in nature constellations to see the supposed "influences and disturbances from the surroundings" as phenomena that belong to the constellation itself, the more I am astonished at the rich and precise contributions from the environment. Today I believe that the environment steps in and co-directs, if the intention of the work is clearly oriented towards a balance in the system and if we ask for such support in the beginning of the constellation.

How Contributor Came to This Work:

First Encounter. The intricate living organism of the alpine forest, the immense forces that act upon it (avalanches, rock falls etc.) and the demand of human's impact on these forests make the mountain forest a very complex and dynamic system. I have learned that to conceive and describe this system is limited with the analytic methods. Searching for methods that unite instead of separate, I discovered systemic constellation work in 1998. I realized in a constellation with my future teacher Dr. K.H. Rauscher that this approach is suitable for analysis and solution-oriented work on problems concerning our environment. Then I did a training in organizational and family constellation work in 2000 and 2001 to increase my skills.

Experiences and Developments in a Team. During my training I invited friends on weekends and we did experimental nature constellations. On the last day of the Würzburg Conference in 2003, in the Open Space session I and two other people proposed the subject "nature constellations" or closely related themes, which were all combined into one group. Twenty-four people attended the meeting and out of this the "sixth-sense-in-service" team (SSIS) was created: (Erna Alexandra Jansen [Netherlands], Christine Robert [Germany], Chrisjan Leermakers [Netherlands], Johannes Schmucker [Germany], Kenneth Sloan [USA] und Berchthold Wasser [Switzerland]). This team we organized and conducted a series of nature constellation workshops from 2003 to 2007. The consolidation of our experiences and training, the impulses from the team and the mutual work provided much form and power for the nature constellations. During this time we received an invitation from Albrecht and Brigitta Mahr to present a nature constellation workshop as part of their Würzburg Conference in 2005. This was our first public appearance in which we shared our emerging approach to nature constellations..

Important Impulses. The SSIS team work with nature constellations was developed through public seminars and project meetings at locations where we were invited to investigate problems of one kind or another. There were also experiences flowing in as members of the team offered their own workshops and from experiences at seminars of other constellation facilitators. I myself received many impulses from the events of Francesca Mason Boring and Daan van Kampenhout. To these and many other powerful experiences, I owe my conviction that nature constellations really function and have effects in the world. I also know that other resources have influenced how I facilitate constellation work significantly, such as my Buddhist Dzogchen practice (Tsoknyi Rinpoche, 2003), which has had a crucial influence on my presence while facilitating constellations. Due to the Dialogue as David Bohm described and taught it, I can understand many aspects of constellations (Bohm, 1996) that are otherwise

The Sixth Sense in Service Team - Oberdurenbach, Germany, January 2005
(from left) Chrisjan Leermakers, Johannes Schmucker, Christine Robert,
Erna Alexandra Jansen, Berchthold Wasser and Kenneth Sloan (picture by Kenneth Sloan)

mysterious. My qualification as a trained mediator helps me primarily focus the introductory talk to discover the real question being asked.

Case Study 1: Between the Fronts

A Constellation during a workshop about the topic "Landscapes and Humans in Dialogue" in the Emmental Valley (Switzerland).

The Story. The issue is a current problem from Peter's job-related activity. Peter is a biologist. He is co-owner of a planning and consulting office in Austria. Besides other projects his current task is to mediate between the interests of the owners and the claims of the nature conservation agency in a valley situated in the Alps. Peter received a mandate from the nature conservation authority of one Austrian state where he had already been working for some years. So far this task has been very challenging since this valley is, from the perspective of nature conservation, very valuable - in some parts it is still unspoiled countryside and half of it lies in a national park. For the owners, the valley is the basis of their existence. Here their cattle graze and here they produce their milk and cheese. For centuries their ancestors have removed the stones from the pastures and cleared the woodlands to make fertile ground. During a severe storm with exceptionally strong rainfall, large areas of the fertile Alps, the most important street and some bridges were destroyed. It is clear that any significant effort to restore what was lost will only be possible with the help of the government. For the residents of the valley the incident was traumatic and they clearly want the infrastructure and as much land as possible to be restored. They also want the affected buildings to be protected from possible future natural disasters by the construction of dams. The Nature Conservation Agency on the other hand saw this incident as a chance for the natural dynamic to operate and in this case re-create wilderness. They didn't want any more human intervention there because the alpine region is so heavily used by tourism and nature has scarcely anywhere to be able to naturally unfold. It stands to reason that Peter's position was difficult due to these various demands. The situation was extreme: when Peter voiced even understanding for the position of the conservation agency, one of the owners threatened that Peter would be killed if he continued to represent such views.

The Issue. Peter wishes that he will be again accepted and supported by the Nature Conservation Agency and by the residents of the valley, so that he can bring their concerns together to a win-win solution. From the constellation he hopes to obtain clear hints that support him on the way to this goal and to see what he himself can do for it.

Representatives. Peter / Nature Conservation Agency / Residents / Valley / Man who expressed the murder threat (Attacker)

Approach. Peter decides that the constellation will happen "blind". This means that the chosen representatives do not know who or what they represent. (Please remember this when reading the next paragraph.)

Constellation Description. Peter brings the representatives one after the other into the circle: the representative for himself, the representative for the valley, the representative for the Nature Conservation Agency and the representative for the residents. The person that expressed the murder threat (attacker) was not yet chosen and is not yet standing in the circle.

Peter feels weak and insecure, the valley is restless and begins to shiver, the residents are stable. As they are brought in and confronted with the Nature Conservation Agency, the agency turns away and watches from a distance.

Peter looks at the valley and the valley at him; this connection is good for both.

The Nature Conservation Agency is very unsettled and changes its position. Peter is now standing between the agency and the residents. For the residents it is unpleasant not to be able to see the Nature Conservation Agency. They would have to lean over to see it and that is too demanding for them.

The Nature Conservation Agency becomes weaker and weaker. It asks for a chair to sit down. The residents remain unaffected by this development. The system stays without moving in this arrangement for a while longer.

Now the person who expressed the murder threat (attacker) is introduced into the circle. He feels stable. His body sensation concentrates completely on his stomach. He looks at all the persons present and doesn't feel close to anyone. The attacker thinks Peter is "pathetic" and the wistful quizzical eyes of the Nature Conservation Agency seem repulsive to him.

After a while the attacker tries to get between the agency and Peter. There the agency tries to reach out to Peter's hand, so that the attacker cannot get between them. That tempts the attacker even more to get between and he says it is his stomach that wants to push forward in this direction.

Through this provocation, the Nature Conservation Agency is awakened. Slowly it stands up, then strikes the attacker in the stomach and pushes him forcefully to the side.

The attacker offers resistance. He does not want to be pushed to the side so easily. As soon as the fist of the agency is gone, he comes back and tries even more obstinately to step in the gap. Through this, the agency becomes even more activated and pushes the attacker back even more strongly. This sequence repeats several times.

After the third defense of the Nature Conservation Agency the attacker realizes that the position where he wanted to stand is now not possible for him, because the Nature Conservation Agency is now really strong and present there. But it is also no longer that important for him, since Peter has found another position during the conflict between the attacker and the agency. The valley feels that the Nature Conservation Agency is more powerful now and that feels extraordinarily good for the valley. Peter, the valley and the Nature Conservation Agency now form an equilateral triangle.

This new constellation obviously also pleases the attacker. He changes his position and now he can see Peter from a new perspective. From this perspective he likes him much better.

Between the positions Peter, valley and agency there is now eye contact and goodwill. The valley reports that power is flowing from it to Peter.

The attacker is now facing the Nature Conservation Agency. His concentration on his stomach has become less. Now his attention is more in his head and he says to the agency, "from time to time someone should step on your toes" and then he immediately does. As this leads to no change in the system, the attacker retires and watches the whole scene relaxed from a distance.

The facilitator brings now the "real" Peter to his representative, whom he asks to stand behind Peter for a while and to share his current feelings with him.

The attacker now gets behind Peter: His intention is to give him encouragement. For Peter this isn't right, he does not feel supported through that. But on the other hand Peter feels connected with the valley and the Nature Conservation Agency. He would have liked to hug both of them and he feels energy flowing between the valley, the agency and him.

The attacker is changing his position one more time. He is now facing the Nature Conservation Agency. Valley, attacker, Peter and the Nature Conservation Agency are now forming a circle. The residents have already retired to one side.

Attacker and agency look directly at each other for the first time. Their relationship is clear and relaxed. Valley and Peter also look at each other. The valley is grateful that it is seen and it feels power flowing from it to Peter. At this point the constellation is finished.

Evaluation. This evaluation was made together with Peter shortly after the constellation and then reviewed after one year. The criteria for the evaluation is the issue as initially formulated by Peter.

-> The anger and the threat of the most-concerned owners is effectively not directed towards Peter, but against the Nature Conservation Agency.

-> As the agency is weak and hiding behind Peter, he is perceived as a representative of the Nature Conservation Agency.

-> When the Nature Conservation Agency is directly confronted with the strong emotions (gut feeling) of the owners the result is aggressive conflict. That is unpleasant for all involved at the moment it occurs. But as a result the Nature Conservation Agency becomes stronger, as it is now clearly embodying and defending its position. And also Peter can now finally take his place, the place of the mediator, as he wishes.

-> If Peter has a clear distance from the Nature Conservation Agency and is completely in service to the valley, he is perceived as strong and capable. In this position he even has the support of the owners who had threatened his life.

-> Clear and intrinsically strong positions lead to mutual respect and finally also to reassurance.

Three weeks after the constellation there is an orientation meeting. The person that threatened Peter's life (attacker) and his sister are also present. The meeting is very constructive. The man who threatened Peter avoids eye contact. The sister of the man comes up to Peter and thanks him for being so dedicated regarding their future.

Eight months after the constellation Peter visited the family of the man who had threatened him. He was received as a friend. The man who had threatened him said, "You are the only one who stood with us through all of this. Thank you."

Case Study 2: Water Quality

Constellation during the workshop "Naturaufstellungen am Lech" in Upper Bavaria (Germany).

The Story. Claudia is writing her master's thesis about the meaning of water in countries with a surplus and in countries with a scarcity of water. She is particularly interested if and how humans perceive the quality of water. She considers the spiritual quality of the water in addition to its utility.

Issue. Claudia wants to see what meaning the practical value and the spiritual value of water has for people in countries with a lot of water (for example in Middle Europe) and in countries with less water (for example Sahelian zone of Africa).

Representatives:

System A = Country with a lot of water: humans -> (AH), quality of water for use -> (AU), spiritual quality of the water -> (AS)

System B = Country with less water: humans -> (BH), quality of water for use -> (BU), spiritual quality of the water -> (BS)

Further elements that join the constellation later: ecological technology that cleanses the water -> (ET), Blockage of the north-south dialogue -> (BD), transforming power -> (TP)

Approach. It is Claudia's wish that the constellation starts with both systems in place at the same time. But she wants to be able to clearly recognize what is happening in both systems. To make this possible the circle is divided in half. The system with less water will be set up in the southern half, the system with lots of water in the northern half of the circle. Additionally, there is a chronological order set. First, everybody will be introduced in their representations. Then system A in the north begins with movement, while system B is resting. Claudia selects all representatives and brings them into the circle.

Constellation Description.
System A. The water for use (AU) feels abused, polluted, dirty. As a result of the contamination it also lost contact with the spiritual quality. The representative is deeply affected and sad.

The spiritual quality (AS) feels pure but at the same time very weak (the young woman that is embodying AS is still a girl, very delicate, and shy, an ideal embodiment of the quality described above). She is walking slowly towards AU but is not really able to support her.

The humans (AH) are turned away from both of the water qualities. After a while they turn towards the water, but cannot really connect. They realize that something is wrong. But at the same time they feel helpless and they don't know what they should do.

System B. The water for use (BU) directly drops to the ground and lies there crouched. It experiences itself as under and not above the ground surface. It does not want to be used more than it has been.

The spiritual quality (BS) representative is big and strong and his feelings correspond to this.

The humans (BH) bow first before BU and then before BS in a deep and reverent way. BH is standing next to BS. Both are looking into each other's eyes.

The water for use (BU) wails. It says it can hear the humans say: "We know that you are only little but we need you to survive."

A new element from the outer circle: A women says that she is feeling pulled into system B. She gets permission to enter the system. She walks to the water for use (BU) and explains that she is a technology which can clean the water in an economical and ecological way (ET). Now BU moves and after a while is even able to get up, which allows BS and BH to come closer.

Interaction between the systems A and B. Now again the elements of system A receive full attention and the permission to move. Claudia wants to take away the rope that was dividing the circle into "north" and "south".

This attempt is promptly prevented through another element. A man who was sitting in the outer circle jumps into the circle, steps on the end of the rope and shouts out, "The border must not be taken away." This action leads to global confusion. After a while the new element (BD) says, "There must be no north-south dialogue. This kills the profits. (After the constellation this representative reports that he felt very mighty and powerful in this moment and had among others visions, images of Nestlé, a multinational food company and its practice of buying mineral springs worldwide.)

Relieving Movement. I ask Claudia if she wants to choose and introduce a representative for herself. Claudia affirms that and chooses Barbara. Barbara is immediately present, but not as "Claudia", but as a "transforming power" (TP). TP immediately approaches BD. BD grabs a stick and threatens TP (later on after the constellation the representative of BD reports that he saw inner images of African child soldiers in this moment). TP stays relaxed. She turns slightly in a circle around BD and seduces him to a kind of a dance (in the sharing round the representative for the transforming power reports that she knew that every attempt of violence would have been counterproductive). Amazingly BD quickly loses its severity. TP takes the stick away from him and BD is noticeably relieved (BD reports later on about that scene that he felt the part of the child soldier who was finally allowed to be a kid again). He walks to the rope, pulls it away and says, "The dialogue between north and south is good. Don't allow it to be interrupted through profit seeking." Then BD retires from the circle and observes the rest of the constellation from a distance, sitting under a tree. Also TP leaves the circle. She says, "My task is done."

The reactions in the systems A and B: While the process between BD and TP was running, the representatives (BH, BU, BS) in country B were moving more and more together. BS was the central element supporting the others.

After BD went away, there was an awakening in country A. AU and AS reached out with their toes over the former border.

Now, as the blockage is gone and the water qualities of north and south meet, connect and touch each other, the spiritual quality of the south starts to cry with tears of relief.

The humans in the north are still confused. But it is obvious that only they can really change something. Slowly they start to perceive the water qualities in their country. It is as if they really see them for the first time, especially the spiritual quality (AS). The humans in the north place themselves next to the water qualities AU and AS, and together they look towards the south.

I ask the representatives in the south to risk the attempt to look north. They face the representatives in the north. The glances meet and everyone is touched. In this position the constellation is finished.

Evaluation. After the constellation, all representatives and the people in the outer circle are very moved. Obviously, the water issue touched something that everybody feels deeply, as our origin is in the water. And maybe also because our body consists of 70% water.

Claudia is grateful for what she could see and experience.

-> If we remember Claudia's issue. (What is the meaning of the water qualities for humans in countries with lots and countries with less water), we see that in countries with less water the qualities of the water are much more clearly perceived and honored.

-> In countries with less water the spiritual quality is stronger and more important for the people. Or the other way around one could say, the shortage of the water reminds the people how immediately they are connected with the fate of the water.

Once the relations between the humans and the water qualities in the subsystems "north" and "south" have been seen, one could have ended the constellation because the answer for Claudia's question had already been found. What happened afterwards was more like a glimpse into the future, coming from the system itself.

-> The contact between countries with an abundance and countries with less water seems to be an important requirement for a change in the relationship of the humans to the water qualities. The contact seems to bring changes to both sides.

-> The border between north and south was an economical border at first. It was interesting to see that holding on to the border was no longer important when the actual desire of the blockage was fulfilled, to just be allowed to be (a child).

Further Development

The above sections indicate how broad the possible applications of nature constellations are. They show important possible contributions for problem analysis and solution. I am convinced that the potential of nature constellations to heal conflicts and re-establish connections is enormous. Right now we can only see the first steps of this method. My belief in its future is based primarily on the experience of the representatives in a nature constellation, irrespective of the specific theme or issue: that is, the powerful experience of belonging to the specific system and to nature itself. And secondly that this belonging depends neither on any special achievements nor on specific characteristics - it is just there, just present. This experience of belonging unconditionally is what a lot of people are searching for.

Although this experience shows that nature constellations can accelerate planning processes and bring rapid turnarounds to conflicts it will take a while until nature constellation work becomes an established tool for project management. The reason is that this is a radical experiential approach very much in contrast to scientific studies, analysis, reasons and arguments. In the constellation participants have to let go of their intentions and ideas. This is not easy to do. In addition, neither the way nor the goal are determined or assured. Who would want to leave safe ground in important projects or conflicts? Such a person would have to be crazy or desperate or very curious. Of course, these then were the same kinds of people who first took the chance with family constellation work.

It is the way of letting go, that we have to go, if we want real solutions. David Bohm presented this in a very clear way. He had shown that clinging to positions and arguments only brings us deeper in crisis. He developed a method that unites instead of separating (David Bohm 1996). Fascinatingly, nature constellations also have the exact qualities that Bohm described for the solution process of being open for new information and impulses. As mentioned above, nature constellations are also attractive and useful for the participants. But what does this mean now for future development? On one hand we see the unfamiliarity of the method and the courage that it requires to embark on it and on the other hand there is the great potential for project planning and project realization and, above all, an approach that really resolves conflicts and does not disconnect.

I believe for now it will be only the pioneers that follow this path, expand it, improve it and establish it. Therefore case studies, workshops, seminars, trainings and publications like this book are important for progress in this field. In addition, it is important to network and connect with other areas of study like scientific approaches that are investigating and proposing models for the effects of constellation work, environmental education that uses nature constellations in lessons, conflict resolution that uses the approach of constellation work for mediation, and everyone who is open and ready to try out new paths to find new higher-order solutions to old problems.

I do not know if there will be a speedy evolution with this. My hope is that the quote from Victor Hugo, "Nothing is more powerful than an idea whose time has come" fits here. But undoubtedly - regardless of the strength of the idea - there is a lot of ground work to be done before this approach can mature enough to find wide usage.

Bibliograhy:

Bohm, David (1996): On Dialog; Lee Nichol (ed.), Publisher Routledge, London and New York

Tsoknyi Rinpoche (2003): Fearless Simplicity; The Dzogchen Way of Living Freely in a Complex World; Rangjung Yeshe Publications, Boudhanath, Hong Kong and Esby

Zita Cox (MBACP: Msc; BA hons; Dip Counseling; Dip.H) is an experienced facilitator of Constellations. Her interests expanded in the 1990's to include eco-psychology and training in family systems constellations with Albrecht Mahr in 2000. This combination led Zita to extend and pioneer the application of the constellation technique to issues relating to the environment.

Zita has worked for 24 years as an integrative counselor, psychotherapist and supervisor both in private practice and in the National Health Service. Zita has worked as coach and consultant for managers in both the corporate and voluntary sectors and facilitated environmental constellations for individuals, organizations, environmental campaigners, lawyers and as a Team Development and research and educational tool.

Zita's first degree is in Philosophy. Zita has facilitated environmental constellations in Europe, California, and New Zealand. She has presented environmental constellations workshops at over twenty conferences for many different professions. She has written an article on Environmental Constellations, 'A Different Kind of Field Trip', published in 'The Knowing Field' January 2007. She did a research paper into Bystanding and Intervention in extreme situations, contributed as a chapter in 'Balancing Acts: Studies in Counseling Training' edited by Hazel Johns (Routledge 1998).

E-mail: zita@zitacox.com

Website: www.environmentalconstellations.com

Offerings: I offer individual sessions, for personal or professional issues. Group work, such as team development, strategic planning for lawyers. Re-visiting the field, through constellations for researchers in biology, naturalists, marine biologists, climate scientists etc. Education workshops for students of biology, geography, natural scientists. I have also worked with management students, enabling them to expand their thinking about an issue to include the environment and sustainability. Workshops for: movement practitioners, dancers, or movement therapists, eco-psychologists and anyone interested in self- development.

Picture Credits for this chapter: Zita Cox

CHAPTER FIVE

Another Kind of Field Trip

by Zita Cox

Abstract: Human beings have become increasingly influenced by philosophies and religions which set us apart from nature and by splitting us off from nature allow us to develop economic systems which exploit the natural world, reducing all life on Earth to a means for money-making. The idea that consumerism and growth can sustain our societies looks increasingly barren in the face of climate change, mass species extinction and the devastating inequality between rich and poor. Constellations are a wonderfully versatile method, a new language for communicating, deepening our understanding, aiding our empathy and exploring and accessing embodied knowledge. This new language can put us back into our animal place, in systemic connection to the rest of the natural world. It is a method to creatively solve problems and deepen our relationships. Constellations can therefore contribute to imagining a different way to form our societies and relate to other life on Earth, which at times can feel impossible. To find again "the beach beneath the street" before we have consumed or polluted all nature's resources and all there is beneath us is ocean. Constellations can help us think our way out of this rut, inspire us to dream, help us "think impossible things" as the Queen said to Alice. Alice laughed: "There's no use trying," she said; "one can't believe impossible things." "I dare say you haven't had much practice," said the Queen. "When I was younger, I always did it for half an hour a day. Why, sometimes I've believed as many as six impossible things before breakfast." (~ Lewis Carroll from Alice in Wonderland.) Below are a few vignettes from my nature constellations journey.

Note: I published an article with similar content under the same title in The Knowing Field Journal, Issue 9, January 2007. Some material and the title are reused here with the permission of The Knowing Field. More info, to subscribe and to order back copies: www.theknowingfield.com

Audience:

I work with individuals and groups with both personal and professional issues who wish to understand their relationship with nature in a new way. These include lawyers, (both corporate and environmental), management consultants, biologists, physicists, climate scientists, dancers, horse owners and trainers, and campaigners for political and environmental change.

Issues:

My work is varied, from deeply personal concerns to environmental, organizational and political issues, and at times all these combined.

I have constellated questions on personal themes such as deepening the relationship the questioner has with a particular place - for example their garden or home, how to design that garden, how to sell their house, how to find balance in life or further their career, and asking their question of non-humans and places to which the individual feels a strong connection.

Questions may be personal, but also have a larger context such as an individual's fear of a particular river or the sea which has flooded their home. Constellating this question shifted the questioner's understandable fear of water, giving them insight into the nature of water and a desire to renew their relationship with the river and sea. They no longer perceived the water as aggressive and predatory in flooding their homes but having to expand at times outside its usual boundaries: this is its nature. Interestingly this was in Holland and Chrisjan Leermakers was present and able to tell us that the department in Holland responsible for sea defenses had began to think in a similar way about the nature of water, and to protect themselves from flooding by taking this into account.

Questions concerning animals, at times personal issues about a particular horse or dog, at other times more political and environmental, involving campaigns to protect a particular species, such as the Orangutan, or to reintroduce a species for example a wolf.

Questions about the destruction of habitats as a result of commercial interests like defor-estation, mining, oil drilling, laying of pipelines.

Questions involving concepts such as "Can capitalism be non-depleting of the earth?"

Educational questions such as what is the difference between a birch and a beech tree, or the difference between a wild wood and a commercial wood.

Desired Outcomes for the Work:

My interest is in offering a new way to see whatever is of concern to the questioner: to expand thinking to include the other than human world, so we can see an issue in a larger context, to gain empathy and understanding for other beings - human and other than human, to resolve conflicts of interest, and to reduce the fear that is often the consequence or cause of conflict.

To think systemically, to see the pattern an issue makes when it includes and embodies elements, which are often left out or excluded.

To extend the ability we have to think, from the left brained analytical to the right brain and to include embodied knowledge, to gain unexpected insights and solutions. To find a new vision - a shift in the field - and to support the paradigm shift needed in these times of increasing inequality and climate change.

How the Work is Done:

I begin by listening to the questions each participant brings, the quality of the question and how "burning" an issue this is to them. In a circle of people where everyone has something they wish to constellate something seems to stand out around the person who is most ready, almost as if the air goes still around them and becomes dense. Though I have learnt that does not always mean they are ready to leap in and be the questioner, it does mean they have a great deal of feeling about the issue.

Walking the Heaphy Track

If I am with a group of people who have never participated in a constellation before and cannot imagine how to go about finding a question for an Environmental Constellation, then I often do a very brief exercise to facilitate them finding a question. I keep the exercise as brief as possible or there is a danger the question is answered during the exercise!

I invite people to ground themselves by sitting quietly in their chairs, closing their eyes and connecting to their breath, after a moment or two of this I invite them to think of a place which is important to them or let such a place come to them, it might be a place they know well, their garden or favorite walk or it might be somewhere they have only been once on holiday. I then ask them to think of a question, something they would like answered and ask the place or a being, animal or plant, or element that is in the visualization, giving them only a minute or two to do this second part. From this exercise the initial constellations come; once the group has experienced constellations then questions come easily.

Listening is the single most important element in facilitating a constellation. Listening to the question, getting a clear picture of the elements involved. I start with the smallest number of representatives possible, adding in others as their presence or lack of it is felt, listening not only to the words but listening kinesthetically as well. It might seem odd but I think I also listen with my eyes, I am taking in information and weighing it alongside my intuition, my kinesthetic experience and the knowledge I have from past constellations and then waiting a fraction longer to see/feel what happens next. In the traditional way of constellations I will ask representatives for what is happening for them, invite them to follow movements they want to make, express sensations in their body or feelings. From all this information a pattern emerges, as each representative relates systemically to the other representatives.

I recently worked with dance and movement therapists where the constellation became more like a dance. I felt like a choreographer!

When I first began to experiment with ecosystem constellations I decided it was important to stay very open to what might unfold. I wanted to hold lightly in mind the fundamental ideas from classical family constellations such as that everyone has their rightful place in the system, but not to transpose what I had learnt about the orders of love from family constellation. I wanted to let things arrive through evolution in a particular order but not to presume what that order will be or presume anything about what "natural" means for other than human beings. That is, I did not want to impose ideas from family constellations or science or even everyday "common sense."

In one constellation I facilitated, the Earth repeatedly expressed a desire to leave; of course a part of my mind popped up with the thought and image of the Earth in the solar system and how could it leave? However, I suggested the representative followed this movement; two other representatives followed the Earth out of the group. A little later checking in with the Earth, the representative reported the feeling of convalescing, and being engaged happily with the two representatives who had followed the Earth. This caused consternation in the group, as they seemed to think the Earth shouldn't have left but rather lain down, because how can the Earth leave?

A constellation gives us an opportunity to put aside our assumptions and suspend our beliefs and listen and allow something other to emerge. We can then live with that, and if necessary suspend our disbelief and see what happens next. Listening to a constellation allows us to know things, to gain insights we wouldn't otherwise find. It is important, I believe, not to be constrained by our left brain thinking or what we assume is the truth of something or we will miss the very thing which may give us the means to break out of our assumptions, our restricted view.

On reflection it seemed to me the Earth could certainly leave, it could leave its relationship to human beings, could become inhospitable to us while it convalesced from our consumption of its resources and pollution of its habitats.

I am watching and listening and thinking, looking for where the energy is stuck, or conflict arises, or where there is flow and ease.

Over the last 12 years of facilitating constellations I have noticed certain themes emerge, I do not make rules out of them, but hold these themes as possibilities. One such theme I have witnessed frequently expressed in different constellations by different representatives for the Earth, the Rainforest, or an endangered species is the desire to be seen, witnessed, sat with by the human beings - this being with and being seen is what is needed. Later in this chapter I will describe the Rainforest constellation in more detail to demonstrate this more fully. Alongside this emerged the difficulty human beings have in doing this, we want to act, to fix, to do. I am not saying doing is unimportant, I am saying we find it difficult to stop and listen and be with and that is often what was asked of us in constellations, where the question had been "What can I do to save the Rainforest?" or "What can I do about climate change or mass species extinction?" Doing nothing but being with is a courageous act, to sit with how things are to stop consuming anything which is depleting the Earth, is a revolutionary act, and puts the person who does it at odds with a society which values people who have the most more highly than those who have little.

Dealing with environmental issues, unexpected solutions do emerge but at other times the constellations show how things are rather than offering a solution or resolution. I think this is valuable learning to stay with what is and see it embodied. It is hard for individuals, organizations and governments to fully grasp what is happening to our planet, business as usual is such a powerful driver of behavior and attitudes.

In a constellation about the recession, all the participants were focused on the representative for recession, the Earth's representative noticed this and attempted to get the attention of the group saying I am what is important I am all there is, look at me. The people could not take their eyes off recession, they appeared mesmerized, the representative for recession reported a sense of growing bigger and stronger with all the attention. Meanwhile the Earth's representative was completely ignored and felt a certain amusement watching these human beings who she found faintly ridiculous. It seemed impossible or uninteresting for the human representatives to listen to the Earth or even see her and realize the truth of her statement, the Earth is all there is, all the resources we use, the air we breathe the water we drink, every manufactured or man-made product has its origins in the Earth and is inseparable from a healthy Earth. Often in constellations human representatives are seen to have restricted vision like a horse wearing blinkers. They cannot see to left or right, they can only see the track in front of them, they only see each other.

I give plenty of time for people to stay in their representative energy as one of my aims in facilitating Environmental Constellations is to encourage empathy for the other than human beings and to raise awareness of our interconnectedness with all life.

As one participant recently said

"Often it's where I've been a representative that I've been most deeply touched and held onto a memory. This seems especially true for environmental constellations - I remember one about the planned Donald Trump golf course in Scotland (I represented the sands and am still a member of a group that opposes him!) and also a constellation about the tar sands in Canada where I also represented sands, was deeply pained, and now contribute to a Native American group that works against the tar sands exploitation."

Generally at the end I put the questioner into the constellation in place of their representative so they can stand in the constellation and feel the changed system.

Recently a participant described my work in this way:

"You wait, seemingly so patiently, and without appearing fazed by the strangeness of what is happening or being talked about. It seems with Environmental Constellations that so many strange possibilities can appear, you couldn't possibly understand or be ready, except in the accepting and listening and trusting that you do."

How Contributor Came to this Way of Working:

In the early nineties I moved into a flat without a garden. The loss of a garden was a deep grief and the longing for a garden kept growing inside me until it deepened into a longing for something wilder. Alongside this was a growing concern and interest in environmental issues, deforestation, mass species extinction and climate change.

I was working as a Counsellor and Psychotherapist at this time and the longing for a garden took me on a search for some new way to practice. I needed to be outdoors, I needed to contribute to a change in attitude towards the Earth and all its beings human and other.

At the same time I was first coming into contact with Family System Constellations and was fortunate to count amongst my friends and colleagues Vivian Broughton and others who were interested in training in Systemic Constellations. Vivian organised the training, bringing Albrecht Mahr over to Bristol.

As I racked my brain for some way to find a means to do some work for the environment which didn't involve retraining as an environmentalist, I kept thinking there must be some way to use my existing skills but make a different use of them. I remember sitting in my consulting room in London, trying to work out what I could do. I remember sitting on the white sofa beside the large sash window and thinking about why people make changes, about the guilt inducing nature of much environmental campaigning and thinking that if people could relate with more love and empathy to the other than human world, this might give them more incentive to look after the environment. Later an idea came to me, the image

I have is of ideas on wires running along above my head and that I had simply reached up and pulled one down. The idea that came to me was that if we could look at one system like a family why couldn't we constellate other systems, ecosystems in particular. If participants could feel in their bodies what it is like to be a tree or tiger or a polar bear just as they feel in a family constellation what it is like to be a particular member of that family, then they might begin to see these beings differently. They might find empathy and love for the other than human beings. Constellations might be a new language through which we could have cross -species dialogue.

The principle that everyone within a family system has a rightful place in that system and that exclusion causes problems seemed to logically extend to the whole Earth system. Whenever I participated in family constellations I became increasingly aware that we were focusing in a restricted way, like a horse wearing blinkers or blinders. I remember in one particular venue being increasingly aware of the trees outside the building, and how excluding we were being of them.

I remember the excitement of this but also the nervousness that people would think I was mad. I began to experiment with friends to see if this idea was possible.

In 2003 I went to a very large conference in Würzburg where I met up with a group of people interested in Nature Constellations - Germans, Swiss, Dutch, and even an American. I was amazed. I had colleagues! I had also heard from Albrecht Mahr that in a previous conference in Würzburg, an American, whose name I don't know, had set up a constellation with many different animals represented. He had simply taken large pieces of paper and written names of species on them and participants had moved around from place to place experiencing these various representative energies.

I was about to leave on a long awaited sabbatical so when others in the group decided to meet up and experiment with Nature constellations I wasn't able to join them. However on my return I met up with Chrisjan Leermakers. He came over to England to an Ecopsychology summer camp and I went the following year to Holland and we shared our methods of working with Nature and Environmental Constellations.

Case Studies

The energy of an Environmental Constellation varies considerably depending on whether it is based on the knowledge of a naturalist asking a question such as "what is the difference between a managed wood and a wild wood" or a campaigner asking "how can I save the Rainforest" or an individual consulting the elements to find balance in life or deepen their relationship to a particular being. The first two can have a more practical feel and concrete outcomes, the personal can at times feel very dreamlike and as one participate recently said, "I feel like surrealism suddenly makes sense to me in day-to-day life in a way it never did before!"

In this section I will offer some vignettes from each of these perspectives.

I also I want to do justice to the amazement I see in people when they come across this work for the first time,

"It was for me the most remarkable experience… To communicate with the mountain, the river, the trees in such an intimate manner is an honour."

Case Study: Environmental Campaigns and Environmental Law

I have tried to stay true to the constellation described below and the representatives whilst anonymising the company and the particular campaign we were seeking to assist. My aim is to show that using constellations in this way can help people, campaigners, and environmental lawyers, and the other-than-human world fight for the right to control and maintain their community.

This constellation deals with a company attempting to extract a natural resource from the Earth which would lay waste the human community, their sacred land and the other than human life living there.

The question was how to prevent this extraction. The representatives were the mountain, the river, the indigenous people, the consumer, the company, the UN, the lawyer, the ancestors, the mineral, the missing link.

The mountain said "I am so much more than a mountain." The people said, "We are a small people, we and the mountain are one, the mountain is sacred to us and we need to revere it, without the mountain we cease to exist we are nothing." There was no compromise the people or the mountain could make with the company.

The river: "There can be no compromise of the sacred site of life… I was very aware of flowing through all things, being imbibed, being the substance of people's bodies, passing through all living things. I made no judgment of the mineral as 'poisonous', feeling, kinship and love for this fellow part of the Earth, and knowing that my own fate and the fate of the mineral were intertwined."

The missing link was experienced by the representative "I felt moved to sing and felt that the missing link (understood by me to be 'great spirit' and the connecting power of prayer) has a very important role to play."

The consumer: "I was brought bit by bit into facing the reality of the indigenous people, finally to communicate with them; half a minute or more of looking into the eyes of the people was a powerful moment."

Company representative: "All the approaches that attempted to literally weigh the company down failed- literally as the bodies pulled me to the floor – I remember looking away and staying looking away, refusing to engage with any of the aspects of the constellation. The key for me was the finality of it for the company, it had to be killed."

Neither side of the dispute were able to compromise, the movement came from the consumers and the lawyers. "The river became very important and it became apparent that the river should become central to the campaign; I had an image of a poster with the river as the dominant image."

One of the insights from the constellation was that the company had grown out of poverty and for the CEO the thrust for money and growth was intrinsic, which seemed to be connected to being born out of "depression" and poverty, it seemed clear that as long as the founder was in charge there could be no change, the company had to be killed, which happened finally when the Law stopped the company. Is this the basic motivation of all capitalism?

In the resolution, after the death of the company, the individuals from the company found their place within the constellation. The result of the constellation was the insight and empathy the representatives gained for the beings they represented.

One participant, a lawyer, had a creative insight as to how the law could be used by the indigenous people to stop the company taking their land and he was then able to meet with the barristers representing the people and share this idea. This legal action was relevant for this group and others in similar circumstance.

Another participant, an Environmental Campaigner, realized the significance of the river for the campaign; the river could connect the consumers and shareholders with the indigenous people.

Two weeks later we heard the indigenous people had obtained legal protection from the aggressive commercial interests of the company. This was not a final defeat but it was a battle won.

In constellations involving law and campaigning it is fairly typical for there to be solutions and ideas generated.

Case Study: An Educational Method

What is the difference between a managed and a wild wood?

This was a "snap shot" constellation where the purpose is for the participants to gain knowledge through an embodied experience.

With a biologist at Bath University as the questioner I set up two constellations 1) all the students were placed in position as different species of tree in a wild wood, with a a representative for one human forest dweller. Each representative's experience was different and reflected the qualities of that species of tree. One was very unstable and felt very insecure, later we learnt he was representing a tree which is coppiced. The forest dweller felt at home in the forest.

In the second constellation they were positioned as in a commercial wood, all the same species in rows. They reported feeling rigid and facing front unable to see clearly as other trees in front of them blocked their view. Only the representative who had previously been the coppiced tree felt happy, glad to feel secure.

The forester, who had previously been the relaxed forest dweller became nervous and rather paranoid and worried by being in the wood. The biologist later described their experience "the students very much appreciated it, and I think they were very surprised - even shocked - by how strongly their bodies responded to the different situations, 'Listen to what your body has to say, if you want to be ecologically aware', was therefore a 'take home message' for them. The biologist also commented that he hadn't thought of trees having a front previously, but that it did make sense to him.

Case Study: The House Sale

One of the first constellations I did was for a friend who was having difficulty selling her house. Anna had completely re-furbished the house and, having lived in it for a while, wanted to sell, but there were no buyers. We constellated the house, the garden and Anna asking the question "why wasn't the house selling?" The representative for the house was happy and willing for the sale to go through. However the garden was aggrieved that the house had been completely refurbished and nothing at all had been done to nourish and bring back to life the garden. The garden was unwilling for the house to be sold before this happened. The garden was very specific about what it wanted Anna to do. Clear an area at the bottom of the garden and put some chairs down there and enjoy the space.

In the morning Anna and I followed the gardens instructions and afterwards in the cleared space we sat drinking coffee and reading papers in the sunshine. It was a delightful spot. There is a small stream running along the back of the garden beyond the low garden fence and hedge of trees. Four people came to view the house that day, all of them walked to the bottom of the garden and all of them put in offers. The house was sold that day. Whether it was the garden who spoke to us or an unconscious desire on Anna's part to sit in the spot we cleared, I don't know. But the constellation resolved the house selling issue.

Case Study: Five Horses and a Woman

Jenny was concerned about one of her five horses.

At the resolution what emerged was the need for each horse to have its place and be acknowledged by her in the order she had bought them. They also needed her to assume her place as leader; otherwise the horses would compete among themselves for that role.

As the constellation evolved, a few things stood out. The representative for the newest horse in the stable would pop in comments about Canada, for example noticing they were standing in the same configuration as Canada geese fly. After the constellation Jenny told us this horse was from Canada. The representative for this horse had also found it very difficult to get close to the others and even at the end when the most harmonious order had been found, kept a slight distance. Afterwards we were told that this horse had been beaten up as a foal by other horses. It was fine in a stable or being ridden but was too frightened to be alone with horses in a field.

The following day Jenny re-arranged the stabling of the horses, so that they were in the order arrived at in the constellation. Later she took me to meet her horses. The horse she had been concerned about allowed her to put an arm across his shoulders. He stood stock still, though the effort it took to let her touch him was clear, as all his weight was on the two legs furthest from her and he looked as though he were gritting his teeth. This was the first time he had let her touch him in the several months of owning him. When she came to feed the horses she went to feed him first, because he always kicked up such a fuss if she didn't. I suggested she follow the order arrived at in the constellation and feed him last. She started with the horse longest in her care and ended with him, the newest. All was peaceful!

It is apparent that Jenny's conscious knowledge of the horses was conveyed to the representatives in the course of the constellation. Her unconscious knowledge of the system was revealed in the unfolding of the constellation and its resolution. The real horses then responded in ways which we have seen in family system constellations.

Second Cut

Case Study: The Rainforest

The question: "How can I help save the rainforest?"

Amongst those represented were the rainforest, the questioner, and the politicians.

The questioner's experience:

"Before doing the constellation I would have imagined my role would have been to engage with politicians and with politics. It was not what I expected. It was a surprise - I thought I knew what the answer would be. "

I realized the politicians, the establishment couldn't bear to look. The sense of them being disconnected from their feelings and being unable to look at what was happening evoked pity in me rather than anger."

"The Forest said: 'there is nothing you can do to help, you just have to be here with me.'"

The message was about respecting nature, honouring and metaphorically holding the Forest's hand. It may be too late to put it right; we can't necessarily fix everything.

"It is important to honour what is and to grieve for the past and what might have been - to honour the healing power of grief. I took away a different idea of what I would do. My feelings of how to engage were somehow bottom-up, starting with nature rather than looking at the political will.

It seemed very authentic and it felt true. It wasn't what I thought."

The experience is at a seminal, physical level, so you have a deep-level experience, and change your view at this deep level. You believe it. You are not playing at it; this shifts your belief, whether you want it to or not."

The representative for the Rainforest described her experience in the following way:

"I was in my first environmental constellation workshop and was chosen to represent the Rainforest. I forget now exactly what the issue presented was but, almost a year later, the feelings and experience of standing in the place of a Rainforest have stayed with me and encouraged me to learn more about how we can use this work to face environmental issues.

Once placed it wasn't long before I felt very heavy as the Forest; something was clearly wrong. I started to lean over, struggled to stay standing and then gradually and painfully lost my balance as if the root system that held me in place was just giving way underneath me. I had absolutely no control over this. Eventually I toppled to the ground with a sense of confusion and distress.

What stayed with me was the awareness in my body that the human community in the constellation was far away from me; they seemed unaware of what had happened. From what I remember they were fussing about what they should be doing to help this or that environmental issue but they weren't including me. From my position, whilst I had no language that they could understand, I remember feeling that all I needed was to be seen and that I longed for their presence with me, for contact; exactly as I was, wherever I was, falling or dying, uprooted or destroyed; I just wanted us to be in relationship. There was no judgment at all but a wanting for myself and them to be near each other. It seemed both extremely simple and also somehow impossible."

What the Rainforest was requesting was not action but reverence. As all the representatives in the constellation came and knelt around the Rainforest in silence, respect and grief, it slowly died. Most unexpectedly life immediately began to shoot or be re-born from the dying Forest.

This provides a different perspective, which is difficult for our action-orientated society to make sense of. How can doing nothing be a solution to the destruction of the Rainforest?

It is just this kind of perception that I think is useful. A fundamental change in our attitude is called for: a knocking down of the walls of our present perception. The do-nothing approach is a surprising answer - particularly when coupled with the profound feelings and experience of the representatives in the constellation - to blow a hole in our pre-conceptions and make a new space - a space that might allow in something previously unthinkable.

Morning Light Doubtful Sound

Participant Responses to Individual Constellations:

"The Constellations work has left me with a very powerful sense of the interconnectedness and aliveness of everything. In my gardening work, I felt very strongly I could connect with the plants and space I was in and pick up information they were communicating, that we were in communication. I have always had a sense of this, but it was greatly amplified and I now feel it as a given, a fact. It is very strong. I need to learn to listen much more in order to pick up what is being said. "

'"The whole process was a demonstration of the power of constellations to create an emotional dynamic that feels like a powerful truth. The experience means you can't go back to disembodied living, or "business as usual".

"A fascinating technique for slipping past the self-imposed limits of "logical" thinking into the communion of participation."

" I was in my first environmental constellation workshop and was chosen to represent the Rainforest ...a year later, the feelings and experience of standing in the place of a Rainforest have stayed with me and encouraged me to learn more about how we can use this work to face environmental issues."

"It is difficult to explain the experience in words, other than to say that it involves less of a conscious effort and more of a natural progression of feelings and intuition. The answers to our questions came to light in a way that seemed honest and true, on a deeper level than usually results from a mental process of factual analysis. I can see very definite advantages

in this process for resolving conflicts and unanswered questions, be these environmental challenges or otherwise."

For another participant being the representative for a tree had given her an experience of strength and groundedness she had never had before, she told me how profound this was for her, she could now call on that memory and find those qualities in herself.

"Environmental Constellations is an extraordinarily supple (and subtle) approach, as well-suited to illuminating intimate and personal situations as it is to revealing the dynamics of multi-layered business, legal, diplomatic and cultural situations."

I will end with this quote from biologist Alan Raynor on his experience of constellations.

"I think that the most significant aspect is it provides situational awareness and therefore enables you to bring to mind a whole variety of factors that are significant in appreciating the context of a natural ecosystem.
"For an ecologist this is very hard to realize, especially if you are trying to visualize it without being in the field. It's a different kind of field trip where the subject can speak to you. It's an aid to empathy and provides situational awareness."

Summary:

Facilitating environmental constellations is an immensely enriching experience. I have been touched by the insights and empathy of participants and by the power of this experiential and embodied method to transform people.

Witnessing representatives for trees and polar bears, sun, moon and Earth speak and feel has opened my mind to possibilities. I do not know what exactly is going on in a constellation when the Earth moon and sun laugh and laugh at the grandiosity of human beings, how close to the 'truth' these representatives are or not is an important and interesting question that doesn't seem discoverable or provable but it clearly opens up one's mind to possibilities and insights I can think of no other way of discovering. A constellation can make our vision a little less restricted and human centric, breaking us out of the 'homosphere' we unknowingly live in. Cormac Cullinan aptly describes our restricted vision in his book Wild Law (2002)

"It is easy to see from the outside the delusional nature of apartheid in South Africa, the belief that white people were God's chosen people....We have rejected the biosphere into which we were born and have erected in our minds a vast, hermetically-sealed 'humans only' world. We have lived so long within the contrived 'homosphere', breathing in the myths of human supremacy, that it is now more real to us than the Earth." (pp. 52-53)

Through this work I have met many interesting people and been inspired and touched by them. Every constellation is an intense and memorable experience; sometimes an adventure or exploration, at other times a creative experiment or means of research. Thank you to all my fellow adventurers, explorers, researchers and experimenters who have participated in constellations with me or provided opportunities for constellations to take place. As I write this so many constellations and individuals crowd into my mind and I am sorry I have only been able to touch briefly on a very few. I am happy to have so many powerful and interesting memories.

Peter deVries has been deeply immersed in the constellation approach, both as a teacher and a student, for more than ten years. He extends heartfelt gratitude to all his teachers of this work, especially, Bert Hellinger, Hunter Beaumont, Gabrielle Borkan and Victoria Sneh Schnabel. He uses constellations as a counselor and mediator for couples, families and corporate clients and has extensive experience in trauma healing and the healing arts. His private practice is in the San Francisco Bay Area and he teaches workshops and trainings throughout the US, Europe and the Caribbean.

E-mail: peter@constellationworks.com
Website: www.constellationworks.com

Beth Murray, CCH is a certified classical homeopath for both humans and animals. She lives in the San Francisco Bay Area and has a private practice for people and sees animals at several veterinary clinics there. She pioneered a program that provides homeopathy to zoo animals. She is also a poet; many of her books play with the capacity of language to represent the natural world and animal experience.

E-mail: beth@myanimalhomeopath.com
Websites: www.myanimalhomeopath.com
                     www.wholehomeopathy.com

Picture Credits for this chapter: Beth Murray

CHAPTER SIX

The Animal Experience

by Beth Murray and Peter deVries

Abstract: We created The Animal Experience as a forum for doing constellations for animals that are patients in Beth's homeopathy practice and at the local zoo. Having these animals' human guardians participate in the constellations has very much deepened their relationship with their animals, and shown them the extent to which their own state affects those of their animals. We have learned that representing animals can be quite different than representing humans, as animals do not have the mind/body divide to the extent that most humans do. It has been quite profound for us to experience the magnitude of love that animals can feel for their people in these representations.

Audience/Participants:

The participants in The Animal Experience have been almost exclusively people whose animals are my (Beth's) homeopathic patients, both through my practice at local vet clinics, and through my participation in an alternative treatment program at the local zoo.

Presenting Symptoms, Issues or Questions:

People consult me for their animals' physical, mental or emotional issues. Perhaps the most common issues I treat are cancer, skin issues, and behavioral issues. In my practice, whenever I feel that there are issues that are unclear that prevent me from perceiving the remedy the animal needs, or when I feel that the situation of the people the animals live with is deeply affecting the animals, I recommend that the people do a constellation for their animals

Peter had wanted to extend his constellation practice to encompass new fields, as he had been steadily representing human clients in private, family and corporate settings for over ten years. He came to the Animal Experience wondering how it would differ from his work with people.

Desired Outcomes:

We were hoping that the animal constellations would more deeply connect people with their animals and increase their awareness of the influence they had on them. Before I had the forum of constellation work, I would often perceive that the animals' mental and physical health was very much influenced by their people, but in the context of a veterinary clinic, where people often just want "a pill" to fix their animal's itchy skin or aggressive behavior, they are often not prepared to embark on the kind of understanding of their animal's mind and body that constellation work can provide. Prior to constellation work, I felt that I was a "lone voice," telling people about the effect they had on their animals, without a context to support me. Since The Animal Experience, clients are able to directly experience how their animals feel, the effect they have on their animals, and how all of this affects their animal's physical symptoms. This experience very much deepens their understanding of their relationship with their animal.

Additionally, homeopathic prescriptions are based on a being's physical and emotional sensations. Because animals cannot narrate their sensations, animal homeopaths are generally working with a great handicap, and for this reason we have to hone our intuition in order to perceive the animal's sensations, but even with a developed intuition, we often still don't get enough information about an animal's sensations to find a good remedy. For this reason, homeopaths often have to try many remedies before finding one that will help an animal, and many clients discontinue homeopathy before the remedy is found. I began doing constellations for animals in the hope that the representations of animals would give me more information about the animal's sensations. Not only have I found this to be the case, but we have also developed the practice of actually "testing" the remedies that occur to me during the constellation. We do this by either writing the name of the remedy on a piece of paper and having the representative put in their pocket, or by choosing a new representative to represent the remedy. Generally we continue to "test" remedies, until we find one the representative feels greatly alleviates the condition of the animal.

How We Work:

Peter devised the format for the Animal Experience. To start the investigation, we do the "walking in your shoes" (or in this case, "walking in your paws") exercise of Chris Assel. This is a solo constellation where the representative walks, rather than stands. We feel that this kinetic form approximates "animal experience" more closely than static forms. While his theories of animal consciousness are not our model, there is something helpful in Aristotle's theorization that desire always leads animals to locomotion, as differentiated from humans, for whom reason can stall locomotion [1]. We feel that the kinetic form of "walking in your shoes" more closely approximates the embodied animal experience where desire and sensation give rise to movement.

Generally we work completely "blind," which means that the representative does not know anything about the animal besides his/her name. Because Beth usually knows the animals and Peter does not, generally Peter initially "walks" the animal. We let this proceed for about fifteen minutes, until a picture of the animal's main concern has formed. At that point, we ask the animal's person if any of what they have seen resonates for them. Frequently by then, the person is deeply moved by the being they recognize as their animal represented so vividly by someone who "knows" nothing about them. At this point we may pose a question, either from the animal's person or from us. We may also introduce other representatives in order to create a richer picture of the animal's environment. The people the animal lives with, the other animals in the house, and the animal's parents and siblings are all frequently represented, but we have also represented concepts such as "the animal's trauma," or "what is causing the skin to itch." As the representative of the animal, Peter is often specifically drawn to the people who live with the animal sitting in the circle surrounding the constellation space. He may find himself attracted to the scent of these people, wanting to hold their hands, or rub up against them. At other times, especially when we want to investigate the influence of the people on the animal, we choose representatives for the animal's people. As in human constellations, the actual person being represented is often asked to replace their representative towards the end of the constellation so that they may completely embody the experience and be spoken to and speak directly to their animal. We have found that this moment of "stepping in" to their own role and being spoken to by their animals and speaking back to them is quite powerful and the source of ongoing transformation for the person.

Frequently, when the person is able to perceive both the love that their animal has for them, and the nature of the animal's dilemma, the person adjusts to accommodate the animal and the symptoms that the person has originally inquired about recede as time passes.

When the unfolding constellation resembles the physical and mental symptoms of a particular homeopathic remedy, we may introduce this remedy to the constellation, either by writing the name of the remedy on a piece of paper and having a representative put it in his/her pocket, or by choosing a representative to represent the remedy. Very often we will try different remedies until we come to the one that provides the most resolution to the constellation. We note this "resolution," as a kind of energized serenity in the representatives. As a follow-up to the constellation, the animal might receive the remedy used in the constellation.

Beth's Dog Laney with Water Ripples and Shadow

How We Came to This Way of Working:

Eight years ago I, Beth, was introduced to constellation work and immediately began using it for animals. My first animal constellation was for a family of boxers. Upon starting the constellation, all the representatives began to giggle. Initially, I thought they the representatives weren't taking the constellation seriously because it was a new idea to represent dogs, but I quickly realized that these giggling beings WERE the dogs. From this first constellation my understanding of and appreciation for constellations for animals has grown considerably. Over the last several years, in the presence of their keepers, I have done large constellations to represent zoo animals. Over two years ago, I teamed up with Peter deVries who had been my mentor in constellation work, and together we began regularly conducting "The Animal

Experience."

With over ten years of almost daily constellation experience, Peter has found The Animal Experience to be quite welcome. Immediately he was struck by how different it felt to represent an animal than a person. When we represent animals, we both experience an open-heartedness that is unlike any other representing we have done. We find that dogs especially embody this open-heartedness.

Generally, the people who come to The Animal Experience to have their animal represented have never experienced constellations before. Many approach it with some skepticism. Because of this skepticism, we feel it is important to show the participants the power of the knowing field, that force that connects us all, and to which we all have access through constellations and other meditative forms. For this reason we generally work blindly to avoid prior bias. We find that when a person sees a representative move just like their animal, or ask for the food their animal would ask for, or exhibit the relationship with another animal that their animal has, these people are much more engaged and trusting than if they are left wondering if the representation is a product of what the representative was told about the animal.

Vervet

Case Study: Vervets

We did a constellation to look at a group of vervets at the zoo; (vervets are a type of monkey.) We wanted to look at why the vervets would attack each other, and if there was anything that could be done to lessen the attacks. We assembled a group of experienced representatives and invited their keeper. The keeper was the only person who knew the history of the vervets, which was that they had been used as research monkeys in a lab. At the zoo, some of the monkeys were receiving homeopathic remedies; this had lessoned the aggression, but the aggression was still severe enough that a submissive monkey had to live separately from the group in order to recover from the severe physical beating she had received from the most dominant females.

The representatives knew only that they were going to represent monkeys. One by one the keeper chose representatives for each monkey, naming each monkey as she placed the representative. She also chose a representative for the person who worked in the lab. As the constellation began, the monkeys all had a severe aversion, and for some, a very strong anger toward the person who ran the lab. The monkeys who the keeper knew to be more aggressive were running up to the edge of the enclosure and taunting the representative of the lab keeper, who himself felt disdain for the monkeys. The monkeys who the keeper knew to be more submissive were hiding in the corner. I myself was representing a monkey I did not know well. I had no idea that this particular monkey had a fixation with the door, and would escape whenever he got the chance. But the minute I was placed in the role I began looking toward the door and eventually ran out of it. The keeper had chosen two men to represent the only two male monkeys in the group. The dominant male monkey was challenging the lab keeper to a fight. The submissive male monkey was sitting in the corner, saying, "Why should I try? I won't be able to actualize anything." The keeper felt that this was very much the experience of this male monkey, who was artificially kept with a group in which he could not breed due to his position in the group. In the wild, he would have most likely left the group. As the tension in the constellation mounted, the more dominant monkeys began to attack the more submissive monkeys. The keeper suggested that we erect a partition between the two of them similar to the partition she used when violence escalated at the zoo. The representatives of the monkeys felt somewhat relieved by this partition, and this was helpful information for their keeper. We also introduced into the constellation the monkeys' current keeper. They reacted affectionately to her, and expressed that they were quite affected by her own feelings. When she was upset, they felt upset. She was experiencing a difficultly in her personal life. The monkeys' representatives felt that it was better for them if she talked to them about her difficulty, rather than trying to hide it from them, as this only increased their perception of it. By this point in the constellation, the keeper felt quite disheartened. There seemed to be little resolution, and though the keeper loved the monkeys and wanted to do the best she could for them within the zoo setting, the situation from which they had come was so horrible that there seemed to be little relief for them. At this point Peter suggested that we introduce into the constellation a resource for the keeper. With the resource standing behind her, the keeper felt heartened, which in turn positively affected the monkeys and brought more harmony to the group. We also introduced into the constellation a remedy made from a "wild vervet," in order to connect the monkeys to their wild ancestors and reduce the influence of the selective breeding. This also had a calming effect on the vervets. At this point we brought the constellation to a close.

In the months that ensued, I tried to find a remedy made from "wild vervet," but was unsuccessful. Then Kathleen Aspenns, who is a member of the team that practices holistic modalities with me at the zoo suggested that we use remedies from the "Ugandan Series[2]" by David Dalton. David went to Uganda and the essences he made from plants and trees there bring healing to situations of injustice, as these plants and trees live with the atrocities perpetrated since the rise of the Lord's Resistance Army. Kathleen made individual formulas for many of the vervets that included essences from this series, for example, she used his "Hewittia", which allows the release of trauma from witnessing abuse as a juvenile and his "Orchid Tree," which fosters leadership through the regeneration of tribal wisdom.

I would like to say that since the constellation and the use of these essences, the violence among the vervets has stopped entirely. While this is not the case, I can say that no more vervets have been forced to live separately due to the violence visited upon them by other members. Part of the keeper's "resource" has been her own homeopathic treatment, and that rather than having to hide her stress, her realization that her animals can be confidants for her. Much in the way that ancestors' secrets live on in future generations, I have found that when people try to hide their anxiety from their animals, the animals often somatize it, but when people talk about their anxiety with their animals, the animals are less likely to hold that anxiety themselves. We would like to thank these vervets for allowing us to expand our understanding of constellation work, flower essences and homeopathy through our work together. As often the case with constellation work, the link between the work and future consequences is penetrating but subtle.

Daisy, an Old Hound Dog

Case Study: Older Hound Dog

To another recent constellation, we invited two women who care very diligently for an older hound dog who has entirely lost the use of her back legs and has numerous physical ailments. These women have devoted the majority of their lives to caring for her, doing several loads of laundry a day, as she lays in an area covered with blankets and sheets that is frequently soiled due to her incontinence. One of them has delayed her retirement so that she can continue to produce income for this dog's holistic vet bills, and the other one stays home and cooks four meals a day for her. It was not clear to me that this dog wanted to continue in this fashion, and I invited these women to do a constellation, suspecting that the constellation might reveal that this dog was ready to pass. I was secretly hoping that the constellation would enable these women to let her go, because I believed that might be the most compassionate response to her situation.

Peter represented this dog, and immediately he experienced a field of incredible love. He was drawn to the two women sitting at the periphery of the constellation space, and held each of their hands, stating that this was the only place he wanted to be. He experienced what could almost be called swooning from the incredible field of love that he felt for these two women. When I asked if he had any plans to pass, or desired to pass, he stated that he wanted to remain with these women as long as possible, and that when he passed it would be a slow "dissolving." It became very clear that this dog was exceedingly happy in her current position, despite the state of her body. Knowing this brought great peace to these two women, who had dedicated their lives to her, and convinced us that euthanasia is not always appropriate for animals who have lost the use of their limbs. For days after this representation, Peter felt affected by the incredible love he felt in his heart during this representation.

What we Have Found Representing Animals:

In our flier for The Animal Experience we write,

> *"We are finding that it is very good for people to 'represent' animals. This is because animals do not wear any masks; they live in the now, experience unconditional love and do not second-guess or judge their impulses. Living as we do in a psyche that is often split between mind, body, emotion and spirit, representing an animal that has a more unified system can be a profound experience."*

Though there are exceptions to this, we have found general differences in representing cats and dogs. True to common perceptions about them, we find that cats tend to have a stronger sense of their individual being and are strongly connected to their sensual desires. This particular hound dog was an example of the nature of many dogs we have represented who have very large heart fields and great devotion to their people. We have also represented many dogs who have a great need to move and who feel frenetic and unsettled. We believe this is partially because they do not get enough off-leash running time, but also that it is a response to their surroundings or to a shock or trauma they experienced prior to coming to their present home.

As a homeopath, it has long been my perception that many cases of skin and irritable bowel syndrome have their root in anxiety that animals take on from/for their people. It has been interesting to see this validated in the constellation work. When their people are experiencing anxiety, dogs' need to move is heightened, and if they do not get to move enough, the anxiety often leads to itching skin. The representatives for these animals often find themselves pacing, as the animals may in fact do. I have also found myself walking "stereotypies" while representing animals. In her book, Animals Make Us Human, Temple Grandin[3] talks about how walking the same route over and over can be soothing to an animal that is in an untenable situation. These repetitive pacing patterns are called "stereotypies," and include behaviors such as repetitive digging. She notes, and I have seen, especially at the zoo, animals who pace the length of their enclosure or who walk the same circle over and over. I have even seen a bear whose nails were worn and he was developing muscular-skeletal problems from always pacing a circle in the same direction, so that the side of the body on the inside of the circle experienced a different kind of repetitive stress than the side of the body on the outside of the circle. In representations where we have been compelled to pace or stereotype, we have felt that moving in this way was our only option, that it was our only way to self-soothe. We also have noted that we have very little perception of our bodies when we are stereotyping; and that we have no time-perception. In one representation, I was pacing a shape like an infinity sign, which I felt was an apt representation for this kind of timeless, un-embodied quality, as well as a shape that enables the pacing to continue uninterrupted. Peter notes that these representations have some commonalities with representations of humans who have been traumatized: that the representatives have a distinct lack of bodily awareness, common to traumatized people who have had to close off awareness of trauma held in the body in order to continue daily life. We also note that when these animals are connected to healing resources, they stop pacing and begin to again feel emotions and sensations in their bodies. But given the traumas of dislocation and severance from those they love, conditional acceptance from the people who care for them, and the lack of connection with nature and other soothing environments that many animals experience, pacing and other stereotyped behaviors are the best way for their systems to respond to the trauma experience.

In representing the zoo animals, we find what the keepers have noted, which is that these animals are not entirely "wild" animals, but like domestic animals that live separately from their people, such as horses in stables, they are highly keyed into the daily routine, and seek routine and a connection with the people in their environment who are compassionate toward them. This may be because routine is a soothing counterpart to the trauma they may have experienced either in transport from the wild, in early breeding environments, or in their current situation. They do have a connection with their "wild" counterparts via instinctual behaviors and flight responses, and I believe they also have an awareness of the importance of representing their species to the visitors to the zoo, an understanding that in living there at the zoo they are helping their species by increasing humankind's compassion for and ability to protect that species.[4]

Peter notes that in animal representations, the predator/prey relationship is not unlike the perpetrator/victim dynamic, with one BIG difference: animals are completely surrendered to their roles. Bert Hellinger says that we all serve some purpose in life or that life takes us in service of something. We believe that the same is true for animals, that they are in service of life, and have a vast capacity to surrender to this service. By contrast, humans often struggle with our experience, monitoring and judging it. Prey animals know how to freeze when they are caught and die as a service to the life of the prey animals who rely on them. This stands in sharp contrast to many humans who get stuck in victimization and traumatization that goes back generations. In homeopathic "provings," we discover what homeopathic remedies can do by giving them to healthy people and recording the mental and emotional symptoms they develop as a result. The symptoms that are common to many participants in the proving become known as the symptoms that remedy can cure. From our provings of remedies made from various animals, we have some understanding of the mental and emotional symptoms that for example, the remedies made from wolf or rabbit's milk can address. While this is a vast topic worthy of another paper, suffice it to say that in these provings we don't find that the remedies made from wolf's milk carry guilt about killing their prey. We believe that the predator also kills as a service to life. Representing animals helps us get in touch with this surrendered place. It is a place of not knowing, of deep, spiritual experience, and experience of Basic Trust.[5] Most humans have lost touch with Basic Trust. Basic Trust is a bit like Buddha Nature, the state of absolute enlightenment and indestructible bliss that all humans are born with, but tend to lose access to unless they have a spiritual practice to support access to it. In our representations of animals, we feel quite in touch with this Basic Trust.

Additionally, good representations only happen through trusting the impulse of the representation and abandoning the judgment of our ego about what we are representing. So, in this way, representing requires a similar form of surrender.

Further Development:

We feel that representing animals should be a requisite for people learning about representation because these representations help people get in touch with not knowing and Basic Trust, two requirements for good representations. We even believe that the animal representation could be built out as a device to help transform the dual nature of mind, the separation between embodied experience and the judging mind that humans experience. We know that people with depression and loneliness are helped by the presence of animal companions. For example, the people who survived the 911 attacks said that helped them more than the human trauma experts; they felt that the animals regulated their system the most.[6] Similarly, Ellen Kaye Gehrke used a measure called Heart Rate Variability to study the influence that people and horses had on each other. Heart Rate Variability, (HRV) is the time between heartbeats. When humans and animals experience positive emotions, their Heart Rate Variability becomes more even. When they experience negative emotions it becomes more erratic. In this study, the HRV of humans and horses were measured prior to coming into contact with each other. After being in compassionate contact for a while, the heart fields were again monitored and found to "cohere" or move in balanced patterns. Interestingly, the humans picked up the horses' HRV rather than vice versa. However the study also found that horses were attracted to people with balanced HRV regardless of whether they knew that person or not.[7] It would be interesting to monitor Heart Rate Variability in people representing animals in constellations! We propose that representing animals could be very helpful for people with psychological imbalances, to help people jump-start a mental/physical/emotional connection that they may have lost.

In one of the Animal Constellations, we asked people to represent two dogs who were experiencing health problems. The representatives of the dogs showed that the dogs had very little interest in life because of the degree of control they experienced in their home. Initially in this constellation, we asked a representative to represent "off-leash runs" as a way of bringing joy and freedom to the dogs. While ultimately the most healing element for the dogs turned out to be a representation of an ancestor dog who lived a life herding and living closely with his people, after the constellation the person who represented "off-leash runs" wrote us with these remarks:

"I represented the 'unleashed run' concept which was an incredible bodily experience. During the representation I fell down which I did not think/feel much about it at the time. But I did manage to injure myself as the keys in my pocket had jammed into my quadriceps and somehow my right side of the upper right leg/hip were torqued. . . . now here comes the juicy part - afterwards, the healing experience and sensations of recovery were like nothing I have ever experienced in my life. I know (and I felt) I was released from my role ... but for the next couple of days I was aware of the pain and discomfort and at the same time I could feel this sensation of healing/rejuvenation/recovery/energy starting from the deepest core of my (I can call it marrow, cellular, ... but I really have no words for it) physical being and emanating to the surface of my body. It was the most unusual sweet sensation of recovery in the midst of discomfort. ... and within a few days all the symptoms of discomfort were gone. I don't want to necessarily label or categorize or even understand what I experienced, at the same time it was somehow related to and inspired by the constellation or the magic of its field."

This statement echoes what we have found to be true; that these representations of animals, natural elements, and even "off-leash runs" can be profound experiences.

We find that animal constellations almost inevitably show that the issues of the humans they live with affect the animals. Animals pick up the issues of their people just like children pick them up from the adults they live with. Generally, both animals and children are the most sensitive members of the family field, and will reflect it's disturbances and shape themselves in such a way as to bring the most harmony to the family field. They do this out of service to balance the family field, but in so doing, take on imbalances of their own. Both children and animals do this out of love. We often see that people new to constellations who have come to have their animal represented for the first time require constellations to look at their own issues, as these issues figure so heavily in the representation of the animal. In homeopathy, Beth often finds that if she cannot find a remedy that will help an animal, if she treats the animal's person that the animal's issues resolve. We would like to conduct workshops that allow for both the representation of the person's own issues and those of their animal. This would require a longer time frame and most-likely day-long workshops. It also requires the cultivation of a client-base that is interested in delving deeply into the connections between their animal's issues and their own, but our experience has shown us that the rewards of this work are quite substantial for those who undertake it.

Footnotes:

(1) Aristotle, De Anima

(2) Though a description of the Uganda Series is not published, they can be purchased from David Dalton at www.deltagardens.com. A short description of one of the essences in the set appears in his Late Autumn 2011 Newsletter at http://www.deltagardens.com/delta-gardens2011/index.php?main_page=page&id=10.

(3) Grandin, Temple and Johnson, Catherine; Animals Make Us Human: Creating the Best Life for Animals, Houghton Mifflin Harcourt, 2009.

(4) I have brought several people to the zoo to conduct intuitive readings of certain animals there, and independently, several of the readers have perceived that the zoo animals feel a connection with their species in the wild and a sense of the importance of their representing that species to humankind via their presence at the zoo.

(5) A.H.Almaas, Facets of Unity, Diamond Books, Berkley, CA, pp. 21-32.

(6) Therapy Dogs Played Part in 9/11 Recovery, Rob Hedelt
http://fredericksburg.com/News/FLS/2008/092008/09112008/409775/index_html?page=2 and Little Known Heroes: The 9/11 Therapy Dogs, Ernie Sloan,
http://www.dogchannel.com/dog-blog/ernie-slone-blog/little-known-heroes-the-911-therapy-dogs.aspx

(7) Gehrke, Ellen Kaye, PhD, *The Horse-Human Heart Connection: Results of Studies Using Heart Rate Variability*, published in NARHA Strides, Spring 2010.

Sara Fancy. I was born in 1962 in Surrey Kent, although I grew up in Herne close to a city called Canterbury that is famous for its Cathedral and Canterbury tales. Our bungalow overlooked a large recreational field surrounded by woods. As a child I spent as much time as possible outdoors playing on the swings, climbing trees, running free on the grass and exploring nature.

My early adulthood was filled with immigration to the United States and success in the arena of professional body building. I enjoyed music and painting. I encountered the beginning of a different kind of discipline and opening through meditation.

As an adult in my late thirties, I studied Dr. Stone's Polarity Healing Arts and Upledger's Cranial Sacral Unwinding with Gary Strauss graduating in 2003 as an RPP (registered Polarity Practitioner). I provided Equine Therapy through a local business for 7 years, after which time I founded my own business, Silver Horse Healing Ranch (SHHR). Sometime later I studied Constellation Therapy with Francesca Boring and graduated from her training in 2008.

Silver Horse Healing Ranch is my business which provides various courses for both children and adults, including the following:

- Dancing with Horses
- Shamanic Horse Workshop Intensive
- Mentorship Program
- Horse Constellations

I combine the skills I learned in the healing arts with my knowledge and experience of horses and how horses willingly support healing movements. In 2012 the work at the Silver Horse Healing Ranch was featured in Depaak Chopra's "30 Days to Intent" YouTube Video Series.

E-mail: sara@silverhorse.org
Website: www.silverhorse.org

Picture Credits for this chapter and portrait of Sara: Leigha Hodnet lhphotographs.com (except of Silver which is by Sara)

CHAPTER SEVEN

Silver Horse Healing Ranch

by Sara Fancy

Abstract: I facilitate a space where humans and horses come together to bring balance and harmony to challenging situations. This work follows the principles of Family Constellation and utilizes the help offered from our ancestors and nature. The horses willingly participate instinctively knowing what to do in order to support the healing movement of the focus and group. A Horse Constellation is similar to a Family Constellation except that it is done outdoors within a round pen with horses. A Constellation clears energy in the past that is affecting the present. A horse is invited into the round pen along with other people to participate in the Constellation. The horse assumes a role and will demonstrate what it is that needs attention. In a Horse Constellation we are outdoors exposed to other life forms such as birds, insects, rabbits, coyotes, dogs, trees, elements etc. Many times these other additions become part of the Constellation and we find ourselves being supported by nature. The horses hold a neutral energy, they are not invested in the outcome of the Constellation or worried about how well they are representing yet they do have a propensity to find balance and ease. I also provide table top constellations for individuals using horses as the figures for representatives.

Audience:

The people who come to me for Horse Constellations are approximately 80% women and are generally attracted because of the horses. The groups Constellations + Horses are for adults only. The topics and intense emotional releases are in my opinion too much for children to integrate, although obviously constellations can be performed for children who do not have to be present.

Horses represent freedom and power and people come because they are seeking these elements in their lives. They are in a job and/or relationship that is destroying them spiritually, mentally, emotionally and/or physically yet they are tied because of the security offered in the situation.

This work is helpful to whoever has the courage and openness to look at what is present for them in the moment and what it is that is inhibiting their wellbeing. If someone is terrified or allergic to horses then this modality would not be recommended.

There are horses that are not appropriate to do this type of work. An abused horse that does not trust people would need to be rehabilitated before offering themselves to this work if at all. Green horses, (horses without any initial training) would not be a good idea to use as they can startle easily if someone moves suddenly or displays predatory behavior.

Issues:

People come to receive this work for many different reasons. One example is people suffering from depression who love horses; another example would be people who are in crisis regarding their path in life.

Desired Outcomes:

People come because they are curious as to how horses can facilitate their healing. Their previous experience with horses, if any, has been in a traditional context such as riding or jumping.

Horses themselves benefit from Constellations. If a horse is having a hard time integrating into a herd a Constellation could bring insight to what it is that is in the way. Also physical symptoms can be set up in a Constellation for a horse to show what is missing.

How Contributor Came to this Work:

I've been asked numerous times by people if I grew up with horses. The answer is no, I didn't.

As a young child I had a few uneventful lessons with an old, sad horse at a local barn.

At forty years old I adopted my first horse, Silver. Now, ten years later I have seven horses and a business called Silver Horse Healing Ranch. That ten years involved something of a journey for me, of course.

Not long after, I moved to Topanga Canyon, a small town in the mountains, and began my journey into the healing arts. I reconnected to animals by adopting a cat, a dog and then another dog. Living next to horses I took some riding lessons, discovering how much I thoroughly enjoyed being in the company of horses. After graduating from Polarity Healing Arts school I had a sense of what it was I wanted to do. I knew horses had to be involved, I loved being outdoors and I was ready to be of service.

I was told about an Equine Therapeutic Ranch that had recently opened in my neighborhood. I applied for a job and was hired to feed and clean up after the horses. After a couple of months I was promoted to manager of the ranch. Among other things this involved facilitating horse sessions with cancer survivors, special needs adults and children, as well as working with neurotypicals.

I felt I was ready to own a horse and declared this decision in a prayer. Soon after I had a significant dream, in it there was a horse wearing a coat of arms, purple with gold emblems. This horse came running towards me in a panic. He was being chased, and as he came towards me I was worried he would run me down but for whatever reason he managed to stop right in front of me. This horse led me inside a bank where we met and congregated with his other horse friends.

Following this dream I had an encounter with a horse exactly how it was in the dream. It was a new horse at the corral I was mucking out in. He was being chased by another horse, I was directly in his tracks and again he stopped right in front of me. I knew this was the horse I was supposed to meet. As it turned out his owner was looking for someone to adopt him. I was asked if I wanted him, without hesitation I said yes.

This Arabian horse, who I named Silver, has a goofy sense of humor and loves to play. He is extremely sensitive and has an uncanny knack of detecting human weaknesses. He is incredibly personable and knows how to open people's hearts. Because of his willingness and eagerness to engage with people I was able to get him a job at the ranch as a teacher although clearly he is a healer.

Silver

I was motivated to learn everything I possibly could about horses, reading books, watching videos and following horse people from various backgrounds that do extraordinary work with horses such as Linda Kohonov, Klaus Hempfling and Alexander Nevzorov. Through studying their work I was shown how anything is possible with horses; I became excited about how and where my work with horses could evolve.

In 2003- 2004 there was a saturation of Premarin mares on the horse rescue scene. Premarin is a hormone replacement therapy drug which is made from pregnant mares' urine and is prescribed for menopausal women and men with prostrate cancer. Some of the Premarin Ranches were closing down due to a survey that publicized the connection with this drug to breast cancer. It was during this time that I began adopting Premarin mares. In the winter of 2008 I was involved in a communal constellation regarding Premarin mares in Banff, Alberta, Canada which resulted in an article I coauthored with Shannon Fleming (now Dr. Shannon Zaychuk).[1] One of the mares I adopted was Laydee, a Premarin mare from Alberta Canada. She had produced Premarin until she could no longer become pregnant. I saw Laydee mentioned in an e-mail from the Animali Farm (a horse rescue organization that specifically deals with horses from the Premarin Industry). She was about to be sold for horse meat. Laydee works with young kids and participates in the horse constellations.

These mares had little experience and were in need of basic training. I knew it was possible to train horses without the use of metal bits, spurs and heavy saddles. I followed the principles of Natural Horsemanship, which works with the horses' willing nature. By understanding the natural instincts of a horse, it's possible to have a partnership based on trust as opposed to force and domination. I learned a great deal from the mares. There is a prejudice towards mares in the horse world. I've heard people call them moody mares, bitches, crazy mares etc. Unlike the geldings (castrated stallions) mares are complete. I have found mares to be loving, affectionate, nurturing and strong willed. It is usually a mare who is the alpha in the herd.

In 2007 with my own herd of horses I started Silver Horse Healing Ranch.

After Graduating from Francesca Boring Masons Family Constellation training I started facilitating Family Constellation circles in 2008. A constellation colleague who has established a busy Constellation practice in LA suggested I combine the Constellation work with the horses. We tried it out a couple of Constellations and were both amazed. The horses took to this work with grace and ease. This was an area where all the horses were able to participate, offering their services to help people.

I believe that horses are fully aware of our hidden dynamics involving emotional and mental wounding. Being prey animals prone to being eaten by other animals, including humans, they have a built in hypersensitivity and awareness essential for their survival.

As herd animals they are psychically connected and easily tune into the "field". This is why it is so natural for them to participate in the Constellations. What astounds me more than anything is their willingness to help; this is why I consider horses to be "natural born healers".

Perhaps the best introduction to horse constellations is to provide some examples of how subtle and profound the participation of horses can be in a constellation. The following summaries also provide an opportunity to illustrate how involved nature herself can become, spontaneously supporting or being a willing representative in a constellation.

Case Study: Nature's Blessings

Mandy's close connection to nature and love of animals led her to come to SHHR to receive a personal Horse Constellation. Mandy was familiar with Family Constellations but had yet to experience a Constellation outdoors with horses.

Inside the Circle. As a small group of women we sat in a circle and listened as Mandy spoke of her intention for her Constellation. She was aware of how abusive and traumatic behaviors are passed down through family generations and was concerned about the uncontrollable anger she sometimes felt towards her young son. She wanted to expand her family by bringing in an adopted baby and wanted to address her feelings of anger before committing to another child. She spoke of the physical abuse she suffered as a child at the hands of her father. As she was speaking, we were disrupted by a squirrel that ran frantically across a branch near our table. My two large dogs charged at the squirrel barking ferociously. There was a scuffle and the squirrel escaped unharmed. Clearly we were being shown the perpetrator energy that lay waiting for us in Mandy's family system.

The Constellation. I asked Mandy to pick representatives for herself, her father, grandfather and great grandfather. I then asked her to pick a horse out of the seven that were present.

Mandy picked Laydee for the horse, a large Percheron white mare. As we walked towards the round pen the atmosphere felt weighted with an intense expectancy. A small flock of birds flew by and gathered in a tree that stands on the edge of the circle. The bird's appearance was comforting as if they were showing their support by being witnesses for Mandy's Constellation.

Mandy placed the representatives inside the round-pen. She placed herself, father and grandfather in a sequential line about ten feet apart from one other. The representative for the Great-Grandfather she placed to the right of the others. He stood about fifteen feet opposite his son.

The Great-Grandfather stood isolated and stiff, as though he were upholding a horrific story in silence. He was aware of the distance between himself and his family and that the huge white horse did not come near him. He felt powerless because of the intensity of keeping the story to himself. His representative was magnetized to the place where he stood, completely immobile.

As the Great-Grandfather looked at the ground he saw open graves, chaos, darkness and sounds of horror, the vision he saw was eerily reflected back to us by wailing coyotes hiding in the surrounding hillside from where we gathered.

I placed myself behind the Great-Grandfather to be a woman who had loved and adored this man as a baby. Slowly, Great-Grandfather softened his rigidity, about to crumble. He began to fall and just as he dropped I noticed one of the birds behind him dive vertically to the ground perfectly in sync with the Great-Grandfather's downward movement.

As the Great-Grandfather accepted the love from his mother, he was able to look at his family for the first time. He wasn't ready to join them but cared that their burden was lifted and that they were able to make new connections with each other.

Laydee, the horse, moved to where the Great-Grandfather sat; in the Constellation she was the shock absorber, transmuting and dissipating energy that was released from the constellation, her enormous stature and connection to the earth assisting in this alchemical process. It was then that we noticed the bunch of wild rabbits hesitantly making their way into the circle.

Now Mandy's representative, the representatives of her father, and the representative of the Grandfather, were able to acknowledge each other and honor each for their positions in the Family System. Suddenly a loud chorus of Coyote cries echoed around us and continued for what seemed a significant amount of time.

Summary. This is where the Constellation ended. Mandy said later that the abuse she suffered from her father took place outdoors and it was therapeutic to receive a healing amongst nature with the support of the animals for it was them that helped her through this challenging time in her childhood.

Throughout this Constellation I was extremely aware of the participation and support of the surrounding animals and birds and how nature offered us a beautiful support system.

I heard from Mandy a few months after her Constellation. She was delighted to report how she and her husband had adopted a baby girl. She believed that the constellation allowed the space for the baby to come into their family. She also said that her father, who lives in a VA home, had opened up to one of the caretakers at the facility about the abuse he had suffered as a child. He spoke of how his father who had locked him in an attic and then sent him away from the family to live with an aunt while his siblings stayed with his parents.

Laydee

Case Study: Laydee Lucille La Don's

Identifying the Client. At a Constellation + Horses event in December 2011, we had a hat with people's names in it who wanted a constellation. I added in Laydee's name, an ex-Premarin, Percheron mare; she had been dealing with digestive issues and I felt she could use a constellation. A name was picked from the hat, it was Laydee's. We turned around to look for her and there she was watching us from behind the fence inside the round-pen.

The Constellation. One person in the group volunteered to represent Laydee and another volunteered to represent her symptoms. We entered the round-pen and connected to our body sensations, movement and feelings.

Laydee's representative said she felt restless and her stomach hurt. She moved anxiously around the round-pen as if searching for something. The representative for Laydee's symptoms stood motionless with her head down, looking into a mud pool.

Laydee's representative said she felt something was missing. I stepped into the role of what was missing. Instantly Laydee's representative and I came together and clung to each other. We were both overcome with emotion and Laydee's representative was sobbing. The representative for Laydee felt like my mother and I her foal. I felt as though I had been taken away from her prematurely. (A high percentage of Premarin foals are sent to the feedlots to be fattened up before going to auction to be sold for horse meat.)

We held onto each other for quite some time and then directed our attention to the representative for the symptom who was still standing in the same spot looking down into the mud. We walked over and stood on either side of her. The symptom's representative moved her hands in an opening and clutching rhythm reminding us of a foal trying to suckle. The symptom seemed like another one of Laydee's foals who didn't make it, possibly dying at birth. (A significant amount of foals die within days of being born of starvation or exposure).

We all held hands and Laydee's representative said the stomach pains had gone. Then from across the round-pen the real Laydee turned to face us and walked towards us. Stopping in front of us she acknowledged me (her foal) by touching my hand gently with her nose and did the same to her other foal (symptom).

We bowed down to Laydee, honoring her as a mother and for her lifelong service to the Premarin Industry.

Summary. Since this constellation Laydee's digestive problems have cleared up and I noticed how she has become more confident in the herd, joining the mares in the higher ranks and being more assertive with Hank (the omega horse).

The Herd, Sara, and the Dog Zorro

A Last Sharing On Horse Constellations

Horses, dividing their time between the spiritual and physical worlds, navigate the Field with a natural ease. The horses at Silver Horse Healing Ranch enjoy offering themselves to this type of service where they are allowed to move and interact freely at their own choice.

Having horses involved in a Constellation is a memorable experience. The impact of relating with very different beings affects us on a deep level. The presence of the horse in the Constellation brings potency to the healing; being outdoors and in nature creates a therapeutic environment for the Constellation.

Footnote:

(1) Fancy, S., & Fleming, S., (2009). "Horses in the Field." *The Knowing Field* Issue 14, 38-42.

Chrisjan (drs. C.J.M.) Leermakers, M.Sc. I was born in a village in the south of Holland. My father was a veterinarian. I often went to the farms with him to help cure the animals. I went to the Gymnasium and after that I studied Physical Geography at the University of Amsterdam and worked for many years in nature and environmental projects in the Netherlands, among others at the tourist board (ANWB) and the national nature management agency (Staatsbosbeheer). Currently (2013) I'm working at the national organization for water and highways (Rijkswaterstaat). From about 1995 I changed my direction and began taking courses in inner child therapy, emotional bodywork, NLP, geomancy, intuitive training and family and organization constellation facilitating. Over the last 10 years I have a practice as a Constellation Facilitator, Therapist, and Coach. I play in a jazz band in Amsterdam as a saxophonist and I'm the father of a son and a daughter.

Website:	www.systop.nl
E-mail:	info@systop.nl
Offerings:	individual sessions on family, housing, birthplace
	career planning constellations
	group workshops on demand
	in-company-organizations
	environmental constellations

Picture Credits for aerial view: Kees van der Veer

CHAPTER EIGHT

Environmental Organization Constellations for the Buurderij Haarlemmermeer Zuid

by Chrisjan Leermakers

Abstract: This chapter presents an example of how the representation of land and water and other environmental factors in a systemic constellation can provide valuable insights when examining issues of land usage . The energies of the environment can be given a voice that is normally unheard. Such constellations can contribute to acting towards the environment in a more balanced and respectful way.

Audience:

Facilitators of constellations interested in involving environmental features in the constellation work.

For the particular application described in this chapter: Land planners who are interested in new forms of living and working together in a rural environment.

Issues (for this case study):

Exploring new forms of land usage and community cooperation.

Desired Outcomes for the Work (for this case study):

The goal of the constellations was to support the project initiators by providing insight into the elements to be considered for the project to succeed.

How Contributor Came to this Work:

During my study of physical geography and landscape ecology at the University of Amsterdam, in which a holistic approach is essential, I came in contact with landscape phenomenology. What I learned from that is to thoroughly watch the phenomena in the landscape and look for the key elements that form its identity and go along with that.

I would say that in constellation work it's a bit the same. That is, it demands the same attitude: thoroughly watch the phenomena in the constellation, look for the key elements, and then go along with them.

So here I found a similarity in approach and attitude what made me want to explore the possibilities of constellations for getting closer to the essences of our surroundings: the living creatures, animals, plants, but also stones, houses and landscapes.

At a big conference about constellations in Würzburg, Germany in 2003, I found in an Open Space conference session several colleague constellation facilitators who had more or less the same drive and together we formed the investigation group of the Sixth Sense

Buurderij Haarlemmermeer Zuid (2010)

in Service. For a few years we experimented together in seminars that we organized and discovered the Birthplace Constellations and many other exciting new ways of getting in touch with what we also called "our bigger family:" the plants, the stones, the animals. Nowadays I work in Holland with Birthplace and also Living place constellations and next to that I gradually work further on environmental organization constellations, like the ones I describe in this chapter. I do this besides my work as a specialist in nature policy affairs.

Case Study

In 2007 and 2011 I facilitated two constellations around the experiment Buurderij Haarlem-mermeer Zuid (Neighborhood farm or Community farm Haarlemmermeer South) in the Netherlands. The first constellation was at the beginning of the experiment, the second at the end of the first phase.

The constellations showed that this form of work can be a helpful tool to show the underlying dynamics of the process of the development - in this specific case of a completely new form of cooperation in building up new ways of living in a rural community in a Dutch Polder-area.

In the following section I describe the two constellations. I tend to call this type of constellation "organization constellations with a focus on environmental factors," in short environmental organization constellations. The organization is the main focus, while in environmental or nature constellations the environment itself is the main focus, though often directly related to humans on a personal level (such as living place or birthplace).

The example described is the process of development of one of the first neighborhood farms or community farms (buurderijen) in the Netherlands, namely Haarlemmermeer Zuid. The constellations were done at the request of the three initiators: a farmer, a horticulturist and a sculptor.

What is a buurderij? Buurderij is a new composed word which, etymologically, is composed of the Dutch word for boerderij, meaning farm, and buur or buurman, meaning neighbor. So a buurderij in its most simple expression is a farm with neighbors. Or: a farm that deliberately wants to take on board the views of its neighbors. Or a farm that seeks to be of service to its neighbors. It is also a farm that seeks neighbors that aim to serve the farm. The essential value that is key to the buurderij is reciprocity. This reciprocity is expressed in organizational, economic and ecological form.[1]

A buurderij is a new concept for farms that, next to farm activities fulfill tasks for the neighborhood and the surrounding landscape in an innovative way. For example the farm may offer space for a kindergarten, care-taking, recreation and artistic activities. A constellation can be helpful to have a closer look at the often uncertain processes that are taking place in this changing community and environment. Also the land can be given a voice.

The aim of the concept of the Buurderij is restoring the link between agriculture and society and to make use of other potential benefits of agriculture than just the efficient production of food.

Buurderijen, community farms, differ from other enterprises in that they apply new combinations of functions, new forms of participation, new organizational principles, new financial arrangements and take care of a whole region, beyond the traditional limits of the farm. For this reason, developing a buurderij is an undertaking that shakes up and renovates current institutional and policy arrangements. The goal of the constellations was to support this uncertain process and provide insights into the impact of initiatives on the people involved, entrepreneurs and inhabitants, and also on the land and water resources themselves.

To repeat for clarity, the first constellation took place in the phase that the Buurderij was just newly established in 2007 and the second after the first initializing phase was concluded, together with the encouraging subsidies in 2011.

First Constellation at Project Beginning in 2007

At the first constellation in 2007, the method of constellations was quite new for the people involved. Because the initiators were also pioneers in experimenting with a new way of land management, which the Buurderij-concept is (central motto 'reflection, slow pace and awareness in a multifunctional and spatially attractive landscape'), they were very open to this unknown way of working. I had brought with me a couple of representatives: friends and colleagues, and the initiators of the Buurderij brought up their question and could watch how the constellation developed. The constellation took place on the estate of the horticulturist. Unfortunately the farmer was absent.

The question, on behalf of all the three initiators expressed by the horticulturist, was in short:

"The project of the Buurderij has not jet gained enough power to get other parties enthusiastic and join; how can this be improved?"

Next to representatives for the Buurderij and for the government the land was represented as well as water. The Haarlemmermeer is a polder which was gained from the sea in the 19th century. There are many ditches and canals. The soil is very fertile for agriculture. There was also a representative for the neighbors which expressed that they felt not involved. This was one of the insights of the constellation that this should be more the case.

The land expressed that it did not feel that it was respected. The reason for this could well be that the reclamation from the sea was being done merely for economic reasons (economic benefits from agriculture are the main objective). It was clear that the land as such, and also the water, were not being acknowledged as of value for themselves but only as a means for the benefits for mankind.

The good intentions of the initiators of the Buurderij to have an integrated approach with respect to the environment (nature and landscape conservation) and all functions of the land for society involved (such as recreation facilities for nearby cities or water detainment basins) could not diminish this wronged feeling of the land.

The main project consultant of the Buurderij expressed later on that it made clear that the land should be asked for permission in some sort of ritual in order to act much more respectfully in regard to the intrinsic values of the land (and water).

Second Constellation

In 2011 I facilitated on request another constellation for the Buurderij Haarlemmermeer Zuid. This time all three initiators were present. Again I also brought a couple of representatives with me.

The question now was more: "what is the attitude of the government towards the initiative? Are they still interested in the experiment to integrate land use also for community purpose next to the agricultural entrepreneurship from the neighborhood itself.?"

There were signals that the authorities were withdrawing themselves.

It turned out in the constellation that the administration concerned (commune and province) were very divided in themselves. Civil servants were willing to cooperate, but most governors weren't very interested anymore. The processes went too slow and the government claimed new rights to the land such as for high tension electric cables and space for new housing in the scope of the so-called Westflank-area. Next to this there was a policy of retrenchment which were not beneficial to new initiatives like the Buurderij.

The (potato) farmer was angry because of this and also about the fact that the other two entrepreneurs seemed to go along with the demands of the authorities. There was a different view on what should be the best policy. The farmer turned his back to the politicians and faced the land, which was to him the most reliable partner. The land turned out to be more neutral in this constellation compared to the first one. "I'm just the land" it indicated. But it gave the farmer a comforted feeling, there seemed to be some sort of bond between them.

A Year After the Second Constellation

In February 2012, about a year after the second constellation, I had separate interviews by telephone with the three initiators.

The sculptor stated that the Buurderij was developing on a low level. Authorities still didn't support it very much and made their own plans around the Westflank.

Nevertheless the three entrepreneurs kept on doing activities together. The sculptor had made a new statue for the estate of the horticulturist and showed it to the public to express their feelings: the 'hokjesgeest', parochialism, in the polder. As if the land expressed itself.

The farmer had learned in the constellations that they shouldn't wait for cooperation of the authorities, but take more initiatives by themselves and in that involve the neighbors. One of his new activities is to teach school students about potato growing.

The horticulturist had already organized a lot for the neighborhood, opening his estate for events like cooking lessons about the biological fruit and vegetables sold there and giving the opportunity for people to adopt an apple tree and learn how to prune it. He had become a bit skeptical due to the lack of support from the authorities, but was determined to keep on going with the Buurderij-concept together with his colleagues albeit at a slow pace.

They all mentioned the constellations as giving clearance about the motives and goals of the different stakeholders, the reluctance of the authorities to go along with such a new and unknown concept and the expression of the land itself for not being seen in the beginning and becoming more 'neutral' after awhile.

The main project consultant spoke of the goals of the people involved in the Buurderij being the integrated approach based on reciprocity. The intention to work for the welfare of the whole is more important than strict planning of what should be achieved. This corresponds with the turquoise values in the value system theory of Graves. The surroundings are touched by this development and slowly go along with the concept and movement.

Interpretation and Possible Future Developments

To me the Buurderij-constellations are an example of how environmental organization constellations can contribute to the well-being of both mankind and the land.

The constellations for the Buurderij show that it is possible to give the land or the spirit of the land a voice which can be heard and listened to.

The people of the Buurderij were tending to slow their pace as the land signaled that to them, especially the potato farmer who went ahead in this. It seemed at the second constellation which took place 4 years after the first one that the land felt already more respected, being less reluctant and with a more neutral attitude. So it looks like the entrepreneurs at the first constellation had learned some of their lesson in their attitude towards the land. The farmer, who happened not to be present at the first constellation, had felt apparently from the beginning that going along with the pace of the land was the only way to do the project. For him it was not necessary to have attended the first constellation at least in respect to this aspect.

So an important factor is that constellations can help to establish the right attitude towards the spirit of the land (and the water).

Notes

1. Cited from:

Dr. Ir. G.G.A.Remmers, Dealing with uncertainty in urban-rural foodscapes: the case of integral entrepreneurship of buurderij Haarlemmermeer-Zuid. Paper delivered at the XXIV Conference of the European Society of Rural Sociology Chania, Crete, Greece, 22-25 August 2011

2. See on this subject among others the work of Bas Pedroli, such as in:

an interview with him called Landschap vraagt om actieve verwondering, in Motief, magazine for anthroposophy - nr. 45, October 2001; http://www.antroposofie.nl/literatuur/antroposofische_literatuur/artikelendatabase/ms/int/df/motief45-1

Landscape - our home; essays on the culture of the European landscape as a task, 2000; Indigo, Zeist, the Netherlands, ISBN 90 6038 490 3

Berchthold Wasser is the married father of two daughters. For over twenty years he has been the owner and head of a small engineering office in Thun, Switzerland. Since finishing his studies as a forestry engineer at the ETH in Zürich, the forest has been his most important field of interest, especially protection of the forests of the European Alps.

I grew up on a farm at the border of a stream close to the forest and enjoyed lots of freedom there. Nature has influenced me and my life directly and effortlessly. Studying forestry engineering was yet another step towards nature for me. And indeed, this career choice has enabled me to work in and for the forest for three decades.

In my work I have developed a lot of interesting projects and solved challenging issues for forest owners in several Swiss cantons and especially for the Swiss federal environment agency (Bundesamt für Umwelt) in Bern. The consulting service for forest rangers and administration is still my main work today. During my studies, I realized that we are able to answer a lot of questions using the traditional analytic scientific approach. However, in practice I have found that a strictly rational analytic approach often contributes more to the problem than provides solutions, because the objectivity disconnects what essentially belongs together. This realization led me to search for ways that bring things together versus separate them. My work with Nature Constellations is a direct result of that search.

E-Mail:	wasser@naturdialog.ch
Website:	www.naturdialog.ch
Offers:	Training "Naturaufstellungen" in German
	Seminars and Workshops
	Consulting for relevant issues and questions.

CHAPTER NINE

Nature Experience and Nature Theater

by Berchthold Wasser

Abstract: Nature Constellations offer an enormous potential to provide individuals with direct perceptions from the perspective of elements of ecosystems or of individual elements outside the framework of a particular ecosystem. This potential can be used in any educational context to supplement other forms of instruction or learning. It is also useful for any individual who is simply interested in exploring his or her "larger identity" as a member of Earth Community. This chapter explores some of these applications.

Audience:

Pupils, Students and Teachers: Since the representatives in Nature Constellations immediately experience the peculiarities of animals, plants, mountains and rivers, the relations in ecosystems and the interaction between nature and culture, this method is a promising tool in environmental education.

Everyone Who is Interested in Who They Are: Since the representative's perception shows that we can step out of our everyday identities and experience unknown roles very easily, our beliefs about who, what and how we are can be expanded.

Issues:

This form of Nature Constellations work is not primarily issue-oriented, but it can be most effective if students or workshop participants can have their experiences within the context of either a specific ecosystem question or a specific personal intention. Without some energy or interest by the participants, exercises do not bring much. An exception to this is Nature Theater or Nature Experience for children, who usually have an immediate and intense interest quite spontaneously especially if they are introduced to it incrementally and in a playful way.

Desired Outcomes:

Letting go of Concepts and Self-Concepts: Whoever really embarks on a representation in a Nature Constellation abandons or forgets his ego for the time of the constellation, at least partially (ego means here the sum of all concepts and beliefs we have of and about ourselves). This process is so common that it often remains unnoticed. But the meaning of this simple process could be much greater than we can imagine at this time (see section: Further Development).

Discovering Resources: After constellations, representatives often report perceptions that there are resources available that they hadn't experienced before in daily life or at least not in this intensity (example: in the representation of a big oak tree, a women is experiencing herself as tremendously stable and connected to the earth). My interpretation of this phenomenon is that such little known or unknown perceptions must lie within the realm of being of the representative, although suppressed or dormant. Usually we don't speculate, after a constellation, "what just happened to us?" Since I have often seen these casual experiences pointing to important resources, I consider it useful to remind people of these experiences after the constellation, to talk about them and to anchor them through repetition. An example: A shy reserved young woman in the representation of a garden weed experiences how she is able to naturally take her place and expand joyfully. This experience is very inspiring for her. She realizes that she actually carries in herself the potential for a more liberated and free life (Case Study 2).

Revision of Moral Values: We interpret observations in nature (example: a fox attacks several chickens) against the background of human experiences and first of all on the basis of human moral values. So the fox that is biting several chickens to death in the same incident but is only eating one, becomes a "bloodthirsty" fox. In Nature Constellations or in the Nature Theater the representatives often experience something completely different from what we expect based on our moral and hierarchical beliefs.

Change of Perspective: Whoever stands as a representation always experiences a change of perspective. The representative is brought into the new perspective through the focus and very importantly is directly perceived by the other elements of the system as that which he or she represents. This circularity is very meaningful because in the same way as we are confirmed or fixed on who we are as a person by others in daily life, the representatives also get confirmed and held in their roles through the other parts of a system.

This also happens in Nature Constellations and in the Nature Theater. And since there are often not humans but plants, animals, mountains, rivers or houses represented who actually get acknowledged by the other parts of the system, they experience the system truly from this perspective.

Many behavioral scientists have experienced that other parts of a system are really ready, through adapted behavior, to acknowledge the representative as a belonging part (for example: Konrad Lorenz with ducks and graylag geese, Werner Freund and many others with wolves, or Dian Fossey with gorillas). They have learned a lot from the perspective of the animals about the behavior of animals.

According to this line of thinking, the change of point-of-view in Nature Theater and Nature Constellations can enable us to open to a new perspective on the system and therefore a new and extended understanding of the perceptions and mental states of particular parts of the system. We might finally understand our dog, for example.

Observing Oneself: Every family or organizational constellation allows the focus (the person with the question for whom the constellation is performed) an unusual outer view. The focus has the opportunity to observe the system he is normally embedded in from the outside (if he can really see and accept what he is seeing is another question). In Nature Constellations and especially in the Nature Theater this is also valid. If we cast the position with "the human" or "the human of the western world," we have the opportunity to observe ourselves from an external perspective. And if we are really ready for it, we will be able to see that our behavior is less rational or reasonable than we generally assume.

How the Work is Done:

As a "side-effect" in any Nature Constellation. Every Nature Constellation provides specific and often significant nature experiences. In addition to the specific purpose or intention of the constellation, these experiences can be very important educationally and in development of a larger and more environmentally-connected sense of self.

Specific Formats and Exercises for Experiencing Nature. We have developed formats that are not oriented towards the solution of an issue but on learning from nature and the nature experience itself. The focus of this chapter is a basic model of simple exercises, the Nature Theater, and the use of Nature Constellation work in teaching.

Nature Experience Exercises: I got to know the basic model of these exercises with Daan van Kampenhout for the first time in October 2002. The simplest form is the partner exercise. One person is asked by a partner if he or she is willing to represent a certain plant, animal or an element of a landscape. The partner can tell the person which animal he or she represents but the exercise also works if they don't talk about it. If the person agrees, he or she is brought by the partner to a place that feels right for in this moment. He then searches for a place for himself with a distance of approximately three meters (10 ft) (see Case Study 1). I then usually guide the pairs through the exercise based on simple questions and instructions. First, I lead them into full body awareness. I ask them about the size, the posture, the breath, any tensions etc.. This is followed by questions about the perception of the environment and the point in time when the partners exchange their positions. Then I let the focus search for the proper distance to the counterpart. Usually there is no talking during the exercise.

After the exercise, the pairs have a sharing about their experiences. The participants are often surprised how moving and powerful these simple exercises can be. Not only how the representative is feeling is remarkable, but also the relationship to the counterpart and how it is changing through movement.

A Man Encounters "His Tree" in a Constellation Exercise.

Nature Theater: Since first-hand and body experiences influence us more strongly and more lastingly than what we experience intellectually, I was convinced from my first Nature Constellation experience that this approach could revive and complete nature, biology and ecology studies of many kinds. Since I didn't want to subject children and teenagers to the tragic nature and heaviness that possibly reveal themselves in Nature Constellations, I designed a format in 2003 which allows children a playful participation in the world of nature. I called this format Nature Theater. As in Nature Constellations the children embody the representations of landscapes, plants, animals or humans. This is not about the analysis or a solution for a certain problem but solely for the participation in the natural life cycles (see Case Study 4). The Nature Theater was tested and developed further by Andreas Demmel in his diploma thesis (Demmel, 2010).

Environmental Education: Later on in secondary education, Nature Constellations are suitable to observe and understand systems of our environment from an experience-oriented perspective. In this case Nature Constellations are not utilized to solve certain conflicts but to learn with exemplary cases. Case Study 5 refers to the use of Nature Constellations at a senior technical college for environmental engineers in Switzerland. This method could naturally also be used in high schools, for professional education or at universities.

The Key Mechanism in this Work: the Transformation of Implicit Knowledge into Explicit Knowledge and Skill

One aspect that has not yet been discussed so far is the transformation of more or less casual representational experiences into explicit knowledge and skill. During and after constellations, nature experience exercises and Nature Theater, the representatives are often surprised and touched by what they have experienced. Later on these experiences vanish into oblivion or one remembers them as seemingly meaningless episodes. But what if important realizations and insights want to show themselves? I am convinced this happens often and therefore support the members of groups I work with to reflect on experiences after constellations in such a way that the experience can unfold their personal and collective meanings. Through this effort - that is, through reflection on the experience - new insights are able to emerge.

Georg H. Neuweg in his book "Könnerschaft und implizites Wissen" (Skills and Implicit Knowledge), is concerned with the question of how knowledge comes into being (Neuweg, 2004). He shows that knowledge is normally the result of an examination of previous occurrences and actions and not an expression of theoretical consideration. So Aristotle did not "discover" the laws of logic. They were instead opened up to him as he remembered the sentences from conversations and observed their impact on himself and other listeners.

Contributors Way to This Work:

The description of how I came to this work in general is in the corresponding chapter of my other chapter in this book "Experiencing Ecosystems".

What remains to add is that I - impressed from the beginning with my experiences as a representative in Nature Constellations - had the wish to open this experiential realm to children and teenagers. This was in part because at that time I taught the subject "Forest Ecosystems" in the Swiss Educational Institution for Nature and Environmental Specialists. I knew already that children are very naturally able to go into representations, as I had asked my two daughters to participate in my first Nature Constellation experiments. As both of them were then in a summer camp in the summer 2003 and the leadership was open for an experiment, I designed the first Nature Theater. I owe my conviction that these Nature Constellations could be used as a teaching method to Timothy and Cynthia Cunningham. I participated in a workshop they conducted with the title Eco-Systems Constellations at the Würzburg Conference in 2001 (see Revision of Moral Values section in this chapter).

Case Studies

Case Study 1: Encounter with the Power Animal (exercise with two persons)

Power Animals Accompany the Participants through the Seminar. In the beginning of the seminar all participants took a "card of power". (44 cards, on each a drawing of an animal, all the same on the backside). I had the cards spread on the ground with the image of the animals downward. The participants were sitting in a circle around the cards before they chose their card. Everybody then closed their eyes and was asked to take the animal that will accompany and support them in an optimal way during the next two days. Once all have taken their power animal card the partner exercise begins.

The pairs agree upon who starts to take over the representation of the power animal first. As in constellations, the person leads her power animal to a place which seems now suitable for her. After this she searches for her own suitable place.

Experience Report of One Participant (a man):

> I stand there in front of my power animal, the deer, face to face. It feels good to feel him so close in front of me. He has something upright, strong. And through this I can also experience my greatness, my power, my uprightness. It becomes a part of myself. Through the deer, I have the feeling that I come in contact with my male power and strength. Nothing threatening. A wonderful feeling. A great serenity and dignity. A dignity that has nothing to do with arrogance or false pomposity. I want to feel his heart. Synchronously we put our right hands on each other's chests. I sense that this strength can only unfold its true quality and balancing power over the heart. There is masculinity in myself, which is located on one pole – as a counterpart to femininity – but in its quality is at peace with itself and balancing in the middle. Embrace. Just good.

Experience Report of One Participant (a woman):

> I had never before gathered experience with power animals in constellation work. What touched and surprised me extraordinarily was how fast I was able to embody the swan. Immediately I felt surrounded by water, as in a beautiful lake. I felt the presence of birds and saw reeds in the distance. I swam alone and felt very at ease with it. I had a great need for space (also my counterpart realized this, as she had to back off to feel well in my presence.) I felt "queen-like." I stretched my wings wide and fanned over the water. Again and again the same words came up: "Feel." "Feel." Feeling is very important, exchange feelings, allow space for you and towards others!
>
> I was overwhelmed by this call and felt the urge to tell my counterpart. My exercise partner was deeply moved and felt how much the topic "emotions" lies at her heart and how much she wants to deal with them attentively. The swan empowered her to profoundly trust her feelings and to allow them the space they deserve. It was a quintessential exhilarating experience for both of us.

Both reports, the first from the view of the focus, the second from the view of the representative of the power animal, show how this exercise makes resources accessible. During the seminars, one could see that the support through the power animals really works.

Case Study 2: Pure, Wild Joy of Living

Report of a young woman about her experience as a representative of a garden weed within a Nature Constellation.

The Issue: An owner of a garden had increasing difficulties with weeds in his garden. He wanted to know if there was a way that satisfies both his standards for the garden and the demands of the weeds.

Report of the Representative of a Garden Weed:

A representative for the cabbage was chosen. The gardener himself also went into the constellation (the garden). And the garden weed (a beautiful brunet woman) was already remarkably vivid before she entered the circle. At some point I also couldn't sit still anymore and jumped in as a second garden weed into the circle. Normally, I am more of a serious and calm woman and rarely do I have moments where other sides of me pop up. This constellation was such a rare moment. Something not entirely unknown, but not felt for a long time, exploded out of me, the pure and wild joy of living of a very wild garden weed. I was under steady current, had full energy, was jumping around in the circle, was dancing and shouted loudly into the world. We, the two garden weed sisters, were celebrating a "big party" in the small constellation circle. I could perceive the gardener, but he was not strong enough to set us boundaries. So we took our space, spread and crowded around the pudgy-bulging, virtuous but yet a bit boring white cabbage. I mean he was also a plant, like us, but definitely a completely different kind. We didn't have very much in common. In this wild power and vitality, one thing became very clear for me: "We conquer the world!" There are so many of us, we are free and vivid, we are wild and we do what we want! We know what we like! I was happy to be able to share the experience with my garden weed sister and that doubled the fun. Within the constellation it became clear for me, as garden weed, that the gardener had to become stronger and had to set boundaries for us if he really wanted something to come of his cabbage! I could live with it and would be happy, if at least one part of the garden would be accessible for our play. Also I knew for sure that the gardener could profit a lot from our power and our vitality if he would open himself up to us. That is why we belong in every garden!

And what I also could see was the following: if the gardener protects the cabbage for his own sake, it is love. It is the same love that doesn't want to harm us or even cut us down. But he has to love something. Therefore my feeling was very clear that when I was treated carefully and respectfully that I didn't mind only being limited to one place in the garden. The inner harmony would still be preserved. Neither I, nor the cabbage, played the leading role in it. The key was the gardener and his approach (loving or unloving). So rip me out if necessary, or subdue me, but please do it with love and let me grow in another place!

I received this contribution one and a half years after the constellation. Despite the amount of time that had passed, the irrepressible vitality of this woman was still present and active. Obviously she rediscovered a resource and a helpful clue about a direction in which she could develop herself.

Case Study 3: The Farmer, the Farm and Life

Report of the author about his experience as the representation for a 90 year old farmer.

The Story: On a farm in Switzerland two generations live under one roof: the elderly farmer and his wife - both 90 years old - and their son, together with his wife, both in their mid-fifties. The young farmer and primarily his wife feel very constricted. The mother doesn't accept boundaries and insinuates repeatedly that the "young lady" is doing things wrong. The farm is long since the property of the young people and they want the elderly ones to move into an old people's home.

The Issue: The "young" farmer and his wife both wish for the elderly parents to consent to move into the old people's home and to feel comfortable being there.

Report of the Representative of the 90 Year Old Farmer (I myself took over this representation in December 2009 and recorded it a few days after).

From the beginning I do not really understand what is being talked about. I feel wide and open, I see the images in the room and hear the voices. My wife is standing right next to me and I know that I will support her in whatever happens. I don't feel any resentment and also I don't understand why there should be a problem. As my wife says, we will not go in an old people's home, and I agree with her. We have the right to live here and to move is not an option for me. The things that are being spoken about are far away, they don't touch me. The speaking goes on. Slowly I hear and understand more. I can hear how the son and especially the daughter-in-law say that they don't see any other way for us than to move to the old people's home. I think about it for the first time, how it would be if I would have to move. Pictures emerge: I see the farm, the cat, the grass, the pear tree, the shed, everything I am connected with since my youth, and I know – and that is a body sensation – all of this is my life! It is as much my life as it is my skin and my bones, my voice and my hand. And I know if I go away, then also my life will go away. I cry, but it is not the crying that chokes my throat, there is also no accusation behind the crying, it is what it is. My activity is barely led by thoughts, the pictures on the wall, the gestures of the people, the bright room, the big colorful paintings, the emotions that arise slowly but inevitable from my belly, all that was just present in an immediate way. With open eyes I watch my people, my tears roll lightly. I don't close myself off to the continuing proceedings.

In the sharing, after the constellation I realize how direct the connection of this farmer to the farm, to the plants and the animals is. Since the experience was literally still "in my bones" it was more than bare knowledge about meanings and relationships. It was a certainty that death will come if he is forced to leave his trusted surroundings. Because these are not just his surrounding but part of his life! Of course we see this differently in our culture. Skin and hair form the borders of a person. But is this really true? Where is more of our identity lost, if we lose a leg or if we lose a farm?

Representations grasp us in our entirety, in the body, in feelings and in thoughts. They have a great power of persuasion and therefore the potential to question our daily patterns, concepts and perspectives.

Case Study 4: Nature Theater

Frame/Context: What I report here happened in 2003 at a summer camp for eight to ten year-old children in the Diemtigtal valley in Switzerland. The kids had already been at the camp for three days, the weather was wonderful and therefore they had mostly played at a mountain stream and explored and observed the life around and in the stream.

The Concept: An event with children during their holidays has to be fun and must really be interesting for the children. As children love to play theater and they already were familiar with the mountain stream I proposed to have a Nature Theater play together about the mountain stream. The children could choose for themselves which elements of the mountain stream they wanted to embody. And since the summer in 2003 was very hot and dry and a severe thunderstorm had been in the area in the preceding week, I chose the current weather situation as a driving force for the actions.

Preparation: To give the chance for the children to immerse themselves in their roles, we began in the morning to list elements that belong to the mountain stream. And as there were many more characters listed than children available, all of them could choose one role. Afterwards they had time to draw their roles on a piece of cardboard. Additionally the name of the character was written on the cardboard. The cardboard was punched and attached to a string so it could be hung around the neck.

There is no predefined story line in a constellation, but it reacts and changes direction based on what shows itself from moment to moment. I searched for a useful model for this process. The children should be able to experience how a story line develops itself, without thinking about a story beforehand or studying a text. With this goal we built, painted and labeled simple small wooden ships. Then we went to a mountain lake close by and everyone placed their ship carefully on the water's surface. A light breeze stirred and soon all attention was on the action of the little ships. Despite very little current and hardly any wind a lot happened and when the fish suddenly intervened, everyone was fascinated. The kids understood immediately that an exciting "theater" is also possible without a predefined story, if one is present and ready to follow the powers of nature in every moment.

The Stage: For the theater we chose a quiet place in the forest. With our bags and jackets and additional stones and branches, we built a big circle. That was our stage. The children were prepared for the theater, but were also hungry and therefore we first had a long lunch break and the kids could do as they pleased.

The Nature Theater: The orientation was successful. The kids were now tuned in and interested in what was going to happen. I asked everyone to get into their roles. Then I explained that I would bring them one after the other on stage and that they wouldn't have to do anything other than following their impulses. They should be as free as their little boats on the water. Whoever wants to move should do this, as should the ones who want to stand still, lie or sit down. Only for the beginning, I asked them to stand still while the others were still finding their places. Finally I explained that the camp leader would periodically give details on the weather. Except for in the first few minutes, the kids were dedicated and strongly connected to their roles.

The process then took nearly an hour. Often it was funny, sometimes sad, but always moving. Many systemic correlations were visible and the relevance of the weather on the mountain stream and its residents was very impressive.

Description of Individual Scenes:

Beginning: First I introduced the water – a nine year old boy – into the circle. Standing alone on the "stage" was difficult for him. For the moment he was not in his representation but more a clown for the other kids. This changed as others joined the scene and the first sympathies and antipathies emerged.

Relations: With the appearance of the first animals the "relationship game" started. The mosquito was drawn to the water, the tadpole to the water plant, the dragonfly was afraid of the frog and wanted to escape and the duck child was drawn desperately to his mother. Without waiting for my permission, the kids expressed these affections and repulsions spontaneously with words and also sometimes with body expressions (example: dragonfly shivers terribly as soon as the frog comes closer. The mosquito "feels pain", when the frog is approaching).

Movement: Once I allow movement, the bonding of the children to their roles becomes more intensified. They move decisively, soon a clear aggregation emerges and everybody feels quite at ease in their newly found positions.

Thunderstorm: The camp leader describes a thunderstorm. As soon as the first raindrops fall the system becomes vivid. The tadpole and the salamander are very awake, the fish is chasing the mosquito, the ducks are searching for something to cover themselves. As lightning and thunder set in, all the animals calm down and movement starts in the water. After the thunderstorm, I ask all the characters how it was for them. Only the little duck had felt real fear. For all the others, the thunderstorm wasn't that bad. As the water was moving fast, the stream got excited and the water plants would have loved to have had the chance to enjoy more light.

Dry period: The camp leader describes a long dry period. At the beginning, all characters are cheerful, they are having fun. Then it gets more and more quiet, soon the tadpole lies down, the water plant and the fish sit down. Nobody is standing any longer and suddenly the tadpole doesn't move any more. As soon as the first clouds appear, movement flows into the mosquito, the dragonfly and the ducks. The water animals and the water plants do not start to move until the rain really sets in. Now the water is also moving, everyone is rambunctious, only the tadpole stays lying on the ground. My review shows the dry period was much worse than the thunderstorm for the tadpole. It brought death and the water plant was very close to death as well.

The Appearance of the Human: In the end the human also appears. With the exception of the mosquito, all the animals immediately draw themselves back. The water and the water plants distance themselves, and are skeptical of the human, but the human is only interested in the ducks and the fishes.

Conclusion: Nature Theater is possible and fun with 8 to 13 year old children. In their roles the children directly experience where their characters feel comfortable, what is good for them and what causes them harm. This kind of experience convinces me that children can find a deeper understanding and a greater intimacy with nature through Nature Theater.

Case Study 5: Environmental Education

In November 2006 I was invited by a senior technical college to introduce the Nature Constellation work in the fifth semester of the study course "Environmental Engineering". The leader of the study course had reserved one afternoon and we had agreed that we would work on a current topic from the lessons. The students were between 19 and 24 years old, they had attended grammar school before or learned a profession. Participation was voluntarily. Except for one student, everyone traveled to the little nature conservation center, twenty kilometers away from the school.

Since only two students were familiar with constellation work from their own experience, I began the afternoon with a partner exercise (an exercise similar to Case Study No. 1; the students met a tree that was important for them). During the exercise and also during the constellation, we were outside and, despite that it was really cold, all interactions were very focused. In the following break the conversations about the freshly experienced material continued.

The Nature Constellation:

The Topic: In the talking round after the break it became apparent that the remigration of the lynx was an important topic, not only in the media, but also in the college. Two students who were both trained hunters complained that the multiplying of the lynx is depicted too much from the perspective of the nature conservation in the lessons. From the intensive discussion that followed, the following issue emerged.

The Issue: The students wished for an "objective view" on the system lynx-deer-humans in Switzerland.

The Representations: Through the talk with the group, it became clear that the following elements of the system should be represented:

The lynx

The deer (the deer is the most common wild species in the area and the most important prey of the lynx)

The habitat of the wild animals

The hunter (representative for all hunters and hunter organizations)

The nature conservation (representative for all nature conservers and their organizations)

The human population in the area

Later, during the constellation, another representative was added. It was an element towards which the population as well as the hunter and the nature conservation could orientate. We call them here:

"Free humans" by which we mean people who are able to see and acknowledge what is.

The choice and the constellating of the representatives: To ensure that the system could be represented, preferably objectively:

The issue was discussed long enough for a consensus to be found.

The choice and the constellating of the representatives was set in the following way:

The representative for „the hunter" was chosen and positioned by one of the students who had represented the interests of the hunters in the discussion.

The representative for the nature conservation was chosen and positioned by a student who had represented the nature conservation perspective in the discussion

All other representatives were chosen by myself. They chose their own positions in the circle by themselves.

Phases of the Constellation: Deer and lynx were close to each other in the beginning. The deer perceived the lynx as a threat but did not panic about it. The habitat of the wild animals did not find rest. It was in constant movement. Its restlessness spread to the lynx and the deer. The population was standing in the middle. The other elements were not in their line of sight. The nature conservation followed the habitat and as the habitat finally stood still, the nature conservation was stepping on its feet.

To give the representatives the opportunity to tell their experiences, I asked everyone how they felt and what they perceived.

Lynx: "I am pressured in a very strong way by the human, the hunters are chasing me, the population is leaving very little space for me and the nature conservers occupy a big part of the remaining habitat. The deer is important for me, I feel a love for it somehow."

Deer: "My situation is very unpleasant, I am threatened from all sides, the worst is the ever-narrowing habitat."

Habitat: "I feel totally torn apart. I see that there is space to live basically everywhere, but the problem is the permanent agitation."

Hunter: "I see that the situation for the game is bad. I don't want to be pressured by the population, but supported by it. Actually for me, only the deer is important here."

Nature Conservation: "I stand very close to nature. The problem lies in the hunting and with the population. But I also notice that I like to see deer and lynx, and that there is not really an intimate relationship between myself and them."

Population: "The activity going on here is boring, it's a marginal side issue and doesn't interest me. I am looking for entertainment."

The system did not change any further, the habitat could barely breathe and also could not move any longer and the deer went more and more into a frenetic state.

I asked everyone to look deeply at the system and recall the issue (to get an objective view on the system lynx-deer-humans in Switzerland)

A little later the oldest student reports that he feels pulled "into the system". I allow him to step into the circle and ask him to find his place in the system by himself.

Without hesitation he places himself in front of the population. As the population looks at him it realizes how insecure it is being. He himself felt independent from the opinions of the population, the nature conservation and the hunters but at the same time there was an immediate understanding between him, the wild animals and the habitat. The "free human" came to stand beside the population, and from there could see all of the others. (Later on, the population reported that there, in this moment, a shift happened. She would have loved to turn to the others in this moment). The nature conservation reacted immediately. He found a proper distance to the habitat and to the wild animals. The hunter also found a new orientation through the "free human." It was remarkable that the "free human" did not intervene or give out instructions. The movement emerged through only his presence and probably also because the population respected him. For the habitat and the deer the change was very liberating. They felt much better. Also for the lynx there was a certain improvement, but the situation still feels too limited for him.

At this point I closed the constellation. Together we went into the training room of the center and discussed what we just had experienced.

The representative of the deer was still affected and shocked. I invited her and the entire group to do some breathing exercises. Afterwards she felt calm and was able to talk about her experiences. She spoke about the misery of the deer, about how the permanent stress is changing the deer and finally leads them to untypical behavior for the species.

The report of the lynx was similar. For him it was clear that the habitat in Switzerland would be too limited, even if the lynx were better protected.

The representatives of the nature conservation, the hunters and the population were impressed how one-sided they had perceived the circumstances through their particular positions. The hunters actually felt "pushed to their limits" although they are politically powerful in Switzerland. The nature conservation was not able to see in the constellation that its permanent presence in the wilderness habitat is a problem. Also the representative of the population was disillusioned. He had difficulty accepting his own experience of how unimportant these questions are for the majority of the population.

At this point, I reminded the students one more time of their issue. That they had wished for an objective view on the system lynx-deer-humans in Switzerland and that as far as I could judge the constellation effectively revealed that. I suggested to the leader of the study course and to the students that they could review this topic in their lessons and to discuss it on the basis of the recent experiences and realizations.

Everyone perceived the appearance of the "free human" as an unexpected gift. For the young future environmental engineers it was certainly motivating to see that a positive development is possible and from which direction that could emerge.

Further development

An earlier section listed the themes "Letting Go of Concepts", "Discovering Resources", "Revision of Moral Values", "Change of Perspective", and "Observing Oneself" as desired outcomes. These topics are of great and fundamental importance. If the experience of "Being a Representative" offers a real potential for change, it is likely that this quality will sooner or later be realized by innovative people and brought into their fields of expertise. Here are some examples that show in which directions future developments could go, based on the list of desired outcomes.

Letting Go of Concepts: From a Buddhist perspective, the perpetual agitation of our thoughts about ourselves is one of the greatest problems of humankind. Shantideva, the great Buddhist master from southern India (about 750-850) wrote as following:

All suffering we see in the world, originates from our self-absorbed living, because we only strive for our own happiness. All happiness we see in the world emerges through taking care of the well-being of other sentient beings.

I am repeatedly amazed by how easily we abandon thoughts about our own well-being during representations in constellations and let ourselves get into other sensations and emotions for ten, twenty or even thirty minutes.

After the constellation, we don't feel any loss. Obviously the gap in our egocentricity doesn't harm us. This phenomenon doesn't mean, of course, that through the representation our self-centeredness disappears automatically. But reflection on what is happening each time we represent a part of nature and noticing how simply this occurs may lead some people to find ways to use this phenomenon more consciously for the loosening of deeply anchored ego identity patterns.

Discovering Resources: Case Studies No.1 and No. 2 show how and why representatives can be power sources. Several people have told me that they realized something through certain representations, something they still remember, something that empowers them and helps them with decisions. I am confident that in the future representational experiences with this quality of access to resources will be more consciously perceived, reflected and anchored in daily life with suitable exercises. The first step is giving value to the representation experience. As facilitators we should help the representatives to acknowledge and reflect upon their experiences and the personal meanings of the representation. This can be supported through recording their insights, for example. After nature experience exercises, Kenneth Sloan and I ask the people to share their experiences and we often see that finally through the sharing of the experiences a deeper meaning of the experience is revealed. (see Georg H. Neuweg, chapter 8). In our Nature Constellation work training we asked the participants to write down their experience. Through the writing process, the experience is again remembered and composed into language.

Revision of Moral Values: Here, also, I can only bring in ideas for the future development. To get started, I choose the following example. At the Systemic Constellation Work Conference in May 2001 in Würzburg, Timothy and Cynthia Cunningham conducted a workshop with the title "Eco-Systems Constellations". They chose representatives for different animal classes (crawlers, reptiles, fishes, birds, mammals etc.) and then asked the representatives to place themselves in order of their significance. The most important animal classes in the front, the less important ones at the end. And what could we see? The system didn't come to rest, the animals didn't know where they belonged. First one animal was in the front, and then suddenly another one. It became obvious that there was no order of priority from the perspective of the animals! Even as we are more careful today with the interpretation of animal behavior, our language seduces us again and again to the wrong attributions. I believe that we are able to realize, with the help of Nature Constellations or with Nature Theater, where we are especially confused through our language and moral values. And if, with this, we would be able to lift the anthropocentric veil just a little bit, it would already be significant in its impact. Following the example of T. and C. Cunningham, one could introduce this approach in nature and ecology study lessons. Biology students could conceive hypotheses on the basis of Nature Constellations and ecologists could examine the impact of planned nature protection actions.

Change of Perspective: The change of perspective is the aftermath of letting go of concepts. If we leave behind the trusted patterns and concepts and surrender to the feelings in the representations, we change our perspective and are able to see the system from a new position.

Berchthold and an Old Oak Tree

The change of perspective is very important in conflict resolution. If conflicting parties really succeed in seeing the perspective of the other party, the understanding for their views becomes possible and a good base for conflict resolution is provided. Therefore, purposefully applied constellations could be very effective in mediation processes. Because many delicate conflicts between humans and animals, plants and whole ecosystems are taking place, I hope that through the application of Nature Constellations the perspectives can be changed and more peaceable and balanced solutions can become possible.

Observing One's Self: By this I mean the external view of human collectives and their impacts on the environment. This is a special case of changing perspective. From the perspective of the system theory it is not possible for parts of a system to adopt an external view. But constellation work allows the focus an outside view on his system. Since this perspective is so uncommon, the focus is often not able to acknowledge what he sees as reality. That is why the words of Bert Hellinger "acknowledging what is" are so important and meaningful.

To give this special change of perspective the possibility to unfold its effect, it needs trust beforehand that we as a collective truly have the possibility to observe our actions in ecosystems from the outside. This trust grows when there are enough well documented case studies to confirm this. Nevertheless, we have to find solutions along the way to ideally reach a state of "neutrality of the facilitator." Meant by this is that the facilitator himself is also a human being, and therefore not normally neutral. It is not really possible to avoid this problem, but it is possible to alleviate its impact through suitable arrangements. A bigger obstacle is then to acknowledge what is. Often the focus in family systems is fixed on certain beliefs and patterns and therefore is not able to understand and believe what he can see in a constellation of his family. We are equally fixed as a collective when we look at our beliefs and impacts with regard to nature.

To acknowledge the impact of human societies on their environment would probably be very depressing but also very healing. I believe that Nature Constellation work can be an important help in this process.

References

Demmel, Andreas (2010): Naturaufstellungen; Eine Methode zur Stärkung der Beziehung zwischen Mensch und Natur im umweltpädagogischen Arbeitsfeld; Diplomarbeit an der Kath. Stiftungsfachhochschule München

Neuweg, Georg Hans (2001): Könnerschaft und implizites Wissen; Zur lehr-lerntheoretischen Bedeutung der Erkenntnis- und Wissenstheorie Michael Polanys; Waxmannn Münster / New York / München /Berlin

Kirsten Love Lauzon. I am a dreamer, writer and artist who believes in the power of love and the primacy of the heart. My passion is paleopsychology: a study of the evolution of human consciousness whose practice emphasizes the importance of our innate indigenous wisdom in the emergence of conscious, collective evolution. After studying eco-psychology, conscious dreaming and other shamanic practices for many years, my life changed forever after my first constellation experience in 2003 with G. Dietrich Weth, of Frankfurt Germany.

I began facilitator training with Dietrich in 2004, continued my training with Mark Johnson from 2005-2008 and have been facilitating constellations since 2006. I began studying as a Facilitator Trainer in 2009 and have been training students since 2011. I have also had periodic training and workshops over the years with Dietrich Klinghardt, Ursula Franke, Sneh Victoria Schnabel, Dan Booth Cohen, Ed Lynch, Johannes B. Schmidt, Francesca Mason Boring, and Vivian Broughton, among others.

Since 2006, I have facilitated many workshops and have offered large-scale Community Constellation experiences in Seattle and San Francisco. In 2013, I am offering a Monthly Systemic Constellation Workgroup, where participants of all experience levels learn about the work or practice their skills in an ongoing group.

I also serve as Program Director for the Seattle Constellations Institute (SCI), as well as Facilitator/Co-facilitator for various SCI events and co-trainer in SCI's Systemic Constellation Facilitator Training Programs.

E-Mail: kirsten@healing-earth.net

Website: www.healing-earth.net.

Offerings: I am passionate about supporting individuals, couples, families, communities & larger collectives as we emerge into increased conscious and collective awareness together.

Offering One-to-one and Public or Private Group Sessions:

• Eco-Healing: Sessions in Nature & Elemental Support • Family, Inter-generational & Ancestral Healing • Emotional Intelligence, Heart Wisdom & Relational Mentoring • Imaginal Intelligence, Archetypal Assistance & Dream-Tending • Ritual Design: Cultivating Sacred Space with Loving Intent

• Systemic Constellation Facilitator Training and Mentoring

Picture Credits for this chapter: Kirsten Love Lauzon

CHAPTER TEN

Dream Constellations: In the Nature of the Psyche

by Kirsten Love Lauzon

Abstract: The following chapter is a basic guide to exploring and engaging with our individual and collective Dreaming Natures using the Constellation process. If it is true that we are the Earth becoming conscious of Herself - then our dreams are none other than the dreams of the Earth

The Dream Constellation Process is a method of direct communication within the systems of our conscious and unconscious Selves, including the Selves of Gaia and of the Cosmos. The basic function of dreams is to bring into consciousness the unseen aspects of the psyche. Dreams, by their very nature, reveal the precise wisdom necessary for our continued individual and collective evolution in relation to the Earth.

I firmly hold that working systemically with dreams is one of the central ways we may conscientiously participate in the unfolding of human evolution in harmony with Nature and the Earth.

Audience:

This work is for anyone looking to strengthen their relationship to the numinous, the magical, the creative and the divine. It is recommended for very experienced dreamers as well as those who don't remember their night dreams at all. Most who attend these workshops are interested in cultivating their dream life and some aren't sure exactly how to access or apply the wisdom they know is there. Many are intellectually aware of or curious about the personal and/or global benefits of community dreamwork.

Dream Constellations are appropriate for Adults, Adolescents, Children, The Aged, Sick or Dying. The simple embodied experience of a key dream can unlock whatever is needed for healing to spontaneously occur…for a young one to transition into adulthood, for a mother to face her biggest fear, for a beloved elder to make a final, peaceful passage into death. As mentioned in the abstract for this chapter, Dreams are a crucial entry point for engaging in healthy ways with Nature and the Earth. As such, included here are those who wish to make positive use of the wisdom of their dreams of Nature or the Earth in their waking lives, in community or in the context of other collectives.

Issues:

Seekers in this work are usually interested in exploring a specific sleep dream that has captured their attention in some way. The presented dream tends to contain a strong charge for the Dreamer, challenging them with the integration or resolution of its content. Usually the Dreamer is aware that there is important information contained within the dream and is seeking assistance in identifying, clarifying and utilizing it.

Specific issues and concerns include: complete or partial lack of dream recall; recurring night dreams or nightmares; waking life synchronicities with a dream-like quality or strong impact; irrational fears, delusions, visions or illusions; recurring or obsessive daydreams, themes or images; persistent symbols, beings or locations from meditations or journeys; any combinations of these.

Desired Outcomes:

Most dreamers seek meaning. The most basic function of dreaming is to bring unconscious material into the light of consciousness. The unconscious mind speaks in the language of symbols, archetypes, images, emotions and experiences, so we often feel at a loss, from the perspective of the ego, as to what the dream really means.

Sometimes the Dreamer is already clear about the meaning of the dream and has a more specific outcome in mind, such as: cultivating deeper relationships with specific symbols, beings, places or archetypes; continuing the dream onward or on a parallel trajectory; integrating new information; making unconscious impulses conscious; resolving conflicts; reclaiming excluded parts of the self; resolution of past trauma; releasing stuck or blocked creative energy.

One of the most basic and inherent outcomes of the Dream Constellation Process is the integration of collective material into the individual psyche and vice versa. Dreams are holographic in nature, and the wisdom and principles gained apply both within and without the individual psyche.

How the Work is Done:

Introduction: This work is the culmination of a six-year process of designing, experimenting with and endlessly tweaking the elements of the dream constellation process, and continues to unfold as I learn and grow. Following are just a few of the basic tools in the dream constellation tool-bag, available as needed on a dreamer-by-dreamer basis. What comes up in the moment is more important than following any guideline or process. Having a fluid, adaptable and open approach is best, and following the dream is of essence.

A Physical Container for the Work: The setting in which the work is done can have a direct effect on the outcome. If a space is too small or too cluttered a dream can feel fettered. If there are too many external distractions a constellation can lose its focus quickly. A quiet, private, comfortable and open space where dream constellations can fully unfold is a gift to the Dreamer, the dream community and to the dream world itself.

Calling in the directions, ancestors, totems, and other allies: For constellation work I usually do this before participants begin to arrive. There are many different methods for opening (and closing) ritual space and calling in support for the work. I highly recommend becoming familiar with the art of ritual leadership.

Long Form and Demonstration Considerations: Below is a detailed description of various elements in the Dream Constellation Process. Using all these elements during a single constellation is ill-advised and unnecessary. Facilitating a shorter demonstration of the Dream Constellation Process requires a deft sense of what steps to include and which can be abbreviated, combined, adapted or left out, as well as how to keep the introduction to a reasonably brief yet thorough presentation that focuses quickly on the core of the dream's wisdom.

Things can sometimes move more quickly in dreams than is possible in family constellation work, but it is important to give adequate time for each constellation to move at its own pace.

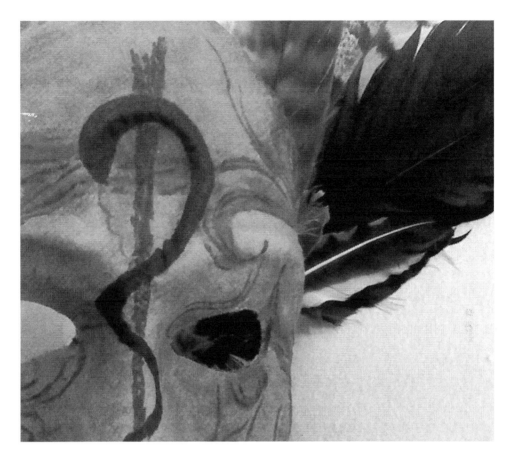

Dream mask of the archetypal wounded healer, created for a dream incubation ritual on Whidbey Island in 2008.

Introduction to Dream Tending: Historical story-telling is a great way to illustrate the power of dreams. Dreams have greatly impacted human history: Albert Einstein's Theory of Relativity, James Watson and Francis Crick's discovery of DNA, Neils Bohr's structure of the atom, Elias Howe's invention of the sewing machine, Harriet Tubman's underground railroad, and Abraham Lincoln's assassination. If there are experienced dreamers in the group I often ask them (with prior permission) to tell a brief story about how a dream changed their life. This is remarkably effective.

Introduction to Constellations: A basic overview of Family and Systemic Constellations is given and a description of how the process unfolds for the participants: seekers, representatives and witnesses.

Basic principles of The Dream Constellation Process

1) Dreams are holographic in nature, bearing truth on both individual and collective levels.

Dreams are a window onto both individual and collective truths: it is important to honor the holographic nature of the dream world. A good facilitator practices holding the space for many (sometimes opposing) viewpoints at once, holding each lightly, and inviting participants to do the same.

Blue Iris Bloom, Seattle, Washington

2) There is great wisdom in the circle, let us be present to ourselves and to others.

Circle wisdom is valued in this process: opening the floor to the participants, when appropriate and with permission, can be extremely beneficial for everyone. We each possess deep insight that can be best shared when we each agree to offer and receive the same respect from one another.

3) The Dreamer is the final author and authority of his or her own dream.

The Dreamer is the owner of the dream and as such has the final say about what their dream means for them. Neither facilitator nor any other participant have any authority over the Dreamer's dream and will refrain from offering direct interpretation.

4) As group dream tenders we will use language and behavior that honors the above.

The use of "I" language when speaking is an absolute requirement. (See more details below under "Constellating the Dream" in Inviting the Wisdom of the Circle.) Participants are encouraged to gather and organize their thoughts before speaking, to be concise and respectful and to listen well to others.

Confidentiality. A sense of safety is crucial in cultivating a space where this work can unfold. Dreams contain deeply personal material and require conscious attention to group confidentiality. Invite attendees to respect and hold others' dreams and personal information confidential by opting into a group agreement. (Participants can gesture or say "I will" to indicate their intent.) Encourage sharing personal learning responsibly by keeping details and identities private.

Collective Presence. At this point the analytical thinking mind can be invited to take a smaller role - we can invite our consciousness to soften into the subtler knowing experiences of the heart, body and soul. Some variety of grounding exercise is helpful: guided meditation, visualization, movement, breathing, chanting, silence, or anything that brings participants into a more present, grounded, heart-centered, open awareness and fully into their bodies.

Group Meditation: Embodying an Archetype. This exercise aids in collective presence and preparation for the representative role.

"Close your eyes and allow an archetype to surface, any one will do. If it isn't the right one for this moment, thank it and allow another to appear. (Have a list of your own handy: Magician, Mother, King, Artist, Fool, Maiden, Hero, Crone, Hermit, Warrior, Wise Old Woman or Man, Child, Lover etc... Allow time for connection.) When the right archetype arrives, invite it to move through you. What does it feel like in your body? If you were to move, how would it move? What would it say? (etc.)"

Stay with this for a few minutes, giving time and space for personal exploration and then guide the group to thank and release the archetype.

Group Bonding and Intent. Group bonding helps participants recognize themselves in each other, increasing connection, compassion and synchronicity. Each participant is invited to speak their name and a word or short phrase that expresses what they're hoping to receive during the workshop or event, for example: clarity, relief, love, a better relationship with the dream world, the courage to move on, facing a dream monster, more intimacy.

Drumming, Movement or Music. Many cultures use rhythm and movement as a portal to the dream world. Used with intent, these practices invite dream images to surface or resurface into consciousness. They also cultivate a quieter mind, allowing the wisdom of the body and the presence of the heart to come forward. When we invite our psyches to speak and open ourselves to listen, images appear - trust imagination.

There are many ways to engage with the wisdom of dreams. The images that arise during the drumming and/or movement might be from a remembered night dream - an epic serial saga begun in childhood, or just the tiny trace of a fragment, feeling, color, or scent ... or a new image might have arisen just now! Notice what arises: synchronistic life experiences, recurring daydreams, meditative visions, notable illusions or sensations in the body.

Round of Dream Titles. Participants choose a title for their dream or image, a single word or short phrase to encapsulate its essence. Pass a talking stick or other ritual object around the circle.

Selecting a Dream. There are many ways to discern which dream is of service to the group's highest good. Allowing the deep needs of the group to choose a direction, working directly with the field, trusting intuition and following synchronicity are just a few. Well-trained and reasonably sensitive facilitators can intuit which dream to choose for excellent group results and may not need a ritualized form of selection.

Regularly using a selection ritual has helped me better trust my intuition in following the group's highest good. I use selection methods more sparingly now, and particularly in groups where there is difficulty bonding, finding shared intent, or where there is little experience in the field. It can be a helpful first exercise for those new to constellations.

An Example Selection Ritual: Everyone who wishes to work stands and finds a place in the circle, representing their dream image and re-entering that space, while remaining still and quiet. A representative for the highest good of the group then moves among them, silently and intuitively choosing the right dream for the group at this time.

Greeting the Dream. Invite the Dreamer to recount the dream in first person present tense: "I am floating down a river and an otter goes swimming by when…"

Clarifying the Collective Vision. Group Q and A: participants ask clarifying questions about the dream, such as: "What is on banks of the river?" "Does the otter notice you?" "Exactly how big is it?"

Choosing an Initial Form for the Constellation. Is the dream brief or can it be condensed into a brief and powerful moment? The reenactment of myth and dream are the very definition of ritual; any dream moment can become a transformative ceremony. Work with the Dreamer to choose and place the representatives in such a way that it reflects the dream as it appeared, as closely as possible, and move slowly forward through the dream.

Is the dream long and meandering? The representatives are placed wherever the Dreamer intuits is appropriate in the present moment in time, rather than as they appeared in the dream.

Representing the Dream. The Facilitator guides the Dreamer to choose the appropriate representatives to begin, keeping in mind that other representatives can be added later. The Dreamer makes eye contact with each representative, stating out loud the symbol they represent as they place each in the circle. In this example, we might begin with representatives for Dreamer, river and otter. The Dreamer takes a seat where they can always clearly see and hear the constellation.

Re-telling the Dream. Invite the Dreamer to recount the dream again after the clarification and set-up. Notice any differences (omissions, additions or variations) from the original telling, as these can be signals of something important emerging into consciousness.

Constellating the Dream

Important Considerations: Dreams are the psyche's best self-balancing processes: what most needs to be seen, acknowledged, and integrated by the conscious mind is revealed. I hold that the spontaneous healing nature of dreams is where dreams and nature intersect. All that may be needed for a beneficial outcome is to provide the Dreamer with a direct, embodied experience of the dream.

Creativity is paramount! Dreams can change direction in the blink of an eye or a millisecond can feel like a million years. Follow the dream's lead: honoring its essence can often require creative and unexpected choices. Below is a list of basic elements to be considered.

Tuning in: The representatives tune into the dream and into the particular archetype or symbol they are representing, closing their eyes and feeling the dream around them as they enter the dream space. Drumming or rattling can be helpful at this juncture to mark the group's transition into the dream's field.

Checking in: Connect with the Dreamer's representative, seeing what she notices, both internally and externally. Inquire of each representative in the order they appear in the dream, checking in alternately with the Dreamer's representative, the Dreamer, and/or the other representatives to see how their experiences of the dream might be changing.

Acknowledging what is: Guide the representatives to speak clear and powerful words, phrases or short sentences that illustrate and encapsulate basic truths as observed within the dream.

Checking in with the Dreamer: Examples: Does this resonate with your experience of the dream? What are you noticing, or most curious about? What does this scene make you think of?

Checking in with the Dreamer's representative: Examples: What are you noticing here? How do you feel in relation to this representative, or this one? What would you do next?

Considering what is missing: Add additional representatives for archetypes or symbols as necessary, but only as indicated by the flow of the constellation. Possibilities include: symbols that weren't included in the initial set-up, weren't previously visible to the Dreamer, or that help provide support for the Dreamer or other existing representatives.

Continuing the Dream Story: Helpful when dreams end or take a sharp left turn just before a significant moment. The Dreamer will usually know what would have happened next in the dream. If not, ask them, "If this were a lucid dream, what would you do now?" The facilitator must be careful that the Dreamer doesn't take over the dream, but instead lets the dream show itself. Reasonably clear archetypal representatives will have some idea what to do or say in the new scenario - the Dreamer's waking mind does not get to determine what the archetypes do or say (even though it will often want to).

Listening as the archetypes speak: Archetypes speak to us from our unconscious mind through dreams at night because this is when we are most available to explore their possibilities. Our ego is its smallest at night while sleeping. Meeting an archetype for the first (or second or third) time can be challenging work while the ego is active, because our ego often bitterly resists. Patience, deep listening and loving care must be taken to phrase or rephrase the Dreamer's queries and the archetype's expressions.

Inviting The Wisdom of the Circle: Each individual psyche has a unique orientation to the archetypes and uses a unique language to express its experiences. This variety of experience can be engaged as a valuable and practical tool. It is important to have the consent of the Dreamer before opening the floor to the wisdom of the group, and to have previously established and agreed upon the basic guidelines of respect, brevity, politeness and intent. (Refer to: Basic Principles of the Dream Constellation Work.) Begin with a brief example, demonstrating the proper use of "I" language: "If I were the Dreamer in this dream, I'd …" or "If it were my dream I would be most interested in …" or "In my dream of your dream I might want to talk to the otter …"

Inviting the Dreamer into the dream: When it feels right (sometimes from the beginning), the Dreamer can step into the dream, standing next to their representative, who can be invited to step into the role of the Dreamer's Deeper Dreaming Self. In some cases it is very important for the Dreamer to face and acknowledge this representative. Cultivating this kind of connection between the Dreamer's conscious and unconscious Selves can be very new. Sometimes this seemingly small step is all that is needed for resolution, or to help an otherwise stuck Dream Constellation begin to flow. Checking in with the relationship of the Dreamer toward his or her dreams (as in the case study "Scary Animals Dream") is helpful especially when the presenting dream is frightening, recurring, or serial in nature.

Concluding the Constellation. Knowing when to end a constellation can be a difficult skill to master. When the dream constellation has come to a close there is usually a felt sense of peace in the system and a knowing that has no need for word or movement.

Releasing the Representatives. Use a short individual or group releasing ritual at the conclusion of every constellation.

Individual Releasing Ritual: Each representative in turn places their hands in the Dreamer's, palms down. The Dreamer says "(representative's name), thank you, I release you from this role." The representative says, "I return to you what is yours." The Dreamer says, "I receive it."

Group Releasing Ritual: The group stands, joining hands. The facilitator leads the group in a call and response: "I have willingly offered myself in service to (Dreamer's name)." The Dreamer says, "Thank you. I release you each from your roles." The group responds, "I, (representative's name) release myself of all that is not mine. The Dreamer says, "I receive all that belongs to me."

The Maryhill Stonehenge, a full-size, astronomically-aligned replica of Stonehenge located in Maryhill, Washington

Honoring the Dream. Facilitate a brief discussion with the Dreamer about honoring the dream's wisdom. Avoid analyzing the dream or the constellation at this time. It is not the intent of this discussion to bring intellectual understanding to the phenomenal experience of the constellation, but rather, to explore possibilities for bringing the phenomenal experience into the external world in a tangible, physically embodied way. This helps cultivate an ongoing dialogue with the deeper dreaming self. When our unconscious mind sees the evidence of its treasures in the external, physical world, it feels heard and valued and is invited into continued exchange.

There are many ways to do this – help the Dreamer find the one that serves their specific circumstances. Be creative! Making art is always a good choice. Write a poem, build an altar, carve a representation of an important dream ally, place it somewhere you'll see it daily and form a relationship with it. Draw, paint, sculpt or build things that evoke the wisdom of the dream. Avoid grand statements or generalized ideals like, "I'll make better decisions regarding my finances." This isn't a tangible objective symbol the unconscious can relate to. A better choice for this dream might be to create a list (or collage or painting) of all the things truly valued in life and hang it in the office as a reminder of what's important.

Making an action plan is an excellent way to accomplish this step. Ask, "what actions or tasks can you list that will help you to honor the wisdom of this dream in your life, family, community or collective?" Then encourage the Dreamer to schedule the plans and tasks, making the wisdom of the dream a reality.

How Contributor Came to this Way of Working:

Developing the Dream Constellation process has been in large part the result of my work in Paleopsychology. Within this framework, I am particularly interested in the knowing ways of pre-historic and indigenous people, how and why these have changed over time, and how we can effectively engage innate indigenous knowing ways as a means to consciously guide our current and future evolution as a species.

We are at an important point in our development as a species: we are in the midst of a global rite of passage the likes of which our world has never seen - a massive collective coming of age. In virtually every culture around the world, and for tens of thousands of years, rites of passage have been integral to culture and survival, and have very real existential consequences. In most cultures, tribal elders guide initiates through the ordeal. The question now becomes: who are our elders in this collective rite of passage? Who will guide us through this collective ordeal?

The work of Paleopsychology is to honor and heed the wisdom of our species' elders by birthing healing modalities for modern humans based on their knowing ways. In this context, I have identified our species' elders as: our prehistoric ancestors, past and present indigenous cultures, naturally wise and open-hearted children, inspiring contemporary figures, and our very own innate inner indigenous souls. In my research I have found two such modalities to be the most unfailingly effective: Dream Tending and Systemic Constellations.

I have always been a big dreamer. Between recurring nightmares and prophetic dreams, I learned fairly early that dreams are real. In my mid-twenties a Dream Bear emerged, bringing me face-to-face with my own latent power.

This experience led me to begin studying Conscious Dreaming with Robert Moss and other shamanic practices with Sandra Ingerman. A few years later, just after receiving my level II Dream Teacher Certificate, I began learning about Family Constellations with G. Dietrich Weth of Frankfurt, Germany, and then with Mark A. Johnson in Seattle, WA. It was clear to me then that the two modalities were deeply connected.

In 2005 I began creating a program at Antioch University Seattle in Paleopsychology. My experiences there, especially with Depth Psychologist Randy Morris, expanded my capacity for phenomenal intelligence and helped inform my current methods. During a "Myth, Symbol and the Sacred" class with Randy in 2008 a dream led me to examine the archetype of the wounded healer. I was gifted with a phenomenal experience of Chiron's birth, life, trials, immortal death and rebirth by standing in as a theatrical representative for the Centaur himself during a mythic re-enactment ritual for the class. This was a cornerstone experience in the development of the Dream Constellation process.

In the beginning, dream constellations were often long and meandering. Through experimenting I learned that it is not necessary to involve every symbol from a dream, nor to accurately follow the dream's linear story-line. I had to trust the dream world's always shifting nature in order to allow fluidity within the structures I was crafting and to let each constellation flow through its own unique combination of possible structural elements.

I am very grateful to the community of dreamers with whom I have worked over the years for their interest in, patience with and support of the birthing of this process. They are my most valued collaborators in this work.

Selected Dream Constellation Examples:

Scary Animals Dream - *How a seeker learned to befriend her dreams - A Dream/Nature Constellation*

The Dreamer recounts: "I am inside a cage and various animals are parading by, scaring me."

Through the constellation, we identified the Dreamer's feeling toward the animals as the same feeling she held toward her dreams. This realization allowed the Dreamer to respond to the situation more consciously. Through exploration she found the cage unlocked and useful as a protective tool; a shield to keep her safe as she assessed the different animals. The safer she felt, the more curious she became about each animal, allowing the cage to eventually transform into a powerful tool: a Shaman's staff. This dreamer reported that her dream life had blossomed since the constellation, and she recently reported no longer being troubled by scary dreams.

Frog Dream – *A Ceremony of Arriving*

Since the seeker in this constellation presented both a dream fragment and a waking life situation, I allowed my imagination to mingle the two and follow my intuition. In sitting with the cyclic nature and water/earth elements of the dream part and the developmental movements in her life, the journey of Frog emerged. After proposing the concept, I arranged several representatives as a beach landscape, explaining some of the mytho-symbolic aspects of water and earth. I then invited the Dreamer to slowly flow, swim, wriggle, crawl, stand, shuffle, walk, and dance from the water onto the land, paying attention to each movement and fully experiencing each transition point. The Dreamer explored many deep insights during the movement and emerged from the experience with a sense of finally being fully grounded and present in her current life situation.

This is a good example of the holographic nature of dreams. This re-enactment of Frog's journey reflected three different levels of evolution: a specific personal evolution for the dreamer, our human emergence from the womb, and our species' early evolution from water to land.

A Pardon for the Perpetrator – *A Dream Constellation becomes a Family Constellation*

This dream begins in a dark basement, the Dreamer hiding in shadows - her mother, now upstairs, having locked her there. The Dreamer recounts that in the dream she understands

Community Dream-catcher Created by Kirsten Lauzon, 2008

and forgives her mother completely. She looks into a mirror and sees a set of sharp menacing teeth.

The Dreamer, her Mother, the Basement, the Teeth and the Mirror were placed in the constellation. The Mirror moved to face the Teeth and the Basement shifted to near the Dreamer's representative. The Mother crouched, frightened and small, hiding near the edge of the circle, so I brought in a representative to help protect and support her. Over time the Dreamer became interested in the Mother's healing process, the Dreamer herself was brought into the constellation, and a more traditional Family Constellation emerged naturally from within the dream space. (Note: this community had never before experienced Family Constellations.) Through this constellation, the Dreamer was able to express her feelings, heal old wounds and open in a new way to the powerful feminine energy flowing to her through her Mother's family lineage. The representative for the Basement was support for the Dreamer throughout while Teeth and Mirror stood as sentinel and guardian to either side as witness to the ritual.

Beautiful Artist Dream – *Meeting the muse and reclaiming creative power*

This dreamer described having met a mysterious woman with a magical book and quill. We set up the Dreamer, the Woman, the Book and the Quill. Through dialogue with each symbol the dreamer was gifted with the surprising realization that he had everything he needed to actualize his life-long dream of being a writer. The woman became his ally in the endeavor and gifted him with the magic book and quill. He reported feeling more motivated and inspired than ever.

Thoughts About Further Development:

I have been playing with the idea of constellating the archetypes for many years. This began when my personal style as a facilitator first began to emerge: I found myself naturally bringing in often unnamed representatives for trees, mountains or animals, usually as supports for the system. I witnessed a natural openness toward these representatives from everyone in the constellation. This awareness has continually nudged me toward further experimentation in constellating inner and outer natural systems.

Though the Dream Constellation Process is currently the most coherent of several ongoing experiments in archetypal constellation work, as I grow and expand as a conduit for this work other forms have begun to take shape.

As I develop I am called to work with larger scale collective systems. For instance, on the Eve of 2012 I facilitated a Cosmic Constellation, which began with a group discussion, determining the most important issue to the group regarding our transition to the New Year. The issue for this constellation emerged as: "How can we honor the truth of who we really are?"

As a group we chose representatives, allowing them to find their places, and adding more as the constellation unfolded: Our True Selves, Gaia, The Sun, Water, The Military Industrial Complex, The Firmament, Fear, Ignorance/Innocence, What is Needed for the M.I. Complex, Death, Those Who Don't Survive, and finally That Which the M.I. Complex Becomes.

Standing with Gaia and the Military Industrial Complex (hereafter MIC) I was surprised at what I experienced. The MIC said to Gaia: "I am so empty and hungry ... I will consume you." I expected to feel concern for Gaia's well-being ... but when I really looked, I knew that she was JUST FINE. Certainly she was going through her own processes, but the firmament was there for her to relax into, and she required nothing from anyone present in the constellation. I then became aware of the flood of anger and blame being directed at the MIC and I felt a deep concern for that place in the system: for the Complex and all it holds - the place where the human species has lost its integrity with itself.

The wounds we inflict on the earth and on the natural environment are first and foremost a terrible self-wounding. This is what I learned: The Earth appears to be entering a period of radical self care, and unless we voluntarily do the same, we will no longer have a choice in the matter. That which we most abhor, reject and judge is that which requires our most conscious and loving acknowledgement: our own collectively self-inflicted wounds. We must allow ourselves to lovingly acknowledge, give a good place, tend and heal these rejected parts of our collective Self.

I recommend further experimentation with these collective scale Archetypal Constellations as a direct means of cultivating a conscious collective evolution. I hope to collect the results of such constellation experiments to help cultivate and share their wisdom. As we listen and tend to the nature of our own dreams, we are also called to tend to the dreams of the world, the earth and the whole of the cosmos.

Recommended Resources

Tending Your Dreams; The Living Image – by Stephen Aizenstat (Unpublished essays)

Dream Tending: Awakening to the Healing Power of Dreams - by Stephen Aizenstat

The Secret Teachings of Plants; The Intelligence of the Heart in the Direct Perception of Nature - by Stephen Harrod Buhner

The Hero with a Thousand Faces – by Joseph Campbell

Field, Form and Fate; Patterns in Mind, Nature and Psyche - by Michael Conforti

Ego and Archetype - by Edward Edinger

Dream Animals - by James Hillman and Margot McClean

Inner Work; Using Dreams & Active Imagination for Personal Growth - by Robert Johnson

Conscious Dreaming; A Spiritual Path for Everyday Life - by Robert Moss

The Secret History of Dreaming - by Robert Moss

Facing the World With Soul - by Robert Sardello

John Cheney. I was born in 1961 in South Weymouth, Massachusetts, USA. I had an interest in music from a young age and received my B.A. in music at the University of Colorado. A life-long study of improvisational music has deeply influenced my facilitating of Systemic Constellations.

I moved to Seattle, Washington in 1995 for professional musical collaboration. In 1999, I was introduced to constellation work by Dietrich Weth from Frankfurt, Germany and trained with him until his death in 2007.

During a workshop lead by Ulrich Bold in 2004, my constellation addressed career choices. The topic of energy work came up, and upon Ulrich's suggestion, I looked into Jin Shin Do Acupressure.

2005 was a pivotal year personally and professionally. It was the year that my Mother passed away, which deeply impacted me and my whole Family. I began my study of Jin Shin Do, which utilizes 5 Elements theory. The idea of doing 5 Element Constellations arose while attending a workshop in Portland at the First US Conference on Systemic Constellations in 2005. An acupuncturist lectured on the use of 5 Elements as a method to support the healing process after doing a family constellation. I found it helpful to integrate my two paths, constellation facilitation and acupressure energy work. Through this combination, the knowing field has become my teacher.

Website: 5elementsconstellations.com

Graphic Credits for this chapter: John Cheney

CHAPTER ELEVEN

Five Element Constellations: a Body-Oriented Health and Wellness Approach

by John Cheney

Abstract: In a 5 Element Constellation, there is usually no story other than the client's experience of some form of imbalance. The application of principles and concepts of Traditional Chinese Medicine allows emotional and physical issues to be addressed during constellations. Representatives stand in for the 5 Elements found in nature (Fire, Earth, Metal, Water, Wood) and report their physical sensations, emotions, and relational dynamics with the other elements as they express the client's overall energetic condition. The constellation process can identify issues and restore balanced intra-systemic communication and stability within the regulatory system of the body's meridians.

Audience:

While most participants in 5 Element Constellations are experienced in classical constellation work, other receptive people tend to be familiar with Traditional Chinese Medicine, energy medicine, holistic health, and energy psychology (Emotional Freedom Technique, Psych-K, etc.). My audience is generally looking for resolutions pertaining to physical health and emotional issues.

Issues:

In addition to issues presented in classical constellation work such as relationship problems, grief, anger, fear, trauma or Family of Origin issues, presenting symptoms can include specific issues such as pain, headaches, asthma, skin conditions, heart issues, low energy, brain fog, chronic illnesses such as Lyme disease, family health legacies, and other medical symptoms.

Desired Outcomes for the Work:

Rather than the classical practice of having representatives stand in for family members, in a 5 Element Constellation representatives stand in for aspects of the overall energetic system of an individual's body. Each of the 5 Elements are related to the client's meridian system and vital organs. Other noted facilitators focus on the desired outcome primarily for the specific client, but I find that it's of the utmost importance to have the client as well as the representatives of the 5 Elements to be in a state of balance and stability when the constellation finishes. That is because they are standing in as an aspect of the client's energy system. If they are not balanced then the client will not be balanced.

In my role as facilitator, it is also important to allow and help all representatives *find their own words* for what they are feeling. This not only facilitates the expression of the system, but provides an added benefit when each person learns his own language of feeling.

How the Work is Done:

The five elements of Chinese medicine are Fire, Earth, Metal, Water, and Wood. In a 5 Element Constellation, representatives are invited to stand in for one of these elements, which taken together represent the whole of the client's energy system as expressed through the body. In order to understand 5 Element Constellations, some background about the five elements as a whole systems model is necessary.

Developed over thousands of years, the 5 elements of Chinese medicine came from observations of nature. Natural phenomena were used to describe the body's energetic system as expressed through the meridians or channels that circulate energy through the body. The meridians help regulate the energetic system of the body and nourish the vital organs. Each element is associated with specific meridians, which are related to and named by the vital organs.

The Chinese are not the only culture that mapped the energy systems of the human body. The indigenous medicine of the Inca's of South America documented the same energetic pathways they called "rios de luz", or "rivers of light".

Character of expression in the human body:

As we have seen in Family Constellations when we set up the Family of a client, they are often amazed that people who don't know their Family are somehow able to personify them. In this same way the Representatives are able to personify the elements without any previous knowledge. I will describe the different attributes or Characters of the 5 Elements and how they can shed light on how an individual's body/mind are functioning. The 5 Elements give a framework to see the character and emotional aspects of a person. When the elements are out of balance they may manifest as a particular physical/psychological problem. This can be an inherited quality (genetic or Family), or our physical or psychological condition, and our tendencies and habits.

Each meridian carries a unique bandwidth of feeling, emotions, drive, flow, and stability.

As we attune ourselves to their means of expressing, we can use them like a prism or magnifying glass to see through, to observe the function and relative condition of the mind/body. I recommend using this structure lightly.

Each individual element may be in a state of depletion, balance, or excess. These states can be observed in the behavior and personal characteristics of the individual representatives as shown in Table 1 below.

ELEMENT	Associated Organs and Meridians	Character, Emotion, Feelings, Sensations			Physical Problems
		Depleted	Balanced	Excess	
FIRE	Heart, Small intestine, Pericardium & Triple Warmer	Exhausted Withdrawn	Joy, Elation, Compassion, Calm	Over-excited, Nervous	Cardiovascular disease, Stuttering, Lupus and hearing issues
EARTH	Spleen and Stomach	Indifferent, Inattentive	Grounded Abundant, Giving, Connected	Worried, Ungrounded, Doubtful	Digestive problems, Anemia and easy bruising
METAL	Lung and Large Intestine	Self-pity, Grief, Cold, Heartless	Structured, Cheerful, Orderly	Prideful, Envious, Defensive	Lung problems, Allergies, Intestinal issues, Slow wound healing
WATER	Kidney and Bladder	Fearful, Frozen, Depressed	Flow, Mysterious, Creative, Deep	Anxious, Audacious, Manic	Back and knee problems, nervous system disorders (cerebral palsy, MS)
WOOD	Liver and Gallbladder	Passive, Low self-esteem	Drive, Motivated, Assertive	Anger, Irritability, Bitter	Vision problems, tremors, headaches and spasms

Table 1 - Five Element Characteristics

For example, Fire is related to spirit. The spirit is called shen, and can be seen in the eyes of an individual. If there is a vacant appearance, the condition of shen might be depleted, or exhausted. We can observe this in a fire that is about to go out. The fuel has been consumed and the flame flickers on the brink of extinguishing itself.

If a person is really strong and present, their shen may show as a bright gleam in their eyes and we might feel warmth in their presence. Like a fire, we may be drawn to them. We could describe such a person as being "warm-hearted". The easiest organ to associate with the Fire element is the Heart (see Table 1 for the attributes of other organs). One could say the "warm hearted" person is a balanced expression of the energy of Fire. Another common phrase is, "the eyes are the gateway to the soul." Much of this knowledge is intuitively coded into our language.

When a fire is out of control, we can see obvious signs for caution. The warmth can turn into an inferno and spread quickly, consuming everything in its path. This can be the case when we are consumed by a moment of rage, when no reason or logic can pull us out of the flames. This is fire in excess.

More in depth descriptions of all the elements can be found on my Website at: 5elementsconstellations.com.

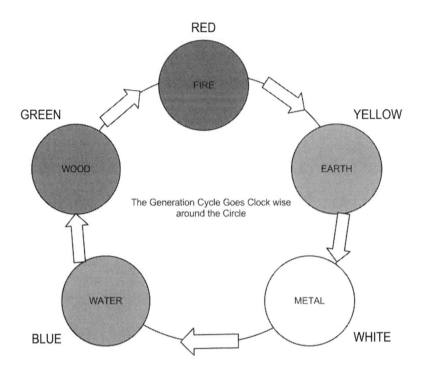

Orders of Flow in 5 Element Constellations

As in family constellations, there are similar "Orders of Love" or "Orders of Flow" within the 12-organ meridian systems as documented in Chinese Medicine. One "Order of Flow" that parallels family systems is: Every Element needs an equal and balanced place.

In other words, if one Element is weak, it will affect the others. The basic flow is expressed in what is called the Generation Cycle.

The Mother of Earth is Fire, and therefore Earth is the Child of Fire.

Earth then is the Mother of Metal, and so on.

If Earth gives too much to the Child (Metal) without receiving from its Mother (Fire), it can become depleted.

An example in nature of Fire generating Earth would be the lava flows in Hawaii that flow to the ocean and gradually create more land. The Heart (Fire) pumps blood in much the same way as lava, and moves the building blocks of our Body (Earth). In addition, Earth creates a place for Metal to form. Trace minerals in Water energize it. Water feeds Wood and Wood feeds Fire.

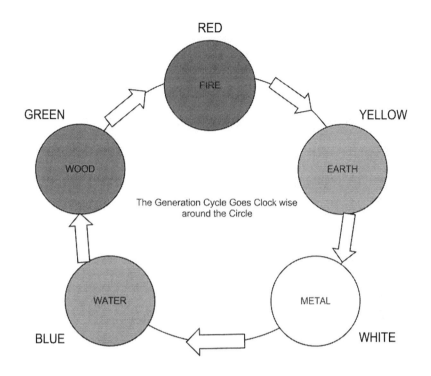

RED

GREEN

YELLOW

FIRE

WOOD

EARTH

The Generation Cycle Goes Clock wise
around the Circle

WATER

METAL

BLUE

WHITE

The Control Cycle

The Control Cycle is the star in the middle of the figure, and the arrows point towards the corresponding Element that it controls.

Fire controls Metal (melting, softening structure, and ideals.)

Earth controls Water, as with a dam (controlling flow.)

Metal controls Wood (trims, chops the over-active wood.)

Water controls Fire.

Wood controls Earth (roots hold Earth in place.)

An everyday experience of Metal controlling Wood could be when we breathe deeply (lung/Metal), we can move through a state of agitation (excessive Wood) by focusing on even and full breaths. Metal controls excess Wood, like metal lopper shears trimming an overgrown tree.

The Control Cycle adds another layer to giving and taking. Instead of uni-directional, which is typical in family constellations (i.e., parents give to the children), the 5 Elements are interdependent, and therefore have multi-directional acts of giving and taking. The Control Cycle ensures that balance is maintained between the elements.

These "Orders of Love" or "Orders of Flow" (Generation and Control Cycles) consistently show themselves in 5 Element Constellations. The beauty of 5 Element Constellations is that we experience these flows for ourselves, and therefore experience the giving and taking in relationship to the other elements. This can be felt through the meridians within our bodies, or as a representative for an element in relationship to another element.

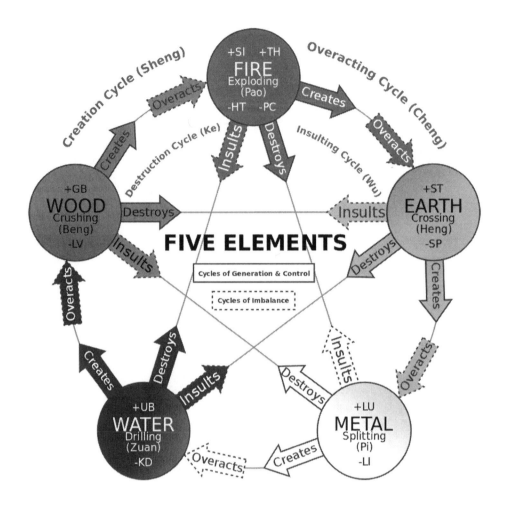

Over-acting and Insulting Cycle

There is also the Over-acting Cycle and the Insulting Cycle. These express the dynamics of dysfunction. A good example in the Over-acting Cycle in the world is humanity over-exercising control on the planet, and the resulting destruction of the environment. This can also be reflected in the organs. If the liver (Wood) is over active, it can de-stabilize the stomach (Earth), causing nausea.

This same example could be applied to a family. Because of their Wood nature and hyper-activity, the family might find it difficult to systemically have a sense of being grounded (Earth), or to simply be relaxed without the constant need for activity to regulate themselves.

An example of the Insulting Cycle could be present if Water fails to flow, causing Earth to be overly damp. Earth is insulted by Water. This may be more clearly illustrated by the lack of will or flow (Water) in life causing a difficulty in focusing (Earth/spleen).

Manic depression could be an expression of excessive energy in the Water (kidney/bladder) element system. An individual with this propensity can get locked into a tidal wave of creativity and not come out of it until they have utilized all available energy. The person is able to dive into a depth of creativity that many would desire, but when the energy is all consumed they are left in a depressed state. On a very simplistic level when an individual is depleted in this area (Water), inexplicable fear may arise in their emotional system. If they are strong or balanced in this area, they might feel courage and easily flow into an area of interest.

These all reflect the character of water:

When stressed, or depleted the river may be running low or trickle.

When strong, or balanced there may be an unrelenting flow, or strong will.

When excessive, the river may be flowing over its banks.

I'm always amazed how these characters express through the representatives so accurately, with very little information to go by.

With this brief background we can now move into how 5 Element Constellations are facilitated.

Facilitating a 5 Element Constellation

In a 5 Element Constellation, the client initially reports an imbalance. This could be a physical or emotional problem, a past trauma, or a Family of Origin issue. I have found there are many ways to take in information during the interview process.

1) There is facial diagnosis, which can give two levels of information:

a. There may be a predominant Element functioning or expressing, illustrated by archetypal facial features.

b. The face also gives clues as to the function of organs (Example: a large bulbous nose can mean an enlarged heart; darkness around the eyes suggests excessive heat.)

2) The organ pulses (found on the wrist) give an indication of the relative condition of the energy system.

3) The tongue can give you clues as to which organs/elements are impacted.

4) The smell that the client generally has can give information as well. (Example: scorched body smell might mean over-acting Fire.)

5) The Organ BioRhythms or Body Clock can be used as well. Example: if the client wakes up every night between 3-5 AM, the lung maybe impacted, which could be a hint towards unresolved grief related to the Family of Origin.

I also rely on the interview process that facilitators of family constellations use, and try to open myself intuitively to what might be expressed at the time.

Representatives are then selected for each of the 5 Elements found in nature.

I use small circular carpets that are the color of the elements.

Fire = Red

Earth = Yellow

Metal = White

Water = Blue

Wood = Green

They are set up in a fixed circle, the shape of the commonly seen 5 Element diagrams, with the five circles in the five colors arranged as shown.

I have the client make contact with each representative, placing him or her on the circle of carpet for the element that each person has been chosen to represent.

After setting up all the representatives, I ask the client to find a seated position so that they may be able to see best. Then I ask the representatives to close their eyes for a moment and focus on any feeling or sensation that they may feel in their bodies.

I generally walk through the circle to observe what I feel in my own body. Based on what is needed, I begin my work. I might give a representative a few words to give language to the underlying feeling. I observe the dynamics between the representatives and ask the client if s/he resonates with any of the language or actions just observed.

Acupressure

I use acupressure to assist and help resource the participants and client (with their permission) during the constellation. The meridians are accessed and stimulated via meridian points with energetic transmission through fingertips and sound (from tuning forks). This helps the system and representative (or element) regulate, so that they may participate in the act of giving and taking between the element representatives.

The act of giving and taking is a reflection of the individual's dynamic of health. If one is too weak, I will do acupressure on the representative of the element or directly on the client. It doesn't seem to matter whether I work on the client or the representative; both experience the beneficial effect.

Acupressure can be helpful in supporting the representatives if they are feeling out of balance, or may be helpful directly on the client as well. I continue this process until the circle has reached a balanced state, and the elements are able to feel the support and relative trust towards each other. Sometimes acupressure will help one element and seem to affect another element adversely, which usually points to the Over-acting Cycle and the Insulting Cycle.

Facilitating the Constellation

Let's say a client comes with a complaint that they are unable to feel stable in the world. They have a propensity to worry about their situation and find it difficult to stand toe to toe with adversity. There is also a bit of hypertension, but on the subtle end. They might have a tendency to have edema in their lower extremities.

Of course this could be addressed in a Family Constellation. Perhaps their father or mother had a similar feeling. What one might find with the elements is that a family dynamic, or a system that has been habitually run down through diet, life style, overeating, or overwork could somehow impact the Earth element.

As I do my intake of information I might notice a crack down the center of the tongue, which could mean the stomach has been significantly impacted. I could ask about their digestion, which they might indicate being on a prescription drug to alleviate stomach distress, sometimes their own assessment isn't very accurate because they have become so used to the condition they are in. They might not be a morning person which is common, because the Earth Elements peak energetic time is 7 am to 11 am. That is perhaps why they say breakfast is the most important meal. In some ways the intake of information is not necessary, because the constellation itself will express what is needed.

The Client sets up the elements and the dynamics are then brought to personification.

As I look at the system as a whole I might see that some elements don't seem to be aware of each other. Let's say as suspected the Earth element is weak in the constellation. It is having a difficult time being present. It is important to say I always try to keep my focus on how the client is being affected by the movement of the constellation. I decide to immediately do acupressure on the stomach meridian, which flows from the head down to the ground. This might ground them, but could have an adverse effect for another element. Let's say the Wood element seems a bit perturbed or nauseated when stomach begins to feel slightly better. Wood controls Earth (like a the roots that grow through the earth), so it may be that Wood is over-controlling Earth. Words or acupressure can be used to help clear Wood's nausea.

If this helps them feel somewhat better I can begin to look at the other elements to make sure they are in a good place. Sometimes the elements are indifferent. Let's say the Metal element is a bit cold and uninvolved. It might see Wood as a tiring nuisance and withdraw from trying to control it. When it looks toward Earth it might see that Earth is in a slightly better place and could be interested in that fact. I would try to get them to speak.

"I've missed you; I need your presence", might be expressed by Metal". So Metal is looking towards its mother for support. Sometimes Metal is a bit distant emotionally and needs to connect with Fire (Fire Controls Metal see diagram B) to warm up to being more intimate. When the warmth is felt in Metal, suddenly Metal can be more present with Earth. This also might help Fire be more present and able to give to Earth. So even though it is called the Control Cycle there is a give and take between the one that is controlling and the one that is being controlled. Metal then might be able to control Wood, which can be a relief for Water and Earth. Water might have been drained due to Wood's demands for energy. Water may complain of leg or lower back pains. I might ask the client "do you feel this?", and they usually are feeling exactly the same as the representatives. So I might choose to work on the client's leg and lower back, and ask the Water Element (and client), "is this helpful?"

Suddenly the relationships of the elements begin to become more vibrant and dynamic. If there are any problems of trust between the Elements they can be worked through with dialogue. I am basically looking for a place of balance and homeostasis. This comes into being when each element is heard, seen, and felt. Then the system is in a state of wholeness and can freely give and take. The process usually takes about an hour.

A Family of Origin issue revealing an imbalance of giving and taking might be that the child didn't like mom's controlling ways. As a result child is unable to take in mothers support. A 5 Element constellation might mirror this family dynamic in the Generation Cycle. The dynamic between mother and child might show itself in that Water (child) will not take Metal's (mother) support (see diagram A) due to Water's dislike of the structural and controlling attribute of Metal. This might be reflected in life, since they don't have a healthy sense of structure due to the rebellion against their mother's control. Sometimes this can turn into an advantage for doing a 5 Element Constellation compared to traditional family constellation: since Metal is not recognized as mother there may be less resistance to having an experience of what taking/receiving support in balance is like.

My observation has been that everyone experiences these imbalances from time to time. It is a part of the ebb and flow of life. We don't need to judge ourselves. When we observe through a detached perspective instead of a sense of ownership, the feeling begins to move. This seems to facilitate a clean resolution as the client doesn't create any unnecessary suffering through self-criticism. ("Why do I have such dark feelings?" "What's wrong with me?")

I have found that it is important to create an environment that includes feelings that we commonly view as unhealthy or undesirable. When we can see the feeling as an object in the field of our awareness, the feeling will have a beginning, middle, and an end. The dynamic field of a constellation can hasten this resolution and release of feeling.

Our likes and dislikes reveal a lot about the interrelationships of feeling between elements, and show many signs about our personality. When elements in a constellation don't like each other, this can be a reflection of the personality of the client. For example: if an individual is timid and seems to be very stoic, it could be that their system is overacting or controlling the Wood element which is the element that represents our active nature. This might be because of a discomfort with aggressive behavior, which might not have been allowed in the Family of Origin.

5 Element Constellations can be a supportive tool for Family of Origin Constellations. When shifts occur in the family of origin's field due to a Family Constellation the body can

take time for the new structure to be integrated. While this process cannot be rushed, it can be a powerful tool to support this integration.

How Contributor Came to This Work:

My constellation experience began in 1999 when a friend gave me a flyer about a family constellation workshop that Dietrich Weth would be conducting. She was prompted to share the flyer after I described a problem I was experiencing with my work. I had been teaching piano in the homes of my students for about 18 months, going to approximately 36 homes a week. At that time, I was having difficulty adjusting to the change or feel of each environment in which I taught.

I would feel focused and at peace in some homes, while in others I would feel my throat constricting and find it difficult to express myself during the lesson. The next house might be consistently distracting. There were many different environments.

What I didn't know at the time was I was entering the field of that family. I was feeling the dynamics that were present, as well as my own issues in relationship to the feelings that were resonating in that field.

The workshop began with a demonstration evening, but since I had to teach into the evening, I arrived late for the demonstration, so I was free of any explanation. I literally walked into the room as a constellation was in progress and sat down. Dietrich came up to me and asked in broken English, "Do you want to work?" (meaning 'will you be a representative?'). I had no idea as to what the process was about and did not expect to feel anything. He set me up in the constellation, and shortly after asked me, "What do you feel?" I was perplexed. "What? I'm supposed to feel something?"

I surprised myself by saying, "I feel like I am dead", and he said, "Yes." Turns out I was someone in that family who had been murdered. It was a bit shocking to be thrown into the unknown like that, but this experience never gave my doubting mind a chance.

I was deeply inspired by this first experience. I attended eight of his workshops and eventually committing to his two-year training. I continued attending his workshops/trainings through 2007 when Dietrich passed from this world.

Dietrich taught us a method of doing "blind constellations," in which the facilitator did not know what the issue was, but would simply follow the energy of the constellation and his inner feeling. We did many constellations of this nature in our peer study group. This method allowed us lots of creativity in our approach to setting-up constellations, giving us a format that allowed each group member to have an opportunity to facilitate. This also mirrored the improvisational approach I had nurtured in music.

What I learned was that the facilitator is just giving voice to what "is." By expressing what "is," a release happens and the system begins to flow. Although it may require expressing what "is" from many different perspectives, the release seems to happen faster when no blame pertaining to the feeling (and to the other person) is expressed. If there is a conflict, there is a feeling associated with it in the field, which is then expressed through the body, and then through words.

This way of facilitating paved the way to 5 Element Constellations. Because we didn't know anything about the issue that we were setting up, we could only go by what the feeling was. This isn't to say protocol (the Orders of Love) and technique are not important. They certainly are, but this allowed a simple starting point for me. Over time, the technique emerged, confirming the basic foundations of how acupuncture classically works with the 5 Elements.

My first experience of facilitating 5 Element Constellations began in 2006 when I seemed to "unconsciously" set up my first 5 Element Constellation. A woman came to the circle with a creative block issue. I felt it might be helpful to see if her heart was really into the creative idea, so I set up the heart, the block, and the creative flow. As I recall, the heart needed to be engaged or be felt in order to begin the process of creation, but support was needed. One representative asked for support of 2 additional representatives. One had a grounding quality, the other an active quality. Only a few days later did I realize that the 5 components in the constellation matched the 5 Elements.

I set-up my first "conscious" 5 Element Constellation in a facilitator mentoring series provided by Mark Johnson. Then I began to organize small groups where I could try out the work and slowly develop the approaches I currently use. I had my doubts and wanted to test the 5 Element Constellations to make sure I wasn't deluding myself.

In an experimental session, I had an acupuncturist and a medical intuitive present. They wrote down their diagnosis for the client that I was about to work with. Then after the constellation, they revealed what they had diagnosed. We found that the central issue in the constellation was the same as their diagnoses. Soon I began using acupressure, as well as dialogue and EFT (Emotional Freedom Technique) in constellations, although I use it less frequently now.

One thing I find important in facilitating 5 Element Constellations is to create an atmosphere in which any feeling is welcome. Most people don't have knowledge of the 5 Elements or the character of each element, which may actually be advantageous.

For example, with a client who had a skin condition, the representative for the Wood element began to jump up and down. I usually advise representatives to tone down the expression of a feeling that springs up. However, this was a good expression that the liver was working overtime and needed to be balanced. The participant had no knowledge of the elements. I was amazed when the constellation was finished that the client's skin appeared much more even toned.

Selected Examples:

Asthma

In a constellation for a woman with a life-long case of asthma, my mind immediately went to the idea that there might have been some systemic grief in her Family of Origin. In the interview process, however, I realized that my idea didn't fit. My mind said grief, but on the feeling level I didn't sense any obvious expression of grief. I was a bit perplexed and yet preceded to set-up a 5 Element Constellation.

As I was walking through the field of the constellation, for a few seconds I felt as if I had been knocked unconscious. I paused to gather my words to express what had just been expressed in the field. Wondering if it were a real experience or my own trigger or imagination, I asked the client, "Have you been in an accident?" I had to re-frame the question several times to get to the actual event. She finally said, "When I was 14 years old, I was hit by a car. I never made the connection that since that accident I have had asthma."

It made sense. The breath had literally been knocked out of her. In the Metal element (lung and large intestine) there was difficulty breathing and a fair amount of dissociating going on. I resourced the participant with acupressure, and slowly the 5 representatives of the elements became stable. The surprising result from the constellation is that the client has been off her medication and free of asthma for 4 years.

This is the woman's account of the situation that led to her asthma:

"I was 14 when I was hit by a car in a cross walk and landed on my left side, with my face suffering most of the damage. I had one fractured rib and needed a lot of dental work. I was unconscious, and a nurse on her way home from work stopped and administered CPR. I was resuscitated and began to scream (people tell me) and then Life Flight transported me to the UC Davis Trauma Center. I was on a respirator and in and out for 4-6 hours.

"That was when I developed asthma and started to use a rescue inhaler in California. I moved to Washington state in 2000 and needed a stronger asthma medication, so I started taking Advair® daily.

In 2006 I started exploring energy medicine. During a constellation in 2007, I felt a tingling sensation along the outside of my right hand while in a constellation, and you explained what it was. Later, when you facilitated a 5 Element Constellation for me, you took my pulses. You walked up to me from the back right side and asked if I had been in an accident.

"My Mom was there and she was completely amazed. At the end of the constellation, I could breathe again. After a few appointments at your home, I remembered that my breathing would get worse at 3 pm, and you said it had to do with my biorhythm. (Oriental organ clock?) After the last time, when you had me scream into a pillow, I felt completely beat up, but I was better and stopped needing my inhalers."

Lyme Disease

I also had a client that was diagnosed with Lyme disease by a naturopathic physician. The client was having limited ability to enjoy a functional life and spent a lot of time in bed and at home. After going through many treatment protocols and months on a restrictive diet he began to doubt his diagnosis. Here is what he wrote after his constellation and the subsequent shift he felt in how he identified himself.

"The efficacy of the Constellation may have been in that it helped me to detach from the crutch of the Lyme label, as it empowered me to frame my health in a way that was much richer. I experienced a connection with my body and spirit in a cohesive, symbolic fashion that was more tangible than my scientific body, which I had often disconnected from my mind and my soul within the scientific, western medical context."

Further Development:

5 Elements as a Model for a Systemic of Wholeness

When all the elements are in a state of balance one could call this a state of systemic wholeness. Where each element has a place, can give and take, control and surrender as needed. There are few models for systemic wholeness. My sense is this could be applied to any system.

I think that 5 Element Constellations can also be utilized in organizational constellations to address the management processes of a company.

For example: What are the energetic conditions of the company with respect to:

Spirit (Fire)

Sense of groundedness (Earth)

Structural, planning and accounting (Metal)

Will and overall Flow (Water)

Active/doing (Wood)

The company as a whole may reveal disturbances in the same way that individuals experience depleted, imbalanced, or excess energy that will impact the inter-systemic communication and stability. If the planning (Metal) and will (Water) to implement a goal is difficult to execute, the company might not have enough support within the elements. Perhaps no one will be behind the plan, or not enough people will be sufficiently engaged to bring success.

There can be many levels to the utilization of this tool. Does the company have the quality of individuals that represent a balanced system? Example:

Are there enough Earth people to provide stability?

Are there enough Metal people to plan thoroughly?

Sufficient Water people to bring will and flow to their respective positions?

Adequate Wood people to complete the actions necessary to finish a given job?

Does the company have a heart-felt purpose and a sense of what is needed to sustain the (Fire) spirit of its employees?

At the macro level, various cultures could also be seen as displaying strengths and weaknesses in the 5 Elements, with blocks in the energy flow, as well as depletion, imbalance, or excess energy in the larger culture. Using this modality and these approaches may help in viewing the societal problems in a broader systemic context.

This model can be used to measure systemic wholeness, from looking at an environment using the Feng Shui utilization of the 5 Elements to the overall energy flow balance of a physical space.

Openness to What Is

As I mentioned earlier, I have found that it is important to create an environment that includes feelings that we commonly view as unhealthy or undesirable. What constellations have taught me is that by acknowledging a feeling and objectifying it, we create an environment of inclusion and stability towards feeling. The mind can relax and yet be present with what is expressing in the moment. At the same time we need not immerse ourselves in the feeling, but just be in contact with it.

Andreas Demmel. I was born in the summer of 1984 in Rosenheim am Inn in Bavaria, Germany. My grandparents on both sides were farmers. Our families had been been rooted in the Bavarian land and had worked that land for countless generations so my ancestral memory was already filled with a strong relation to the earth. In Bavaria it was normal to dominate other beings and then to consume parts ("products") of their reproductive processes (eggs/milk) or even the beings themselves (meat). It was normal to suppress transgenerational traumas from the wars that included domination over the Jews and other peoples and groups. It was also normal to talk about spirituality without talking about the joy of sexuality.

I have lived in Berlin since August of 2011. I experience Berlin as a big melting pot, a large laboratory, where many people - professionals, researchers and magicians - who have explored the issues around global change meet together. I am one of those who have come to Berlin to participate in this. Together we combine our insights to create a field in which everyone immersed and engaged in this topic profits from the nourishing effects of the various approaches and insights.

E-mail: andreas@systembewegungen.de

Website: www.systembewegungen.de

Facebook: Andreas Demmel

Offerings: Single Sessions
                Workshops
                Consulting

Picture Credits for this chapter: Andreas Demmel, Johannes Demmel, Michael Bock

CHAPTER TWELVE

Constellations on Global Change

by Andreas Demmel

Abstract: Nature Constellations are perfectly suited to work with questions and issues of global change. Using this approach can help people understand, integrate and structure their personal experiences of global change while supporting and guiding this process on the physical, mental, emotional and spiritual levels. In this chapter I describe four possible intentions for this work, present my approach to facilitating global change constellations and document three examples. In addition, I present my views about the future of work in this area, particularly my perception that human catalysts are needed to reconnect a world out of balance.

Audience:

As we are all part of the planet and the planetary process, this format is suitable for any audience. But I consider it particularly supportive for people who already feel a special connection to, relation to, initiation through, or mission from the planet itself as a whole.

It can serve, on the one hand, to open people to the many interior and exterior processes around global change. On the other hand, it can help people who have already been opened through meditative practices, spontaneous or induced non-ordinary states of consciousness, visions, dreams and other life changing and ego-transcending experiences to better understand and integrate their experiences.

There is a growing number of people on the planet whose deep self-explorations have gone beyond their gestation, childhood, and present life into the transpersonal realms of the archetypes, the collective and the span of history. These people experience themselves over time as less and less separate from life; they perceive themselves as parts of a larger system, a larger reality, a larger change.

As this collective opening on the planet progresses, it sometimes happens that people open to these larger realities spontaneously and are overwhelmed by them. Usually these people do not get support or understanding from society. Sometimes they fall into the psychiatric system which considers their reports of their experiences to be symptoms of serious psychopathology. And so they themselves come to doubt their own experiences, and are often sedated or even hospitalized. Experiencing a Nature Constellation about global change can help these people to integrate their opening consciousness and to frame and re-structure their prior experiences in a more useful way.

Issues and Questions:

In nearly every group where I have facilitated or participated in Nature Constellation work, sooner or later questions arose about global change. These are questions like "What is the solution to the question of global warming?" Or "How can humankind and nature be in balance again?" Or "How can we reach a relationship in which both the earth and the humans can benefit from the process of change?"

Such questions are consistently met with positive resonance from the other participants. So one could say: It is a big topic, widely shared.

2012 with its prophecies of a major world change arrived. Especially in that year many people were concerned and hopeful about the possibility that there would be a major shift on the planet. Kai Ehrhardt put it as follows:

> "No doubt, the world is standing on the brink of unprecedented, systemic change. New integral and holistic organizing principles are yearning to be born – and you get to live in the middle of it. This can be very disorienting and scary. At the same time it can be profoundly gratifying and exciting to participate in the evolution of a new cultural paradigm."(Kai Ehrhardt 2012)

The experience of working on global change issues in constellations confirms that there are a lot of emotions in this kind of work: hope, fear, guilt and many desires and wishes connected to this global change.

The method of Nature Constellation work is very suitable to work on global change, as the architecture of the method itself already contains a part of the solution. That is, one of the biggest obstacles in the global change is the lack of connection and relationship of humans to nature. Because Nature Constellations enable us to look at these relationships and to re-connect and re-balance them, the method itself and the experience itself is helpful, regardless of the specific content of the constellation.

I have had the pleasure and honor to experience this format in several settings: at a forum for political constellation work, at Nature Constellation workshops in the wilderness, at a small workshop at an improvisational dance festival, to mention just a few in addition to more traditional workshop settings. It has become clear that global change can be viewed from many perspectives and is each time new.

Desired Outcomes:

This format is ideally suited to contain and accompany processes around global change in the four crucial dimensions of a physical, mental, emotional and spiritual experience.

Physical: When these kinds of questions are invited into the constellation space, the people who are standing as representations and those in the outer circle can experience the physical quality of planetary systems directly in their bodies. They can literally feel the heaviness of the situation. Sometimes people who stand for the earth are shaking and shivering, representatives for water feel polluted and a person who stands for re-connection can feel hope and potential blossoming within. These experiences provide a deep anchoring into the physical process of the planet – a "grounding" through felt body experience.

Mental & Emotional: This format offers the possibility to meet the thoughts and emotions around global change directly, with fewer of our normal intellectual filters and less of our emotional armor. Through seeing the larger systems and perceiving how they unfold, our mind and heart are nourished by direct truth. We gain a better understanding of the complex coherences that are unfolding on the planet. We are able to integrate previous experiences of openings by observing perhaps for the first time that within those experiences was the potential for connections and movements which we are now able to follow. That is, in constellation work about global change people can find ways of better framing and integrating previous experiences or impressions.. For example, when people realize that much of the sadness that has been coming through them is connected to the larger process of the planet these feelings can finally find direction and be integrated in a new way. The feelings of sadness become less overwhelming when one realizes they are not strictly personal.

Spiritual: The more we experience the many ways in which we are embedded in larger systems, the more we can see that we are an inseparable part of these processes and that global change is unavoidable for all of us. This initially frightens some people but it also provides the opportunity for the realization that the planet is not an entity that is judging us but rather an extremely compassionate being that is involving us in this enormous and complex transformation for our own good, as well as its own evolution. In a global change constellation we are sometimes able to experience that the planet itself provides the mission, the initiation and the support in this process. It is a true gift when we are able to accept our unique responsibilities and devote our service to its transformation, thereby accessing the support the planet has to offer.

How the Work is Done:

My aspiration is to make every constellation in a new way according to the needs, intentions and desires of the group and setting. Therefore each time I combine various building blocks and approaches in a new way to fit the situation and the participants.

For me, two key aspects of Nature Constellations about global change are intention and facilitation.

Intention

It must be clear with which intention I facilitate a Nature Constellation about global change. Four basic models of the work can be used purely or combined in any way that feels appropriate.

1. Experience-oriented constellations
2. Solution-oriented and developmental constellations
3. Constellations as an ongoing practice
4. Constellations as a vision quest

1. Experience-oriented constellations

This emphasis offers the possibility to experience a certain element in a system about global change. Here one can experience how trees, rivers, nature, humans and the planet feel about everything that's happening right now on and around the planet. (Read more about this in Berchthold Wasser's chapter "Nature Experience and Nature Theater")

2. Solution-oriented and developmental constellations

Here we look at these questions about global change in a more solution-oriented or developmental way. This requires a clear intention of what specific question we want to explore, solve or develop further.

3. Constellations as an ongoing practice

This format is suitable not only to ask a specific question once but as an ongoing practice around an important issue or theme for us. This is made possible by the astonishing characteristic of the constellation method itself that every constellation on the same topic shows a new part of a bigger evolution rather than a simple repetition. People can work together then to explore some theme over time in an organic ever-renewing multifaceted way.

4. Constellations as a vision quest.

The aspect of seeing constellations and especially Nature Constellations as a vision quest definitely deserves attention. There is a cosmic intelligence behind the orchestration of constellations and their representations. These roles, situations and representations are capable of pointing out one's unique individual path in a very clear way.

Facilitation

The first question in facilitation concerns deciding the issue that will be the basis for the constellation. (I am assuming here it is in the context of a workshop dedicated to the area of global change.) An issue can be brought in by one person who has an urgent question in connection with herself and the earth process. A question can also be brought in from several people or from the whole group. If there are multiple issues, overlapping issues, or a lack of clarity I usually take one of two possible approaches: 1) I form small groups where people can chat and find a question together or, 2) if the group is small enough (up to 7-8 people), I go around the circle asking each participant to state their individual question or wish about global change. With the results of this round, or the results of the small groups, I can see where these questions converge or overlap and open myself to the bigger question underneath that wants to show itself at that moment for that group. From this I then develop, in a dialogue with the group, a big common question as the basis for our work together, with a selected person as focus.

The Elements

Usually I first ask the focus and then the group what represented elements we might need for the work. Depending on the emphasis felt by the focus and group, we decide if there will be more elements to give space for nature experience or more elements that carry a question in a specific context. My experience is that in addition to the elements that represent the core problem or issue it is good to also include elements that represent supportive (for example animals, plants, new technologies, sadness, effective microorganisms) and inhibiting (greed, politics, reactionary) elements.

This basic trinity of representatives - the core question, the supporting elements and the blocking elements – establishes a beginning gestalt from which the question in its complexity can unfold by itself. Therefore I take a lot of time in the beginning of the constellation before anything changes suggesting that all the elements feel their bodies and connect to their inner impulses, with trust that what needs to be seen will show itself.

Trust is the most critical element in the constellation; trust that we as a collective have the possibility to observe our actions in ecosystems from the inside and the outside, thereby enabling this special change of perspective to unfold.

Trusting this cosmic wisdom, I then give space to what wants to show itself in this moment through these representatives. Once such a trustful container is established by the facilitator, it transfers itself to the participants and we are all able to let whatever wants to show itself come.

During the constellation I am not as an outside director but rather a representative for some entity that witnesses the situation with a perspective on the whole. I let the entire process run also within myself. I see where it leads me, following my inner movement, remembering the intention of the question and occasionally supporting movements that are already arising. I follow the arch of the events, bring in elements if they are missing and encourage breathing and presence if representatives lose their emotional balance between participation and observation.

When the movement and the constellation comes to a natural end, I invite the participants to feel the echo of the work in their bodies.

After some minutes of focused silence, we come together again to sit in a circle. Then I ask if there is anything left that needs to be shared from the roles that would be supportive to the focus or the group process. Here it is important to be careful not to fall into a round of discussion or interpretation. Discussing and especially interpreting can easily interrupt many helpful processes that are underway in the group at the non-verbal level.

The element of time is very important to me in this work. I strive to be patient, to create the safety that comes when things are trusted to show themselves in their own way,and to work on a deep level where time has a different feeling than our normal hectic. I give time to settle into representations, time to connect to the constellation, time until movement arrives. The creation of a timeless space is a very important resource; there are certain critical movements and dynamics that are shy. They will not show themselves unless there is a sense of "timeless presence" in the room. For that is the space in which they live, and feel at home.

Contributors Way to this Work:

I first became strongly connected to the global process when I was between 16-18 years old. I had in this time a longer period of visions/dreams and experiences of war, the planet and its evolution in the future. These inner visions of other realities overlaid my daily life. It was in the time of both the euphoria of the new millennium (Y2K-euphoria) and the big shock and wave of insecurity that rolled over the western world after 9/11.

Also about then I heard for the first time that there was going to be a paradigm shift, a big change, a great transformation happening on this planet. I became very interested in this topic and have dedicated most of my life and energy since then to research this change, to study with others involved with it, and especially to experiment to discover ways human beings can support this process.

My university studies were in social sciences (social pedagogy) with an emphasis on environment and culture. I became familiar with family constellation work, trauma constellation work and nature constellation work. I realized that constellation work is a useful tool to work on this global shift since it makes hidden things visible and assists these things to move and transform.

I studied methods of constellation work with many teachers and in many contexts. With time , I realized, mostly through inner images, about its potential for the healing of specific geographic areas and landscapes. For example, I was attracted by a landscape about 15 kilometers from my home village. I had always felt there was something strange with this area. (Later I found out that there, on these fields, was the biggest battle of the Napoleonic Wars in about 1800, where the Austrian-Bavarian army lost around 18,000 soldiers in an uneven clash with the French army.)

At the Würzburg Conference in 2008, I found out there was already a group ("Sixth Sense in Service") working with a nature constellation approach. I met Berchthold Wasser and Kenneth Sloan, invited them to show their work in my University and later did the Nature Constellation Facilitation training with them and learned from their experiences.

After the Nature Constellation training, I went on to complete a two-year training in classical family constellation work ("after the Bert Hellinger approach") on a beautiful island in the Chiemsee in Bavaria. There I had the chance to learn from Bert Hellinger's early students, who have been active in this work for over 20 years, and from their various approaches.

I became more and more interested in the actual constellation process, and what factors lead to enabling real changes and shifts. I was also interested in discovering constellation work forms where this change takes place at a personal level, to work with my personal process.

I traveled for almost three years and collected what I needed for what would come later. During this time, I was living in the mountains, learning about gardening, studying nutrition, engaging in dance and performance practices, increasingly working with text as a writer and translator, experiencing community living, community building, discovering my own sexuality and deep desires around it, doing somatic and yoga practice and observing what is happening in the body through my meditation practice.

Now living in Berlin, I have begun to work in cooperation with others to weave these many aspects together in an exhilarating way.

Constellation Examples:

To give a sense of how Nature Constellations on global change "tastes," I have chosen three examples from protocols, descriptions and experience reports. The first one gives an overview of how a Constellation on global change can be structured and how it progresses. In the second example, we learn about the meaning and importance of emotions in this process through the reports of two young women who represented the emotions of sadness and greed in one constellation. The report in the third example is written by a man who was representing the "male aspects" on this planet. There we learn about the changing relationship of men and women within this process. (All descriptions are with permission from the original authors or participants.)

Example No. 1: "How can we reach a relationship where both earth and the human can benefit from the process of change?"

Context: The constellation was facilitated by Ruth Sander in the year 2008 within the frame of "Politik im Raum", an open forum for constellation work about political and societal topics in Munich. This constellation showed so many aspects of Global Change Constellations that I have decided to include it here instead of using a constellation which I facilitated, and Ruth has kindly allowed me to do so.

Representatives: *earth, humans, vision, relationship, change, obstacles, resources, men*; during the constellation the following elements are added: *women, nature, trees, cosmos*; the vision transforms first to *children* then to *child 1*, as a *child 2* enters the constellation;

After the beginning, the *earth* declares that she felt best as long as she was alone in the room. From the *humans*, she can only see the feet that clatter around on her. Also from the *vision* she can only see the feet. *Change* and *obstacles* are perceived as a strengthening by the *earth*. But something is missing for the *earth*: Only two men are standing there, the women are missing. So we choose a further element. The *women*.

The *men* are facing the *earth*, sideways between them the *vision*. The *men* feel alienated, longing for connection and sadness about the alienation. Of all the other elements, besides the *women*, they don't know who is standing for what. The *women* enjoy it, to stand besides the *men* and to be two. They feel powerful through this.

The *vision* would love to connect *humans* and the *earth*, but gets no contact to the sad and exhausted *earth*. Therefore she turns more to the *humans*. The relationship feels connected with everybody on an emotional level.

The *change* is standing close to the *earth*, feels like its mouthpiece, is ready to protect and defend her. The *change* is angry towards the *humans* because they just exploit the *earth*. And he is indignant at the *women* that they bring the word "power" in: "If they don't stop with it I will intervene and make sure that they disappear." The *obstacles* had body contact with the *vision* in the beginning and experienced this as pleasant. As the *vision* is changing its position and the body contact is missing, the *obstacles* begin to be more and more unbalanced until they are jack-knived bent to the front.

The *resources* are standing far outside of the system. They don't feel good. They lean on a table which is standing behind them and declare the table to be *nature*. The *nature* gives them strength and is psyching them up. They are startled about the fact that the *humans* lost connection to the *nature* and to their *resources*. And they wish that the *earth* would come to them.

In the further proceedings the *vision* transforms into the *children* (of the next generation) of *men* and *women*. The *earth* feels even worse through this. ("Even more that clatter around on me!"). She turns away from what's happening. We add the element "*cosmos*", this element only has a relation to the *earth* but not to the rest of the system. The *cosmos* feels responsible for holding the *earth* stable, whatever happens to her. For the *earth*, it feels good to turn away and to only feel the connection with the *cosmos*.

The *men* feel shame and guilt. They don't want to look the *children* in the eye. The *women* however cannot understand why the *earth* has turned away. They ask her to show the beautiful side that she also has. That shocks the *change*, makes him bewildered and angry. Also the *children*, who want to make their parents accessible to their new consciousness, are moved by that. This reaches the *women*. They want a good relation with their *children*. They listen.

Meanwhile a little flirt between the *relationship* and the *obstacles* has begun. They are holding each other's hands and sway to the beat of inaudible music and have forgotten the rest of the system. The *resources* are very far in the distance, still sad but now complemented by the *trees*.

After being asked to follow their own impulses, the *resources* and *trees* make a move. They take up a position next to the *earth* and the *change*, turn the *earth* smoothly around again to face the *humans*. *Obstacles* and *relationship* finish their dance and look at the *children* (*child 1*). Another observer is pulled into the picture. She represents now a further child (*child 2*), the third generation. The *obstacles* are very happy about this *child* of the third generation.

Men and *women* now stand next to each other, opposite from them are *child 1* and *child 2*, behind them *earth, change, trees, resources*. The *relationship* is standing a bit to the side, and wonders why she gets so little attention. She could be so useful. The *obstacles* have now retired far in the background. They proclaim that they are no longer needed now, as long as there is exchange and contact (*relationship*!) and no blaming happens.

But they will be called back into the plan in the moment when the *men* go into the attitude of victim again. Then they place themselves behind the *men* and tell them that it is absolutely important to come out of this role and to get involved. They thank the *change* for its (presence) and its action.

The children still have divergences. *Child 1* has the standpoint that *men* and *women* have done everything they could. They did not know any better. *Child 2* has the standpoint that *men* and *women* have botched it all up and have to take responsibility for it. We don't resolve this disagreement here but close the constellation at this point. (Ruth Sander 2008)

Example No. 2 "What can we as humankind do to support/restore balance on earth?"

Context: This constellation took place within my introductory workshop in Nature Constellation Work during the 1st Contact Festival "Begegnung in Bewegung" in the eco-community Tempelhof in Southern Germany in November 2011.

Representatives: *earth, greed, sadness, (old) human, (new) human, anger, transformation.*

Experience report of Katrin as the representation of *greed*:

> "It hurts, to torture the earth so badly! As greed, I feel disgust, shame, sadness, anger, exhaustion. Greed as a part of the old human. I feel all this, but I hardly move. It is important for women to connect and support each other.
>
> Very present is this disgust, this wanting to vomit. The choking. Being stuffed. The greed turned its back to the scene behind her.
>
> Was it the closed eyes, the shut ears, or just a feeling of "I don't want to see all this"? I remember this abandonment.
>
> Then the disgust, the shame and the sadness. Then anger, then exhaustion.
>
> The sadness that the "old humans" just went out of the room, because they could not stand it any longer... they were shaken by the anger... the anger shouted "wake up" in their ear... they wanted to hear nothing of it ... just close themselves... until they had to stand up and go.
>
> The greed was so sad when two of the old humans left... so so sad ... and finally ... there was only exhaustion... only tiredness... only observing of what was happening... calm and without strong emotions... too tired to sense deeply. Yes... nearly empty!?
>
> It was as if the greed lost all its vitality with the vanishing of the old human."

Experience report of Noëlle as the representation of *sadness*:

> "Earth, humanity, balance and greed are already standing, as I am asked if I want to represent sadness. I want.
>
> Standing up, it becomes clear that I first have to go to the earth, as she is shivering and had to suffer so much. But I also feel my attention for the greed and the human, also, but not predominantly. I cradle the earth, feel my love towards her and trust. I know I help her to heal. I am very calm. As greed becomes louder, the human is feeling pain and the earth is trembling stronger and starts to feel sick. I say, "I am everywhere" and that's how it is. The whole room is filled with grief and sorrow.
>
> Suddenly I have to go to the human, to support him, be there for him, in his weakness, his pain, his guilt. I lay my arm around him, and I know I give him strength. Inner calmness is within me, still. The earth, also sad, I give her my hand. Earth and humanity, I am with both of them. For a while we just stay like this. It is good and right.
>
> As I go, I am not sure if the time is right, but other things happen. I give space to the proceedings. I know I do not disappear yet... only taking two steps backwards.
>
> Fittingly, where I sit now is not far from an observer. She is crying.
>
> The healing gives me a homelike feeling, as if we would be friends.
>
> As the anger urges the human to wake up, there is pressure and density in my chest. I sit on the edge and feel how I am everywhere.
>
> Horrible heaviness and sadness, as the human is leaving the constellation, not able to stand

it any longer, I have the impulse to go back to the earth.

The woman sitting next to me, who is observing, cries and comes in for the new human.

I am there, I am there, calm again… soft and calm. The anger is also standing on the edge. I am behind the anger, which seems to be the right place for me. Behind the anger is sadness.

It is by no means over yet, but the constellation comes to an end.

The closing circle is sad, soft. I feel helplessness, sadness and trust.

After the constellation I have a threesome embrace with two other women, which heals me, protects me.

The whole constellation was very intense for me. I was impressed how deeply it touched everyone, how much emotion was released.

I felt good with the representation as the sadness. It felt quite right. It made me thoughtful.

As I was at dinner later, it was a bit weird, to know that all the other people around me did not take part in what happened in the workshop.

Now two months later, I am still happy that I was part of this.

Now and then I think about the constellation. Very present is the pain and the helplessness, that were released in myself as the human left the constellation. I don't know if this means that humanity will perish, or just that a painful process of transformation will change everything.

Greed is an issue that is on the agenda for us humans, and that the earth will become sick if we go on like this. That is what I see in this constellation.

We did not really pay attention to the trees in the constellation. Maybe there is still potential.

It seems true to me that which showed itself. The human and the earth embraced each other in the end, that felt right.

We are with the earth."

Example No. 3 "How can humankind and nature live in balance again?"

Context: This report is from the representative of the "male aspect on earth" in a constellation that I facilitated during the workshop "Naturaufstellungen am Lech" in 2010, a Nature Constellation workshop in the wilderness.

Representatives: *Male, female, broken parts, earth, sun*

Report from the *male* representative.

> *"During the whole constellation my attention was very often with the dog outside on the grass. He dug and pawed in the earth, for me symbolically: construction site, work, activity and technical progression, only purpose in life: work that takes so much time and energy. Through this distraction I, as the male aspect, am not being attentive to what was going on within the constellation. Also the reaction, the suffering of the "broken parts" was considered by myself as exaggerated and not so bad. – the male aspect was jaded, focused on the digging dog, very apathetic…*
>
> *Through the unification with the "female aspects" and further elements, the change was brought in – the awakening. Suddenly there were feelings and emotions (partly also guilt). The looking away did not work any longer. The facts were put right in front of the "male aspects". The appearance of the sun rounded out the constellation impressively.*
>
> *There still remains a lot to do for the "male" to let the change on earth happen and not to look away and lose himself in other things (sometimes felt like the only things that really existed were work, technical progress, hunger for fame, need for admiration, work work)."*

Further development:

One way to view the possibilities for further development of this format is to examine the phenomena that show themselves through this work and therefore the potential that is revealed through it.

Re-connecting to a World Out of Balance

Observing a lot of Nature Constellations on global change in the last years, several recurring phenomena showed themselves in nearly every constellation. The fundamental theme is that the world is longing for balance, and imbalance is apparent on many levels. I want to mention here three major areas of imbalance that are very important.

1. The imbalance of male and female

The male aspects are still in control of most things. The earth, the feminine and the masculine long for change.

2. The imbalance of power worldwide

A rather small number of people (The "1%") dominate the majority of the planet ("The 99%"). The 99% are already starting to get their power back.

3. The imbalance of giving and receiving

The earth acts like a mother in its ever-giving way. But at one point in history we started to take more than we needed, more than we gave back, more than what we can grow back. Through this, we suffered and continue to suffer from having too much - we feel overstuffed and intoxicated.

If we step back from each of these areas we see that they are not really separate aspects, we can see one big field that is out of balance. A field where more is taken than what is needed. A field where male and female aspects and power are distributed unevenly. Our planet.

As a first step in all of this mess, before even thinking of a solution, there is the process of reconnection. For most people it is much too hard to look at the full dimension of this system at one time. But step by step, at the right pace, reconnection is possible.

There is no greater resource for this than the plants, the animals and the landscape; everything that is so connected to the planet and so forgiving and loving towards us. Our strategy can be to first find our connections to these things, then step by step the larger connections can be experienced without being overwhelming.

Human Catalysts

I have mentioned the increasing number of people who are becoming more open to this process of change for earth. Many of these people perceive themselves as catalysts for the earth process. Each time a new wave of emotion or energy comes in, they feel that it is not exclusively their business but that it is part of a bigger process. Especially for these people, Nature Constellations can become a powerful tool to understand, structure and integrate their experience.

This can also change our view of psychiatric diagnostic categories with regards to these kinds of experiences. From this whole earth perspective, phenomena that are described in diagnoses such as ADHD (wide opening of the senses, issues of power and control, mostly men) or bulimia (wide opening of the senses, issues with taking in too much, mostly women) can be perceived in a totally new way.

Once people's systems open for larger processes, they often become disoriented and confused when they experience the "normal world's" craziness, intoxication and helplessness at the large system level. It is very helpful then if they can be shown that it is not (at least sometimes not) they themselves who are crazy or confused, but that they have opened

to the dynamics of current human society in general. This phase of the personal journey is challenging but helpful and finally empowering once a person has gone through it.

In the meantime, many of us are convinced that what is happening in psychiatric settings, in which reports of connections to larger processes are considered evidence of pathology, leading to excessive prescribing of drugs and snap-diagnoses, is a serious block to the unfolding of our collective mystical power, in addition to its destruction of lives.

Nature Constellations on Global Change

Here in Berlin, I realize more and more through all kinds of ongoing or beginning projects and groups that the constellation work has the potential to unfold in combination with other approaches that serve the same change on another level or in another way.

As the constellation method is already so diverse by itself, it is able to be connected with a variety of methods. I see a big potential in connecting the work with practices that raise body awareness and activate energy flow in the body (dance, somatic practices, meditation, yoga etc.). The body is already in another state, already activated, by these kinds of practices. Therefore the whole body-soul-mind is close to its truth. This allows us to go into deep levels with the work immediately.

Global change is such a large and complex subject that the best approach seems to be to have a large network of ongoing groups that investigate it from all perspectives. Every group could focus on a certain topic and after that bring their research together.

A great insight from this work is that things want to be seen, and through this they can transform themselves. That is why any cooperation with the performing arts is also very desirable. Through serious investigation, the core dynamics of the field could be distilled and translated into performance compositions, which can then be performed, recorded and made available on the internet, giving a bigger audience the possibility to participate and link up in a more conscious way with the process.

Unification of Heaven and Earth

The dissect-and-analyze thought models of old materialist/fundamentalist science have led us far away from our vivid nature and from the mystical world, archetypical principles, stories and dreams. I am optimistic that Nature Constellation work can support the process of bringing the so-called real world together with the nature and dream world to support a reunification of heaven and earth. Bridging between these two extremities, we are called to work on all levels beginning within ourselves, connecting and supporting the energy flow between our upper and lower body parts, learning more about how the lower and upper regions can work together, how airiness can work together with groundedness, and how sex and mind influence and nourish each other on their path towards creation.

Through all this, we come step by step closer to becoming one with creation through the process of dissolving time and space, reconnecting with the movement of the big soul, the greater system in which our planet is an evolving part.

Kenneth Edwin Sloan was born in 1946 in Decatur, Texas. He moved often while he was growing up and continued to do so as an adult. His most important childhood experiences were in the jungles and beaches of Oahu, Hawaii, where he began a life-long love affair with the mystery and power of the natural world. After a career as a manager and management consultant in large organizations he has dedicated his time since 2003 to projects and offerings for individual and collective self-discovery and reconciliation. He has been a student of Stanislav Grof since 1983 and was certified to offer Grof's Holotropic Breathwork in 1997. He was trained and certified by Albrecht Mahr to facilitate systemic constellations in 2005. Kenneth lives alternately in Steinen, Germany and Pagosa Springs, Colorado with his partner Petra and their two daughters.

E-mail:	synergeist@gmail.com
Website:	www.synergeist.com
Offerings:	Constellation Workshops
	Holotropic Breathwork Workshops
	Training for Facilitation of Nature Constellations
	Publishing (Stream of Experience Productions)

CHAPTER THIRTEEN

The Birthplace Representative: a Bridge to Membership in Earth Community

by Kenneth Edwin Sloan

Abstract: Beyond our personal identities based on membership in families, re-ligions, races, genders, tribes, or nations, we are all members of the earth com-munity of beings born on and nourished by planet earth. In contrast to these other memberships, our connection with the earth is critical not only to our well-being but to our existence - a few minutes without air and we die. In fam-ily constellation work we can experience how important it is for us to be con-nected with the resources of our human family systems, especially the love and life energy flowing to us (or not flowing to us) through our parents. From this resource-oriented perspective the focus is not so much on identifying and re-solving or accepting difficulties in our histories, but instead on recognizing and receiving the resources that are available to us, above and beyond the apparent difficulties. Could it be that our membership in Earth Community, with our birthplace being our direct link to the Earth, provides a similarly critical re-source of love, energy and wisdom for our lives? The answer to this question is a resounding "Yes!" This chapter describes a simple constellation format that can be used to show a person's relationship to their birthplace as a step towards closer integration into Earth Community.

Note 1: A version of this chapter was first published in the January 2008 issue of The Knowing Field Journal, Issue 11. Republished here with permission. More info, to subscribe and to order back copies: www.theknowingfield.com

Note 2: Although it was written and edited by Kenneth Edwin Sloan the origi-nal publication included Erna Alexandra Jansen, Chrisjan Leermakers, Chris-tine Robert, Johannes Schmucker, and Berchthold Wasser as coauthors since all contributed to the creation and development of this constellation format. The use of the term "we" in this chapter refers to the members of this group, the Sixth Sense in Service Team, that was active from 2003 through 2007.

Audience:

Since everyone has a birthplace, a birthplace constellation or the use of a birthplace repre-sentative in a constellation can be useful to see the nature of any individual's first connection with the earth.

Issues:

There are several possible presenting issues or questions that might suggest that a Birthplace Constellation, or the inclusion of a birthplace representative in a constellation with some other aspects, might be useful. Examples are:

- Where there is a clear relationship of an issue to place, especially when a person's relationship to place has been problematic (moved 12 times in three years for example).

- The person seems stuck in a place and expresses a desire to leave it but has not been able to do so.

- There is a sense that some important resource is needed in the life, which has so far not been seen or accepted.

- An individual is having difficulty in "grounding" themselves in a particular context.

- An individual has never felt at home or welcome in this world, regardless of where they go or who they are with.

Desired Outcomes for the Work:

Work with Individuals

To summarize our findings to date, the inclusion of the Birthplace Representative in a constellation is an effective way to explore the relationship of an individual person to the earth, as viewed through the lens of that person's relationship to his or her birthplace. This then indirectly provides an indication of the individual's relationship to other places and to all of nature. This parallels the way in which an individual's relationship to his or her parents colors all of their relationships to other human beings. The Birthplace Constellation provides a starting point for movements over time towards valuing or reclaiming our individual membership in Earth Community and through this connection towards living more happily and responsibly in the world. The importance of our connection to our birthplace as a resource and the positive or negative effect of this on our lives appears at times to rival the importance of our relationship with our parents. If this observation is even partially true, then this direction of work is important and deserves attention.

Work with Groups and Peoples

We have also seen some evidence in this work that what is true for an individual about his or her relationship to the Earth may also be true for collectives of people such as tribes, members of a religion, citizens of a town, and/or the ancestors of such groups and their respective "birth places." So constellation work that includes the "birthplace" of the group at the group soul level either for living groups or their ancestors, may enable those groups to connect to a resource that has been lost and find peace and healing as a result. (For more on the subject of working with ancestor groups see "Tears of the Ancestors" by Daan van Kampenhout, 2007). Many conflicts between groups in our world seem to have their roots in disputed land or specific places, such as holy or sacred locations or relocations of peoples to places other than where they have traditionally lived or some other form of "turning away" from traditional places. So this work may have more than personal value and may be helpful in supporting group work. We are following this thread of inquiry in our continued experimentation, but our results are much more preliminary and tentative than our work with individuals and so are not reported here in detail, except to mention that it appears that a disputed place (usually) acts like the "good mother," who is ready to love and accept all who come to her and that the roots of the conflicts reside with the groups and not with the place. More about this subject was included in the presentation by Christine Robert and Johannes Schmucker at the 2006 Wuerzburg Congress, Collective Intelligence in Large Group Conflicts – Challenges and Solutions (Robert and Schmucker, 2006).

How the Work is Done:

The question or issue for which a Birthplace Constellation is done is usually something of the form "What is my relationship to my birthplace?" This leaves lots of room for whatever is needed and important for the person to show itself. Our experience with more narrowly formulated questions about the birthplace has not been positive since they are often based on assumptions or presumptions that tend to limit what needs to show itself.

The Facilitator of a Birthplace Constellation needs to be well-trained and experienced in systemic constellations, or be directly supported by someone with these qualifications. Although the format is deceptively simple since it looks at the foundation of a person's life on earth it can be very powerful.

In the Birthplace Constellation a person chooses four representatives: the place of birth, the soul of the person, the personality of the person and the person's "power or life force." The person places the four representatives in relative positions in the work area that seem intuitively right, then steps back and sits down. With help as needed by the constellation facilitator, the representatives open to their internal sensations and perceptions of the element for which they stand just as in a normal systemic constellation, with their "degrees of freedom" established by the framework used by the facilitator. It is customary towards the end of a Birthplace Constellation for the individual for whom the constellation is being done to step into the place of their personality to experience directly the relationships and their qualities, but in some cases this does not appear necessary or useful.

There are often questions from the participants about the meanings of the representatives. The roles themselves are not objective – they constitute a particular abstraction of reality that has proven useful in this particular context. Like a map, they are not the territory itself, but taken together they provide a provocative and often useful perspective on the territory and the journey of a soul as it enters the world, and a personality as it encounters its first taste of destiny.

The Birthplace representative is the one which is the most challenging to clearly define, as it can at times appear as a very localized area – a specific house, for example - to larger consciousnesses like "Berlin." It is important to clarify that by birthplace we mean the "Spirit of the place" and not the people who live there, or other entities that may be associated with the place.

The soul is deceptively easy to describe: it is that part of you that existed before you were born and continues to exist after you are dead. For individuals with different beliefs around the soul, or even disbelief, we suggest: "Try it and see what happens."

The Personality is the complement to the soul: it is that part of you that comes into being when you are born and is gone when you die, so it includes your body. A large percentage of people seem uncomfortable with the proposition that part of them at least will die; they may see no sense at all in separating the representatives for the soul and personality or have relatively complex ideas about the various bodies we all possess. Again, we suggest: "Try it."

The Individual's Power or Life Force is usually not problematic to define. It is that energy or power we need to fully accomplish our life's purpose, regardless of our beginnings.

Additional representatives may be introduced from the beginning or during the course of the constellation by the facilitator. It has proven useful not to be too quick with this at either point. As a guideline, additional representatives should be in the form of resources. No attempt should be made to bring "perpetrators" such as: evil parents, siblings or negligent doctors into the constellation. It may be important to work through whatever issues there are around such subjects in a different and more appropriate context. In the timeless dimension of the gestalt of soul, personality, power, life force and birth place, they can be acknowl-

Scene from a Constellation that included a Birthplace Representative

edged when they infringe, but not be given great importance. For example to someone who stands up in the outer circle and says: "I am you mother, I need to be here!" we would say: "Thank you. We have seen that. Please sit back down now." Occasionally they do come in. For such situations one needs intuition as a facilitator, based on solid training and as much well-digested experience as possible

How We Came to This Work:

In May 2003, at the International Congress entitled: 'Passion and Responsibility' held in Wuerzburg, Germany, a group of people came together in an Open Space (Owen, H., 1997) session asking various versions of the question: "What can systemic constellation work contribute to the relationship between humans and nature?"

The first meeting to discuss this question was held in February 2004 with Chrisjan Leermakers, Berchthold Wasser, Christine Robert, and Petra Sloan in attendance. From that meeting, a form of systemic constellation emerged from dialogue and experimentation, which provides clear answers to the question: "How am I in relationship to the Earth?" The participants named this the Birthplace Constellation, based on its inclusion of a representative for the client's birthplace. Since that beginning the Birthplace Constellation has been experienced by a significant number of individuals (estimated at over 500) in many different countries. An early report on some aspects of the Birthplace Constellation has been previously published in German (Wasser, B., 2005). An earlier version of this chapter was published in 2008. In addition to the use of the Birthplace Constellation as a specific form or pattern, the Birthplace Representative has been set up on numerous occasions in other kinds of constellations, with positive effects There were several threads that contributed to the phenomenological emergence of the Birthplace Constellation and appreciation of the Birthplace Representative as a resource.

These threads are:

1. *The regular appearance of countries as representatives in family and systemic constellations*
2. *Observations of the reverence of native peoples for their birthplaces.*
3. *Insights in deep ecology and eco-psychology of the importance of the relationship of human beings to nature.*
4. *The fairytale Snow White.*
5. *The foundations of astrology.*

We will touch on each of these briefly, as in some sense these threads continue to exist in the fabric of the Birthplace Constellation system and express themselves through it.

1) Geographic Elements in Constellations

Geographic elements have been included in constellation work from almost the beginning, especially in the form of a land or country or less often city or region where someone was born or to which they have emigrated. Bert Hellinger often introduced a representative for a country or countries into constellations when there was a question of choosing between countries of birth and adopted countries or countries where individuals ended up living. Many people have been touched by the power and dignity of countries in these constellations led by Hellinger and others; it is not uncommon for countries or regions or cities to come into constellations where the person facilitating the constellation feels they belong. In addition, it sometimes happens that someone from the outer circle stands up at a particularly difficult point in a constellation and says: "I am Hungary. She is one of mine. I will give her a place." or something to that effect. This often has a very positive effect, even if they are not brought into an active representative position. Geographical elements in constellations have been addressed theoretically as well as in practice. In the January 2007 issue of Praxis der Systemaufstellung for example, Dr. Friedrich Asslaender wrote an article entitled: "The Power of the Three Roots – Spiritual, Geographic, and Biographic" (translation of title) (Asslaender, F., 2007) in which he clarifies the importance of geographic as well as spiritual dimensions in constellations, recommending an expansion of focus beyond biographical elements.

2) Reverence by Native People's for Birthplaces.

At least some native peoples have a reverence for the birthplaces of individuals. Christine Robert had noticed a description in the book by Robert Lawlor entitled: "Voices of the First Day," prior to her attendance at the gathering in February 2004, in which Lawlor describes the reverence of members of Australian Aborigine tribes for their places of birth and their practice of periodically returning to and caring for these places. (Lawlor, R., 1991). Touched by this description she visited her own birthplace in Germany and felt a strong emotional and physical response in her body, as well as a sense of a complementary recognition of her by the place itself, which surprised her very much. This signpost from Lawlor and Christine's introduction of her experience into the dialogue at the February 2004 meeting were very important for the emergence of the Birthplace as a Representative.

3) Deep Ecology and Eco-psychology Movement

The deep ecology movement and more recently the eco-psychology work have repeatedly pointed to the importance of our relationship to nature as a felt experience in contrast to an idea or abstraction. Joanna Macy and her coworkers have been pioneers in this work. They refer to techniques to experience and explore our connection to nature as "the work that reconnects" (Macy, J., 1998). Chrisjan Leermakers of the Netherlands, who was at the February 2004 meeting, was familiar with this work and brought this knowledge and experience into the dialogue. The term "Earth Community" in our title has been consciously taken from the "Great Turning" work documented in David Korten's book "The Great Turning: from Empire to Earth Community" (Korten, D., 2006) in which he builds on the work from deep ecology to describe the importance of establishing or re-discovering our individual and collective relationship to the Earth, as felt experiences in our bodies and the potentially transformative effects of such a shift, both individually and collectively (p. 40).

4) The Fairytale Snow White

Berchthold Wasser of Switzerland had been impressed by a constellation in a workshop a few weeks prior to the February 2004 meeting that explored the fairytale Snow White. In the original version of this fairytale it is stated that at the moment of Snow White's birth three colors came together: "Red like blood, White like snow and Black like ebony." The constellation was set up using representatives for the three colors. In the course of the constellation it seemed to be that the red color stood for the life force, white stood for the soul and black for the physical body, all oriented around the birth process. Berchthold brought this information into the dialogue at the February 2004 meeting.

5) Astrology's Emphasis on the Birthplace

Astrology is the last contributing element we will mention in this inventory of the roots of the Birthplace Constellation. In astrology, birth is seen as the entry of a soul into incarnation. The place and time of the birth are keys to the person's power, opportunities and challenges. In the Birthplace Constellation we retain the birthplace and the other elements associated with birth but we do not include the element of time. Our experiments have indicated that time is not helpful as a representative in the birthplace constellation because it limits the view to the moment of birth. With time absent from the stage we enter a timeless dimension that allows great freedom of movement for the representatives through past, present and future. What we observe is that each individual, in addition to being affected by the time of birth, inevitably takes on particular aspects of the place itself and carries these into life, but most fully only when they have recognized and accepted them, which they can do in a Birthplace Constellation.

Constellation Examples

The following examples have been chosen because they each in some way demonstrate the wide range of experiences or some unusual aspects that can be seen in Birthplace Constellations. These are of course only representative and in no way comprehensive:

Childhood Refugee

A German woman in her late 50's complained that she had always been restless and had never felt at home, no matter where she lived. She had always had a great deal of energy, but had difficulty using it wisely. The success in life that she wanted eluded her. She was a psychotherapist in private practice and had done a considerable amount of family constellation work. This work had cleared many issues but it had not seemed to have had any effect on her restlessness and inability to utilise her considerable energy.

In her Birthplace Constellation the personality and soul came together rather quickly but her life force prowled round the room seeking something but never satisfied. The birthplace, who stood alone and peaceful, was ignored by the other three, as if it were invisible. After a considerable time and a gentle suggestion from the facilitator, the personality and soul noticed the birthplace. They discussed the situation together and after an assurance from the soul that it was "probably ok," they approached the birthplace. From their first eye contact, the birthplace responded with a friendly expression. As they moved nearer the birthplace slowly opened its arms in a welcoming gesture. As this movement developed, the life force noticed what was happening and slowed down. Eventually the personality and soul stood immediately in front of the birthplace and the life force joined them, standing quietly and expectantly nearby, next to the birthplace. The woman who had asked for the constellation now took her place where the personality stood. She looked deeply into the eyes of the birthplace, then wept and fell into its embrace, saying: "Forgive me." The soul and life force moved closer and stood beside and behind her, supporting her as well.

After the constellation the woman shared that as a very small child she had come to West Germany as a refugee from a nearby communist country. For various reasons her parents had attempted to hide their origins and become "real Germans." Although the woman knew of her actual birthplace and had even visited it once, it had always been a source of shame for her. None of her current friends knew the truth of her place of origin.

In the year following her constellation many things changed. She reduced her therapeutic practice and started a new career in the arts that gave her much more satisfaction and in which she quickly excelled. She also visited her birth village and took a practical interest in the place and what it needed.

Birth by the Baltic Ocean

A woman had the following to say after her Birthplace Constellation:

> *"Earlier I always focused on the difficult aspects of my childhood and what I had missed. Now I have remembered that I belong to that landscape, to the Baltic Ocean and its smells, to the sun and wind. I feel the ocean in my body. How could I have forgotten it for so long? I have not lived there for a long time but the sun and the ocean nourish me. I carry them in me, even now. I was baptized as a small child with water from the Baltic Ocean. My father insisted on it, overcoming the resistance of the priest. As a young man at the end of the Second World War my father had fled from the advancing Russians across the frozen Baltic Ocean and had always considered it as his saviour. Suddenly I realized that I was also a present for my parents: my birth and my presence had made it easier for them to find a way to settle in their new location."*

Birth on the Site of a Nazi Concentration Camp

Sometimes it is not easy for a person to come into contact with the place of their birth, particularly when there have been traumatic events there. For example, a woman's birthplace was located in an area that had previously been part of a Nazi concentration camp. Some years before her birth many people had died there. The woman's thoughts about her birth had always been difficult and associated with a sense of guilt. So, in addition to the representative for the birthplace, soul and personality, the facilitator placed a representative in the constellation for those who had died in the prison camp. The constellation was done as part of an individual session, using sheets of paper on the floor for each of the representations. The woman herself stood in each position. It was a powerful and healing experience for the woman to stand in the position of the dead concentration camp inmates and feel their goodwill and blessings for her and her birth in this place. At the end of the constellation, the representatives of the birthplace and the concentration camp inmates stood behind the woman as resources and she herself looked forward into life.

Birth in a "Difficult" Place

In a Birthplace Constellation in a public workshop the representative for the soul was immediately insecure and anxious. The representative retreated as far as he could from the centre of the room, finally sitting under a large houseplant in one corner. The facilitator ended the constellation at that point. Only after the constellation did the person for whom the constellation was being done inform the group that defence rockets with atomic warheads had been stationed in the town where she had been born, shortly after the beginning of the cold war. Due to numerous anti-nuclear demonstrations and extensive press coverage the name of the town had become synonymous with the threat of nuclear war. Throughout her life she had avoided letting people know the name of her birthplace.

The birthplace representative, on the other hand, reported after the constellation that he had always been ready to help and support the person, even extending his arms to personality and soul as a sign. But as they took no notice of him he gradually lost interest and in the end was irritated and could not understand the difficulties they were having in approaching him or seeing him for who he was.

The Shock of Coming Home

A Dutch woman in her late forties wrote the following:

> *"Almost two weeks ago I had the opportunity to have my Birthplace Constellation done. It was for me literally an "earth-shattering" experience. Never before had I felt so clearly that I had never felt any welcome to settle fully on this earth, so part of me simply hadn't. In the constellation process I made the decision to go down through this "Gateway to the Earth" and to finally put my feet down fully.*
>
> *When I got home I was very busy. I heard my body telling me to slow down, to put my feet on the earth in a physical way. But I had no time, I was busy, there was so much to do. My body started to speak more loudly, but I ran faster. This was a very familiar pattern for me. This weekend I had a family gathering. I was so tired, but I still worked like a Trojan. But somehow it was different. I was no longer doing it because I needed to earn my place in the family; it was more out of habit. But I also felt more detached from them, that in a way it no longer mattered whether they loved me or not because somewhere I knew that no matter what, I was loved.*
>
> *Today I broke down. I couldn't run anymore. My body simply refused to run any further. My body started to shake. I cried. I decided to clear my agenda for the next week or so and to go outside as much as possible so I could feel the earth under my feet. It was time to really come home to the Earth and myself....for I have finally come to understand that they are the same."*

Tentative Observations

The following are the most important observations that we can make, based on our work with the Birthplace Constellation so far. These are also applicable to constellations in which the Birthplace Representative is included without all the other elements:

Take it Slowly and Ask Questions in Advance about the Birth and Birthplace

Although most Birthplace Constellations run relatively smoothly and require minimal intervention, difficult material can certainly come up, as indicated in some of the examples. We have learned to ask a few questions about the birthplace and the circumstances of birth in the opening conversation with a person about to have a Birthplace Constellation, and to watch for physical reactions to these questions in addition to what the individual answers. If there is a lot of "collateral material" it may be simpler to deal with that in a separate constellation rather than encountering it for the first time in the Birthplace Constellation.

Remember "Resource Oriented Framework"

The Birthplace Constellation is fundamentally about solutions rather than problems - the solutions that can come when we recognize and connect with one of the most valuable resources we have – the Earth itself, through the specific representative of our birthplace. If, and when additional elements are added to a Birthplace Constellation we need to follow this pattern as much as we can. So, for example someone who is struggling might be very well supported by the inclusion of a particular favorite climbing tree that grew in the yard in the house where they were born or spent their early childhood or by the inclusion of an ancestor who had a good relationship with the natural world.

The Purpose is to "See How It Is" and not to "Fix It"

There is a well-known paradox in constellation work. We do the work to assist individuals or groups to move toward wholeness and experience their membership in community. However, within the context of a particular constellation we have as our goal to see how things actually are and to explore what movements are possible within that framework - nothing more. Failure to follow this guideline can lead to considerable difficulty: the person facilitating will tend to not end the constellation soon enough; instead he or she will engage in an increasingly futile effort to bring the unpleasant picture into better balance. Our suggestion is to trust the intrinsic process of the representatives in the constellation and support them in what is trying to unfold and to be very patient. Beyond that paradox we wish you an adventure and great satisfaction should you decide to explore this new "old" territory.

References and Resources

Asslaender, Friedrich (2007) The Power of the Three Roots – Spiritual, Geographic and Biographic in Praxis der Systemische Aufstellung, Issue 1/2007. Oldenburg, Germany (German title translation by Kenneth Sloan)

Kampenhout, Daan van (2007) The Tears of the Ancestors. Zeig, Tucker & Theisen, New York, USA.

Korten, David C. (2006) The Great Turning: from Empire to Earth Community. Berret-Koehler Publishers, San Francisco, USA. p. 40

Lawlor, Robert (1991) Voices of the First Day: Awakening in the Aboriginal Dreamtime, p 156. Inner Traditions, Vermont, USA.

Macy, Joanna. and Brown, Molly Young, (1998) Coming Back to Life: Practices to Reconnect our Lives, Our World. New Society Publishers.

Owen, Harrison, (1997) Open Space Technology. A User's Guide. Berrett-Koehler Publishers, San Francisco, USA. www.openspaceworld.org.

Robert, Christine, and Schmucker, Johannes (2006), Reconciliation with Nature as a Foundation for Reconciliation between Peoples, Congress Presentation, Collective Intelligence, Wuerzburg, Germany. Available at www.nature-constellations.net

Wasser, B. (2005) Geburtsortaufstellung: unsere Wuerzel reichen tiefer in Praxis der Systemische Aufstellung, Issue 2/2005, Oldenburg, Germany.

Susan Schlosser has her roots in the Kettle Moraine and Great Lakes region of Wisconsin. Her fundamental and essential relationship with the Earth was formed upon that land and has sustained her through all the varying streams that have made up her life.

After achieving her Bachelors Degree in Nursing she worked in the Intensive Care and Coronary Care Units, was an in-home Hospice nurse and ran an award winning Wellness Program. She went on to complete a Masters Degree in Applied Behavioral Science and Counseling. Her work has been influenced by Hakomi, the Enneagram and The Work of Byron Katie, and profoundly impacted by her ten year study and consequent integration and facilitation of Constellation Work.

Her deep desire to facilitate the opening of our hearts to ourselves, each other and our Beloved Planet is woven through her perspective and has motivated her life choices and direction. She has a profound respect for our holistic nature and the importance of integrating all aspects of our being to achieve a high level of health, vitality, enjoyment and loving connection with All That Is.

She has been in private practice for 19 years in Ashland, Oregon working with individuals, couples, families and relationships of all kinds, indoors and out. It is through this work that all the tributaries and experiences of her life are woven together. Taking her work into the Wilds of Nature is a fulfilling confluence of her passions. She lives in deep gratitude to her Relations, Ancestors and Teachers of all forms.

Email: wondersus@gmail.com

Website: www.truenatureconstellations.com

Picture Credits for this chapter: Sutra Ray Photography for portrait of Susan and Chaco Canyon, Dominique Shelton for Grand Canyon Water Crossing, Susan Schlosser for all others.

CHAPTER FOURTEEN

The Call of the Wild

by Susan Schlosser

Abstract: Around the same time I represented in a constellation for the first time, I had the great fortune of traveling into what is now called The Great Bear Rainforest in coastal British Columbia, Canada. It was there that I was given the enormous gift of meeting, receiving and being in one of the largest, most pristine temperate rain forests left on the planet. I was so in wonder and awe at the magnificence of that wild land, the presence of the Spirit Bear and its inter-dependence on the salmon and the Cedar trees, some of which are 1000 years old, that I found myself wanting to do SOME thing that would help people realize how vitally important our own interdependence upon the Earth and each other is. I prayed while I was there....out loud in front of others.....something I nor-mally would have never done. I asked these untouched primeval Ancient forces in all their forms to help me know what I could do to help. The answer to my prayer took some years to unfold, and when it did, it happened quite naturally. I love being out in Nature and I have huge respect for Constellation Work. Why not use this work to help open the flow of love with our families and Ances-tors, and with our Mother Earth and Father Sky? Why not put them together? It seemed a natural fit to me. I was intrigued. The thing is, "they" told me it couldn't be done. They (the ones who had been doing Constellation Work longer than me) told me there wouldn't be a container if I tried to do that work out-doors. I listened, I heard that....and yet, I heard a call. A call I had to respond to.

Audience and Issues:

I responded by extending an invitation to others to join me in these outdoor weavings of Constellation work and Nature. Curiously enough, there tend to be more women drawn to these events than there are men. The typical ratio is 1 man to every 3 to 4 women. In general, the groups, other than for a rare 20 or 30 something, have been made up of people in their 40's, 50's and 60's. These brave ones have made their living doing body work, human service and healing; there have been doctors, nurses and nurse practitioners, and many different types of therapists; there have been architects and authors, grad students and teachers, there have been botanists, naturalists and a state park manager, photographers, a maintenance man and some entrepreneurs. Regardless of how they made their living, they all wanted more from life....even if they had retired. Some hadn't camped for years and some had done quite a bit. Some were agile, and some were not.

Desired Outcomes:

Working outdoors with people seemed the perfect place to really see if we could move be-yond the ways we limit ourselves and each other through our thoughts and judgments. I wanted to see if we could actually put the flow of love into practice in the ways we were with each other and the elements. Having worked in human services my entire adult life I have seen many suffer with what I now think is one of the greatest pains....that of aloneness....the fundamental feeling of disconnection and separation. When we believe that we walk this amazing planet feeling alone, we feel disconnected from ourselves and from others. Obvi-ously, this impacts us. It impacts our ability to really see or care for another, it impacts how we treat Life itself and it impacts how we live upon the Earth....the Beloved Mother of us all. With the help of Constellation work I have walked through that pain and out the other side. I want to help others do the same. I am deeply concerned about us two leggeds and the dam-age and destruction that is caused through this fundamental belief that what we do with our life and how we impact the Earth and others doesn't matter. I know that that's not true. How I treat myself on the inner and how I treat all of life does matter. My deep hope and prayer in doing Constellation work to begin with, and then in taking the work out beyond our structures and walls, is that people would be able to know that they're not alone. That they would experience a real in-the-body feeling of love, connection and inter-relatedness with each other, with the elements and with the Ancient Ancestral Ones in all their forms here on this Earth. That out there with the wind, the Earth and the sky the flow of love would open in whatever good ways it could for their family and their family's Ancestral lineage, for each other through the compassion that comes as we step into someone else's shoes, and through our ability to listen and tune into all the forms of Nature that surround us. I want us to know our place. As the representative for the Earth spoke in one constellation "The Earth doesn't need us, WE need the Earth." To me, that speaks of true relationship and our right place.

How the Work is Done:

The gift and the challenge in working outdoors like this means we get to see how good we are at letting go of control. It's not a typical 9 to 5 kind of workshop. Stuff happens, and we can't know ahead of time what that stuff is going to be. For instance on our first trip to Chaco, my intention was for everyone to get there and be ready to begin by 4pm. Well, that didn't happen. For some the journey took longer than they had thought, some got lost along the way, some needed help in getting their tents up, there was trouble setting up the kitchen and the stove, and so on. Being out in the wild this way we rely on each other to make adjustments inwardly and outwardly to accommodate for what is happening. And it's important that we work this way together....whether that be for meal preparation and clean up, to return from hikes when we said we would, or to help save the tents from collapsing or taking off when the wind is blowing at 50 mph....which it did....unrelentingly for three straight days on our second visit to Chaco. It's here in these unplanned-for conditions where people who hardly know each other have a chance to be tested, to see what we're made of when we have to let go of showers and our normal conveniences, when we're uncomfortable and have the up close and personal representative of sand in our beds, and socks and food. Nothing keeps the sand out when the wind is blowing like that. Then we get to see....can we open our hearts to each other and sand, and wind and heat and cold, and whatever else the wild forces of Nature bring our way.

As a way of honoring the sacred opportunity of bringing this work to the people, I like to open with ceremony and prayer. It is important to me to give thanks to Bert Hellinger, to Francesca Mason Boring and to all the teachers and teachings that have helped me learn this work. I like to begin by giving gratitude for all the Ancestors that have come before us.

We open with everyone saying their name and the name of their parents, their Grandmothers and Grandfathers, and give acknowledgement to where they were born. We use what Francesca calls "circle technology" so that everyone can bring their voice to the circle and be heard in an honoring way. That way if they wish, they have the opportunity to share what is going on for them, what they are bringing to the circle in their minds and their hearts. We are given the possibility of really listening and hearing, and through that we get to learn more about ourselves and each other....another opportunity to notice if we're opening or closing ourselves to another.

Throughout the course of every one of these offerings I find it imperative to encourage people to take care of their bodies. As one has shared, "Personally, participating in a series of constellations can be rather emotionally and physically demanding, and at these times, nature can be a nourishing balm to the spirit, allowing for a gentle healing and integration of whatever themes have been revealed." When we're working with the Constellations to help open the flow of love and feel our interrelatedness it seems to me that taking the time to integrate and incorporate the teachings and insights will help people reach their goals for a more fully present, alive, fulfilled self. And to be able to take that time out in Nature could potentially help ground that possibility more deeply.

How the Contributor Came to this Work:

The way I see it, our physical bodies are our own personal piece of Earth. Many of us run around lost in our thinking, forgetting that we even have a body, forgetting or not even knowing that we are all connected....and forgetting that we can't live without our bodies or without the Earth. We can be so preoccupied with trying to make a living, support our families, and get everything done that we don't even notice the beauty of Nature and the magic of Life that's unfolding around us. It's so easy in these days of technology and speed to disconnect, get lost in thought and forget what has heart and meaning. What has heart and meaning is vitally important to me.

I've been a heart resuscitator and I still am. The first heart I tried to restart was my Father's. That happened when I was 15. It didn't work. I didn't realize until some years later, after working as an RN in an ICU/CCU unit, and after having attempted to revive many others, that the heart I was really trying to resuscitate was my own. Even when I was in nursing school back in the late 70's, all throughout my nursing career, and then finally into and through grad school and the numerous other trainings I've been involved in, I would ask the question: What will really help people heal? What will really help us feel connected, and open our hearts to love each other....regardless of our differences? What will help us open our eyes and take care of our precious planet? What can I do to help?

Truth be told, I'm still asking those questions. And I'm watching the threads of my life and work come together in magical ways....in ways that help find answers to those questions. There's the nursing thread....the one that wants all hearts to come back to the fullness of life and to really know love. Then there's my love of Nature.....one of the strongest threads that's been woven through my life. It was being outdoors that kept me sane and nourished through all those years I felt alone and disconnected from people. Nature was my solace, my salvation. I have spent months traveling rural reaches of our planet with my backpack. I have spent days and nights alone, without food or shelter Vision Questing to find myself and some answers. And I spent two plus years with a compass and an aerial photo traversing the forests and clear cuts of the Oregon coast range, up close and personal with the Earth, sometimes crawling on my belly to get through the dense brush, collecting data to find out how the logging is affecting the song birds.

I thank my Ancestors for these opportunities that have made up my life. For without them navigating their way through everything they had to go through, I wouldn't be here. Everything I have been through and everywhere I've been has helped forge me into who I am today; for me They are an alive working part of all of it. And that brings me to the thread of Constellation work. I am so grateful to have this be such an integral and beautiful part of this weaving of my life. Some 10+ years ago I represented for the first time and have been in hundreds of constellations since. The Constellation work has taught me so much. Through this work I have learned to trust myself. I have found real love and deep connectedness as I've opened my heart to myself, my Ancestors, others and the greater Earth Community in ways that I never knew possible. I have grown to trust Life itself. And I have seen how the movements of Love and the wisdom of the Universe are available to us through this Knowing Field.

Example Constellations:

Chaco Canyon

Chaco Canyon, a National Historic Site located in a remote northwest corner of New Mexico was the first place that beckoned. I knew that getting there was no easy feat as Chaco is located 70 miles from the nearest town and accessible only by long washboard dirt roads, the kind that can help your car and your spine lose their alignment. Yet the pull was strong. The Ancient Ones were calling...calling us to that homeland. Would people actually leave the safety of their homes, their towns, their routines and make the effort it took to come there? I had no way of knowing that if I answered this call....and if the people did.... it would work.

As far as we know, the First Americans roamed the land now called Chaco ten thousand years ago. Given the evidence that has been found from bits of basketry, seeds and sandals in the canyon recesses, the earliest habitation there dates back three to four thousand years with the first small pit houses having been built around 200 AD. The more current Americans, brave souls who had answered their own call to do Constellation Work and Nature Constellations there at Chaco, would fashion their housing after something more modern.... tents set out in the wide open space of the group camp site without the cover of a single tree. A place without any privacy, a place where we could hear the opening and closing of zippers each time any one of us went in or out of our tents.....something especially noticeable during the night time bathroom runs.

In opening talking circles the courageous souls that found their way to the Canyon said they wanted to open their hearts more to others, they wanted to feel more connected, they wanted to remove doubts and fears that held them back from life and love, they wanted to feel more empowered, to open more fully to what is and they wanted to better know their Ancestors.

Twice different folks have joined with me to spend four days exploring together over Memorial Day weekend. It seemed to be a fitting time to deepen our honoring of those that came before us. The Ancestral Pueblos, kivas and great houses, the messages left through petroglyphs on the rock walls, the beauty of the land we lived and hiked on for those days, and the magical sky above our heads were constant reminders that our Ancestors were nearby and that we are a part of something much larger. I wanted people to know that. I wanted them to have an opportunity to use the Constellation work to deepen their sense of place in their family while strengthening their felt sense of interconnectedness with Nature.

One of the first constellations we did gave the person who it was set for the opportunity to feel what it is like to experience their Ancestors lined up behind them.....the ones in human form backed by the Ones there in the form of Nature. They felt their love and support and heard the invitation that came from them to lean into them and call upon them when they need help. They felt, for the first time in their lives, that they weren't alone....that the

Chaco Canyon

human Ancestors that came before them are there for them and that there is a much bigger connection available.....a connection that passes on gifts and strengths and wisdom....not just pain and abuse like some have come to believe. With that bigger perspective they were able to open to them and call on them....which consequently, has helped them open more to life, and to love.

Being out in Nature like that, we have to work with the elements. In the heat of the day we took breaks to let people enjoy the shade of the Ancient Pueblos, potentially sparing them from sunburn or excessive warmth. Others liked the time off to hike, or journal or nap. Some constellations we did at night around the camp fire, and we found that it added a magical quality to be out there under the stars... with that form of our Ancestors shining down upon us. We found that lineages could begin to disentangle and people could open their perspectives and feel that love flow in themselves and their families wherever we were outdoors, day or night. As one participant shared "Without shelter we cannot be out in the heat of the day for the extended periods of time required for a constellation. Nature becomes primary. WE adapt to it. We begin to feel subtle messages from the place and the elements and they weave their ways into the constellations. It also helps by graphically giving The Big Picture. The vastness of place and the infinity of the stars at night gives us a perspective that our modern lives diminish."

One particularly visionary constellation happened for a woman of Navajo and Latino descent. She wanted to find her real work and land more fully in her life. Aided by the majesty of the petroglyphs inscribed on the overhanging cliff wall, her Ancestors made themselves known as the Spirit of the Eagle came through her representative to guide her to her true work and a more fulfilling life. She became "Eagle Woman" and since then eagles have become a powerful guide for her life. She has since gone on to find that true work and she feels much more alive and fulfilled in her life.

And then there was the Nature Constellation we were able to do near the ancient walls of a pueblo where everyone received messages from whatever aspects of nature they were representing. Here's the message that was received from a participant that makes her living as a botanist. She was asked by the plants to be their representative and this is what they said:

I was physically placed so that my view gave me a broad vista of the landscape of Chaco so I could see and feel the plants. The plants wanted me to know their combined spirit, energy and vibration. They showed my body and my senses a vast, gently pulsating energy, which stretched out and out, each plant swaying in unison with the others in the whole. It felt like this continued into and beyond the cosmos. They were gloriously peaceful and happy. There was only a profound gentleness and understanding to be felt anywhere, in any of it.

They were vibrating together on the surface of the earth, into the air we breathe and farther out into the atmosphere. Underground, in the earth, they were strongly connected through their roots, fibers and tendrils - in intimate association one to the other - individually and on a collective basis. Their communication was one of sensing - a telepathic effortless knowing, with no energy ever needing to be extended.

They wanted us to know this way of being - light as a spore of a mushroom traveling by air over the land and sea to a far away continent; the swaying - all together - the only feeling perceivable being one of peace, gentleness and joy of understanding all wrapped up together. All that they want from us is to take joyous delight in them, shine out with them in their glory! Their colors - in all their hues; the sparkle of light from their flowers shooting out brilliant colors; the scrumptiousness of their fruits - delectable and succulent; all the fragrances they've concocted to delight our noses and infiltrate our senses; and it goes on and on... No need to worry, they can never be hurt, their joy can never end - no matter what humankind does - they will continue to sway in the joy and peace.

This perspective that was opened for her has changed her life. It has deepened her connection to Nature, her work and the knowing of the interconnectedness of the world around her. She has never again looked at plants in the same way. Her desire now is to know that level of joy and interconnectedness with people....for it has been the ones with two legs that have caused her the most pain. Having felt that intimate connection so deeply in her body that day at Chaco has helped give her a touchstone, it beckons her to what she wants to feel with the two-leggeds.

When we're out in Nature this way, we get to take advantage of the beauty and the opportunities that surround us. At Chaco we got up early and went to the Great Kiva of Pueblo Bonito one morning, and we hiked out to Wijiji another, to sense, feel, listen and receive the silence and beauty of these sacred places at sunrise. Or, for those that were able, we climbed through a break in the canyon wall and up onto South Mesa to do ceremony and offer prayers and gratitude to the Ancient Ones. Up there with a 360 degree view we could utilize the wind to carry our blessings to all the directions before our closing circle.

Mount Shasta:

In between our two magical journeys to Chaco, I felt the pull to Mount Shasta. She was calling and I had to say yes. The desert in May is a very different experience than camping at 7,000 feet during the first weekend of October. This majestic 14,179 foot mountain is known to the Karuk as Uytaahkoo or White Mountain and is considered by many to be one of the most energetically powerful peaks on the planet, a pilgrimage site for people of all walks of life from all over the world. And it's not unusual for winter to set in right about then. Certainly those brave enough to heed this call would need layers.....clothes for warmer days and cold nights, for rain and for snow, and for everything else we might need as we entered the unknown on the shoulder of this snow capped sacred being.

Here, just like Chaco, we needed to work together. We needed the kitchen in good working order and protected at night from the invasion of hungry four leggeds. We needed people to go to the springs and carry water, for there isn't any running water at Panther Meadows. We needed firewood, fire builders and fire tenders. And then when the weather changed we needed all of us to put up the tarps to help keep us, and the altar we set up for our Ancestors, dry during the rain and snow showers.

While up on that Mountain we found ourselves doing a constellation for a young one struggling with the pull to end their life. This precious being had never felt connected with their Mother and hence their connection with life suffered accordingly. I watched this one intently as they would look to that Mountain in a way that seemed to call out for strength and security....for up till now their only safe place had been in places like this, with the mountains and with the Earth. There had been no trust in people...with good reason. In setting that constellation and watching what unfolded through the representatives, with that Mountain standing there to represent herself, we could watch the gifts of this work unfold. We all participated in our way as this person's representative began to soften and allow themselves to feel the beginnings of love and support from the representative of their human Mother. We all saw the resultant ease that radiated from both the face of the representative and the face of the one who hadn't been able to reach out and receive love in this form until that moment arrived, with them now standing in their place in the Constellation of it All.

We set another constellation for someone who had lived near this mountain. Someone who had been able to look at the Mountain every day and feel Sourced and Re-sourced by this proximity. Then they moved and found themselves in a town far from the nourish-

Mount Shasta

ment that came from having this daily visual presence. In this constellation the person that represented Mount Shasta was able to bring the strength and presence this mountain offers directly into the physical body of the person the constellation was set for. She is able, even to this day, to feel the strength and wisdom of that Mountain inside her own being. This presence has helped carry her though some of the difficult times that come with being in life. As stated by the representative of Mount Shasta, "I could feel the message of the Mountain. I could sense it speak through me. At first I was skeptical that a person can represent nature, but it becomes obvious that one can. Through Nature Constellations, I have a fuller connection with trees and other aspects of nature which is alien to how I grew up."

Another participant offers: "I recall my experience of a weekend Constellation at Mt. Shasta. I was given a spirit name several years ago by that mountain, the name is 'Sacred Mountain.' It has been my journey to learn the teachings of what this means. Spending a weekend camping on the mountain and connecting with the Ancestors and Elements through Constellation work brought forth a deeper understanding of what this meant for me. The teachings I received include: feel the fire within and know that it exists even within the exterior of a snow-capped mountain; the mountain has a strong "presence" just like us, one does not always need to do or say something to express this powerful sense of being; it is in who we are that this is reflected, not so much in our words or doing; and Be strength and presence, do not downplay your roll in this life." She goes on to say: "These teachings came through in my participation as a representative in several constellations for others throughout the weekend; the boost to my awareness of my purpose and my confidence in Being and expressing that lives on today. I have learned the Ancestors will bring forth a teaching and follow up with situations in which they can be used. Through this I have been taught to get my "self" out of the way and follow the teachings and messages. A lifelong process for sure."

Being in the amazing presence of that Mountain is a gift in and of itself....and undeniable Presence of the power of Nature. In addition, we were able to walk to the sacred springs where we gathered for ceremony and felt what it was like in our bodies to become the representative of the spring, the meadow and some of the purest water on the planet. We were also gifted with the opportunity to hike to a powerful medicine wheel....the site of many prayers and ceremonies. A place that needs to be tended each year after the snowy stormy winter has its way with it. Here people were able to feel what it was like to sense into the differences of each direction and spend time on or near the wheel in the places that beckoned them. We all found this to be a valuable way to break up the intensity of the work and to help ourselves feel refreshed and replenished by being there and receiving the messages that were there for us in this way.

The Southern Coast of Oregon:

Three times now in the cold, dark, rainy days of winter...a time of year when the weather here can be extreme, a group of us have gathered in the warm shelter of a house on the coast of Southern Oregon. Here these intrepid souls get to experience what it is like to live together... like a family... for a three day Constellation event. Here we have to negotiate who gets bedrooms and who gets to use the couch or pads on the floor. Then there's the line for the bathroom and the flow of making food in the kitchen. We learn to pitch in and navigate our lives around each other. This makes it a great place to test our abilities to do this. How do I respond when someone doesn't do what I want? Do I let that interfere with the flow of love? It's a pretty intense environment, especially if the weather has its way with us. Like the year we had the storm of storms. It rained 8 inches in 48 hours, and the wind was blowing at 100 miles per hour. It was wild. The sea was churned up, and so were the people.... some found it scary being there on the edge of a cliff, for others it was exhilarating. A perfect metaphor for life.

Weather permitting, we've gone out on the beach to give people the opportunity to represent and get to know different aspects of our Earth Community, tuning into what is calling for their attention and their embodiment. Someone might be called to step into what it's like to be the ocean, someone else might become a sea otter, someone else the wind, someone else the rocks or waves, the birds, the shore, a bear, an elk, a loon, the storm itself. Representatives of all types have shown up to bring us their messages. We listen to what these beings, these energies have to say, we watch how they interact with each other, where they feel called to move, each one noticing their place in the Constellation of it All. We have utilized these teachings throughout the weekend and have found them to be important lasting gifts and reminders for the person they were given to and for all the members of our weekend family. Embodying in this way has helped the people discover that we really are connected to Everything and that Life itself in all kinds of forms is there to support and teach us if we open, listen and receive.

The house we've stayed in has ceiling to floor windows overlooking the beauty and wildness of the Pacific Ocean. So regardless of what kind of constellation we are setting, the ocean is a constant back drop, and we use it. As one participant stated:

> "Participating in Constellations at the Oregon coast is an amazing experience. The Ocean is such a powerful presence and teacher. A primary teaching for me there is to allow energy to move; sometimes it is quiet, rhythmic, steady. Other times very forceful and violent. No matter what the circumstance there is always the steady sound and feel of the rhythm of the waters... moving, cleansing, releasing. The elements do not hold onto the present moment or circumstances, they are forever in motion...cycling, transforming....inviting me, reminding me to do the same."

The Grand Canyon:

Another important thread of my heart's prayer and aspiration was brought into this weaving of Constellation work and Nature as I found myself called to the Grand Canyon. I never know how the calls will come, and this one started as a request from someone who had journeyed in the outdoors with me before. Having worked down in that Canyon some 21 years ago, I knew that Arizona Raft Adventures was the company I would want to have guide us. This was a big undertaking....could it really happen? It was a journey of trust all the way.

The trip that was available for us was for 16 days but not leaving until October 22nd.... definitely not my preference. It's a shoulder season. The weather could be warm one day and then snow the next....anything was possible. We would be traveling 225 miles on water that is 48 degrees....it feels really cold even when the temps are over 100. Despite these concerns and others, the trip kept moving forward. I had to trust and move forward with it.

Giving birth to this trip took nine months. If we were going at this time of year I wanted to make sure that the 17 courageous souls that signed up to do Nature Constellations in the Grand Canyon, would have the proper gear. I prayed every day and asked for guidance on how to best take care of the people and their Ancestors that would accompany them. I wanted them to be as comfortable as possible and as prepared as possible for whatever we might encounter. I did research and answered questions. I held meetings and a potluck so folks could share their hopes and dreams, their fears and concerns. I had them bring their gear. I wanted to make sure it was adequate, that it would keep them dry and warm enough

Grand Canyon Water Crossing

as we navigated the huge rapids. There was no staying dry on the Colorado River. I did not want anyone hypothermic, a real possibility any time of the year with water that cold. We shared food and swapped ideas on how to pack everything we wanted to take for all those days in the confines of the little dry bag AzRA provided. Everyone was challenged....though luckily, excited too.

It happened. October 22nd came and all 18 of us got on the bus. There were 3 men and 15 women. Once again, this was the typical male to female ratio for these Nature-based Constellation events. They were aged from their early 40's to their mid 70's....folks that were hoping that this call they had to doing Constellations and being out in Nature for all those days would bring more love, connection and aliveness into their life.

As I felt the chill of that fall morning, I couldn't help but marvel at these incredibly brave souls who had gathered from five states, for when it came to an adventure like rafting down the Grand Canyon, I was the only one who had ever done anything quite like it. Nonetheless, they had signed up and shown up and were now getting to know each other as we traversed the painted desert. We were on our way.

Once we reached the Colorado river, some three hours after we'd left our motel in Flagstaff, we stopped at Navajo Bridge to look down upon Marble Canyon. From there we had a birds eye view of the river we would be floating down. As I stood there taking in the grandeur of where we were and what we were embarking on, an endangered California condor, its wing span measuring close to 9 feet, flew a mere 20 feet above my head.....dipping its wings as if to bless us on our adventure. I took that as a good sign. A few hours later with

Grand Canyon Perspective

our river guides and hopefully everything we needed loaded on those six boats, we pushed off from the shore of Lee's Ferry. No flush toilets and no showers for 16 days.....there was no getting out either....except by helicopter in an emergency.

Being a constellation facilitator has strengthened my ability to listen deeply and I would need that skill in ways I had never utilized before. What I might want to have happen and what the river or the guides might need to have happen could easily be two different things. I've been on rivers enough to know that you can't push them, and that certainly was the case on this one. Here I really had to go with the flow. Before I could bring the group together for opening ceremony and prayer we needed to be steeped in safety and learn the workings of this moving camp. It took some time before we could gather as a group for that opening ceremony. My desires for bringing this possibility of deepening into the sacredness of the Nature that surrounded us would have to wait; first things first. It wasn't until people had some familiarity with the flow of our days down there that we could begin that part of the journey together.

My overall sense for this trip was to focus more on the Natural Community that surrounded us, and less on what we brought from our family. In other words, it felt more right to do constellations that would heighten our experience down there, affording the possibility of moving attention away from thought and the way it can confine us, so that we might bring our awareness more to the present moment....to listen, feel and deeply experience the Ancient rock, the flowing river and the sky that held us throughout our days. My prayer was that our 16 days of being with the Earth and the rawness of the Elements would move us out beyond our habitual patterns and bring us face to face with what lies beyond all that. We would experience in the bones of our being that we are connected to this life that is flowing through it all....that we always have been and we always will be a part of Something much greater than ourselves. I was hoping their lives, their Spirit, and all of the Earth Community, would benefit and be fed this way.

The days in October and November are short. It takes a lot of energy to pack and unpack, set up camp and take it down, stay warm when the cold water kisses our faces and bypasses the velcro we've cinched around our necks. We got worked climbing up the canyon trials, hiking into gorgeous side canyons and paddling the paddle raft. People got tired and I had to adjust what I did with them accordingly. One of the first constellations I did down there amidst those ancient walls was to break the group into groups of four. One person would represent the person setting the constellation, another would represent their Ancestors and a partner would represent the Ancient Ones. I wanted everyone to have a turn at each position.

Here's what one participant said: "It was an evening deep in the Grand Canyon with the walls towering overhead when we were asked to tune into our ancestors. I had never given my ancestors a thought. But I began to feel my father and my grandfather and my great grandfather and mother, all very successful beings who brought support and abundance to their journeys, to others, and to this world. This beginning has had me realize that they are here for me. They are more than willing to lend me their love and guidance. The ancient wilderness brought them to me. The stillness allowed me to hear them for the first time."

This constellation changed the life of another participant who has lived with fear on a daily basis. In the talking circle she told us of her fear of the future, fear of traveling, fear of death, of being injured, and of her fear of the water and drowning. In the constellation, the representative for the Ancient Ones said: "Have NO fear. The Ancient Ones are with you; we are watching over you and holding you." According to the participant, they were so clear and so adamant that she was able to take it in and now more deeply believe that she's okay. She has carried a sense that "my Ancestors want me to be happy and they support this through all their sacrifices and life experiences." She doesn't feel so alone, nor as afraid.

The days were full and I would utilize the evenings to gather us for a talking circle or to set constellations depending on how the group was doing. I encouraged the group to be as present as possible as we passed through the Ancient rocks.....some 1.7 billion years old.... some of THE oldest rock on the planet. As far as we know it is this rock, the Vishnu Schist and the Zoraster Granite, that is found near the core of the earth....truly Ancient Ones.... about as Ancient as we know....certainly Ones to pay attention to. When we entered the inner gorge, the home of this Schist and Granite, we were graced by the light of the full moon~~truly a wonder to watch the moon light play with the Canyon walls. Here I invited those willing to represent this rock, to represent the river and to represent the sky. Here's what one of them shared:

I wrote in my journal: 10/29/12 Full Moon Constellation:

You asked us to feel the rock, the water, the sky and then feel where it lived within ourselves.
ROCK – Vishnu Schist – 1.7 billion years old / Zoraster granite – in me, feels like strong and beautiful, power coming up from the earth. Strong legs, centered in pelvis.
RIVER – in me- felt as fluid running thru my body – lymph, mucous, cerebrospinal fluid, tightness in forehead and temples – fluids pushing thru blockages. POWER
SKY – the moon- in me, felt like reflecting sun, reflecting my own beauty.

Reflections:

Sometimes we would float or hike or absorb the beauty of the side canyons and waterfalls in silence. This stillness would allow people to just be and to absorb what they could from where we were. One traveler noted:

"Being in the Grand Canyon and deepening the experience with the use of Constellations gave me an experience that goes beyond the personal into the transpersonal and ultimately into feeling the presence of the Divine. Recalling this brings tears. That connection is where and how I want to live. It's hard to access that feeling. I have spent my life trying. I felt it down there and I can now touch it more often with my life."

Here's another:

"My experience in the Grand Canyon is somewhat difficult to express in words. Connecting with the Ancestors in what felt to be their homeland and being close and involved with the elements is very much a visceral experience. There was the opportunity to drop away from the mind's workings and be within a depth not available even in an intensive weekend. Some of the teachings I received were:

Go with the flow

The depth of quiet and roar of the Soul are all part of the Journey.

Water, as life, smoothes our rough edges over time.

Be still.

Be playful.

Be mindful of detail and aware of the passage of time.

Be flexible, conditions and plans will change.

Grace is quiet and powerful.

Time and elements move earth up and sideways.

Time passage is measured not by clocks, rather by changes in light, moon, sun on the sky scape and earth movement.

When there is a rough spot. Stop....pray...ask for guidance for peaceful, direct means of communication.

Open to expressions of creativity.

All is well.

Your Spirit Guides and Ancestors are always available......stay tuned.

Be passionate and steady in what you involve yourself in.

All "elements" of this life are important, don't over-focus.

Connect with the rhythms of nature.

Pace yourself.

Compassion...Compassion...Compassion."

And another who had recently experienced the death of her husband:

"When asked what the river meant for me, I could explain about its constant movement and the way it slapped me out of the boat. I needed that help to get back in and continue my life. It taught me yet again that I could get back up, especially with a little help. The sky

offered the ever changing minutes, hours, days, and for me the promise of my life after death watching the stars twinkling at me." She went on to say, "Perhaps the most profound for me was the rock. Walking up side canyons after floating through narrow and wide parts of the canyon carved by the river, was a very profound experience. The rock looks like folds of cloth, enveloping the earth. I felt myself as the mother and the grandmother, and experienced a vision of my life and my purpose. The rock just invited me in, and held me. This deep listening was facilitated by our experiences with Susan as we did nature constellations. I don't imagine it would be possible to reflect as deeply on such a journey without our evening of nature constellations."

One of our special times down there amidst the extraordinarily ancient walls, was Dia de los Muertos. This gave us the opportunity to honor and celebrate those that have passed away. I had hidden a stash of candles in a corner of my dry bag to save for this special occasion. We were camped at a site called, The Ledges, appropriately named for the flat rock ledges that would be home for us for the night. It was a perfect place to do ceremony....to light our candles as we named and remembered our Ancestors. We gave thanks to all those that had come before us. We then stood together in the silence and bore witness as the flickering light of the candles illumined our faces....the ones here, living and bringing forth their lineage.

On our last night in the canyon I invited people to once again represent some aspect of the rock, the water and the sky and then to notice where they felt these in their body and what their messages were for them. I wanted to give them an opportunity to feel more deeply in their body the Presence of where we were and what surrounded us and held us. I wanted them to be able to take that home with them.....to remember the depth of connection available to them so they could draw upon that when they were back in their daily life. Here's a sample:

"ROCK: Vishnu Schist, the oldest shiniest black rock known on earth. Its message to me: "I will survive and you will survive."

WATER: "I flow and I play and you can too."

SKY: The moon in its reflection of the sun – its message to me: "I am a reflection of the sun and you are too."

These are messages that the people continue to carry. At the potluck after we returned home, those that could attend reported how their life had changed, how they felt stronger and more alive than they'd felt in a long time, how the trip changed how they looked at rocks and water, how they felt more rooted in what was most important to them and how they know in a deeper way that we are all interconnected with a Grand Universe that is made up of all different forms of our Ancestors and Ancient Ones, and that they are with us....that they are here to guide and support us and it is our responsibility to open and listen and hear and receive. They felt the flow of that river as a flow of Love and Life. We spoke of what it felt like to have that Source of Life carry us. We laughed and told stories and looked at each other's photos, as we reveled in the experiences we shared. The power of the Colorado river, the Ancientness of the Canyon walls, the elements, the sky, each other, the rawness and flow of life away from our routines, every aspect, everything we experienced....we were all wonderfully and immensely impacted. An impact that is still working in all of our souls.

Further Development:

The way I see it, we have an essential and vitally important call along with a sacred opportunity to live in conscious recognition of our interdependency with each other and with every thing in life. To do that we need us humans to open our hearts and realize, feel, experience and know our interconnectedness and interrelatedness with our Mothers and Fathers, and with our Mother Earth and Father Sky. We couldn't be here, and we couldn't really have life, or love, without them.

In working out in the natural community this way I have found that for those that weren't able to reach towards their own Mothers, being able to reach towards the Earth as our Mother has brought life and more possibility. For those that have been able to open their hearts to their own Mother yet have lived with a fear of Nature, being out in the elements in a good and safe way has helped them open, receive and experience a deeper community of support through our Ancestors and Earth Community. To whatever degree one does or does not feel a loving connection to the Universe and All That Is, I have found that through participating in Nature Constellations and in Constellations out in Nature the felt sense and embodied knowing of this interconnectedness and interdependency has deepened and grown.

New possibilities are beckoning. I'm interested in discovering what's possible in taking this work to places on the Earth that have been harshly impacted by our belief in separation or by our vast ecological footprint. Like the constellation we did for land that had been severely logged, while we were right there standing upon it. There's also more rivers to meet and receive, more places that want us to come, to listen and pay attention, to connect and experience the Love and Wisdom available to us from these forms of our Ancestors and Ancient Ones....The Ones that came before us. Might this fundamental connection with these Ancient Ones be a needed addition to the Orders of Love? Might this important recognition and addition help transform the damage that's occurred from our belief that we are separate and help bring us into right alignment with this vitally important, ancient relationship with our Mother Earth and All Our Relations?

To know of our interrelated and interdependent membership places us in our right place in relation to our Earth Community. This is essential for ourselves, for each other and for all of us in human and non human form...our planet included. The quality of all of our lives, health, and wholeness depends on this. We need this healthy relationship to All That Is to become a loving, life sustaining, fully alive and thriving Community on our planet. It's up to us. We are the voices...and the ones capable of taking action for the Ones who cannot use voices to speak.

Now I hear the Redwoods calling. I must answer their call.

PART III

Opportunities

Opportunities

by Kenneth Edwin Sloan

Each of the contributors have in his or her own unique way explained what this form of work means to them and why they do it. Nonetheless we want to present a short list of reasons that are common across most of the contributions, with a few examples. This list is not complete of course. And each reader will have his or her own points where there is resonance or recognition, or hesitation. But the richness and power of this list helps explain the common commitment of all the contributors to move this work forward and make it more widely known and available.

Completing the Circle of Community

As we noted in the Introduction in our reference to the Council of All Beings work from John Seed and Joanna Macy, completing the circle of community remains one of the first and most fundamental opportunities for this kind of constellation work. With this work we have a way of opening the circle to beings of all kinds when issues in which they are involved or affected are considered. This inclusion alone can bring a new tone to the discussion and to any deliberations. Simply being seen, and recognized as a part of the community is powerful both for those who have been previously ignored and those who have ignored them. But it goes beyond presence to give us the chance to hear their voices, and benefit from their experience and wisdom. Human beings are relatively new as a species. Those looking at us from around the circle, the representatives of the others – the bears in the forests, the whales in the oceans, the mountains and waters, the healing herbs – have a clarity and directness in their eyes that can teach us humans much about how to live. And when they speak, they awaken our own inner awareness of who we really are and what our place in the world should really be.

Experiencing Other Perspectives

The most crucial step in any effort to mediate a conflict is for the participants to experience in some form the perspectives of their opponents or enemies. And one of the most serious conflicts in our modern world is the war of exploitation and devastation of industrialized humanity against nature. In constellation work the chance to stand and experience the sensations, feelings, and thoughts of another participant in a system can be life-changing, and is always a revelation of sorts. I may be at war with the weeds in my garden, for example. But when I stand for awhile as one of the weeds, I will never be able to look at them in the same way again, as long as I can remember and stay connected with that experience of connection and recognition. In the nature paradise of Patagonia, in southern Chile, plans are moving forward to build five enormous hydroelectric dams on two pristine wild rivers, the Baker and Pascua. In a constellation for the project, the experiences of the representatives for the rivers, the forest, and the wildlife there as the dams are one by one brought into the constellation are devastating. None of the participants will forget the depth of tragedy this project represents for the area, and for the world. And so a commitment to activism and engagement is born. The final project approval will happen only after the next elections, in October, 2013. Perhaps there is time to assist those already involved in the struggle to stop the dam project and transfer the renewable energy focus in Chile to solar? But whatever the outcome, it is the experience of the situation in one's own body – the perspective of the Other - that is the most powerful energizer to act rather than passively sit by.

Kenneth's Dog Nemo at Four Months of Age

Finding New Resources

In western cultures there is a prevalent self-image of independence and self-sufficiency. Many people are even alienated from their families and relatives. They may feel little connection to the place in which they live, or to the various elements and beings upon which they are dependent for their existence and well-being. The immutable truth is that we are all extraordinarily dependent on many elements all around us: air, water, soil, light, plants, animals, and a large network of other people who we know or do not know who make our existence possible. Often when we meet another member of Earth Community through this form of work, we are meeting a being that is or has been an important resource for us, even when we did not notice it: the tree we climbed in as a child when we felt sad, and were comforted; the mountain we hiked up when we were discouraged, and felt then ready to continue; the pet that was always there for us, regardless of our circumstances, and wanted only the best for us. By meeting and coming into contact with these resources we remind ourselves that they are there for us, or learn it for the first time. And with each additional resource, with each additional connection, we honor the amazing web of our lives, we can relax a bit more, and we become a little less crazy and dangerous to ourselves, to those around us, and to our world.

Healing Broken Relationships

The origins of family constellation work as well as shamanism have as one of their primary intentions the healing of broken relationships. Systemic constellation work with nature gives us the chance to first of all see more clearly, versus from our own anthropocentric and ego-centric point of view, how things really are in systems of which we are a part. For example, I may think that I have a wonderful relationship to the plants in my garden, but how do they experience me? Was that pesticide I put out last spring really a good idea? With this form of work you can get direct feedback as to how the situation is in general for your garden plants, what they think of you, and exactly how they feel about the pesticide application. If you are really brave you will bring in the representatives for the various insects involved, for the water, for the soil, and get their points of view as well. Whether you change something about what you do in your garden or not based on such a constellation, and even if the constel-lation showed that there are more problems than you had known about, it is a step toward improving the relationship.

Education

How do we learn about the world and our place in it? Partly through experiences, and partly through what other people show us or tell us, or what we read. Constellations with nature offer us the path of direct experience, including the many areas in which verbal descriptions lack vitality or clarity. Once we stand as a plant that is in soil that is too acidic, or too basic for us, and have felt how that is, have tasted it in our mouths, we have a different connection to soil pH than we did before. Once we have stood as a dying honey bee colony, and tasted the metallic plastic taste of the trace pesticides in our mouths, experienced the dizzy fog of our lost clarity, the weariness of the long journey via truck to a new field, the yearning for a stable place of our own where we can simply be ourselves undisturbed, we can no longer watch a honey bee pollinating a cherry tree in the same way. We are changed. We have learned something.

Supporting Decision Processes

How do we humans decide things? Sometimes through some rational process. Sometimes through some emotionally driven process. Sometimes through some intuitive process. Of-ten through a mix of these. What is clear is that in deciding we are best served by knowing about the issue we are deciding: what are the real options, and what are the probable ef-fects of acting on each option? When we are deciding about a natural system, we are often limited because we are aware neither of the full range of options nor the probable effects of each. Systemic constellations with nature can provide a valuable support in such a situation. This does not mean that there is always a clear answer. Often what we experience may be symbolic or expressed in a form – a dance, a song, a gesture – that is hard for us to interpret. Often the only conclusion we can reach is that we appear to have asked the wrong question. But there is often real help available. And nature is always grateful to be asked.

Joy

Often in the chapters of this book there have been references to joy, to exuberance, to pure positive emotion unclouded by thoughts, fears, or hesitations. This in the end is what na-ture offers us: an experience of bliss as we take our place in the dance, and find our own dance, and find our joy in the dances of the others. As we return to membership in Earth Community.

PART IV

Resources

Resources

Internet Site and Online Community

We have set up an internet site for sharing information about Systemic Constellations with Nature. The address is: www.nature-constellations.net. The site is interactive in that it enables persons to join the site and post about their own experiences, communicate with others on the site, and post questions or comments.

The contents of this book are just a beginning. Our hope is that this field of work will expand and become more visible and available; the community site is one way for that to be supported.

The Knowing Field and Barbara Morgan

We would like to thank and acknowledge Barbara Morgan, Editor of The Knowing Field: International Constellations Journal (www.theknowingfield.com - subscription information, back issue contents, and the ability to order back issues are all on the web site). Originally Barbara was a Deputy Editor with the Systemic Solutions Bulletin. She took over the care and feeding of The Systemic Solutions Bulletin as Editor in December 2004. Beginning in 2005 she operated the publication under the name of The Knowing Field: International Constellations Journal. Two chapters in this book were originally published in The Knowing Field (though they have been modified from their original forms) and are published here with her permission.

The Journal has been an international window into developments in Family, Organizational, and Systemic Constellations, including Nature Constellations. Listed below are a few of the other articles included in The Knowing Field which featured elements of Nature in a significant way. Many other articles have included natural elements, indigenous perspectives, or resourcing clients and facilitating in a way which includes Nature. Two examples:

- Mother Earth Belongs, Francesca Mason Boring (Issue 9, January 2007)

- In the Spotlight, Berchthold Wasser and Kenneth Sloan in Conversation with Francesca Mason Boring (Issue 14, June 2009)

Barbara Morgan has been an impassioned and nurturing trailblazer. Her persistent encouragement of many to document their observations and developments has spearheaded the flowering of an extraordinary body of work. She has been determined to give space to every voice. She is a UKCP registered Gestalt Psychotherapist and Family Constellations Practitioner, mother, grandmother, a woman who loves camping, having her hands in the garden, and being replenished by the earth. It is difficult to over-estimate the impact of Barbara's steadfast, more than decade-long commitment to giving voice to the many streams that have flowed from Hellinger's original introduction of Family Constellation and the movements of the soul.

Our dearest thanks to Barbara Morgan, Editor, mentor, and friend!

The Art of Jane Kiskaddon

We searched a long time before we found the right art work for the cover of this book. In the end it was the painting "Sitting in the Forest" by Jane Kiskaddon, - www.janekiskaddon.com that was perfect. Jane graciously allowed us to use it, and it has become a touchstone for the work of systemic constellations with nature for us. There are many more of her wonderful paintings available on her web site. Highly recommended. Thanks, Jane!

Index